RETREAT TO REALITY

RETREAT

TO

REALITY

by Dudley Zuver

NEW YORK

Thomas Y. Crowell Company

ESTABLISHED 1834

Designed by Laurel Wagner

Manufactured in the United States of America
by the Vail-Ballou Press, Inc., Binghamton, N. Y.

Library of Congress Catalog Card No. 59-12501

CONTENTS

1092323

I

INTRODUCTION: TWO INCIDENTS

ANY BOOK with *reality* in its title seems predestined to say something about God. But a book on God is liable to impress as unreal, perhaps as inane. Unless God be conceived as a complete bore, sustained talk about him is bound to be ungodly.

Discourse inevitably deals with an object, whatsoever we think about or talk about being just that—an object. The determination of objects by means of concepts we call knowledge. But God, being no object, cannot be known; or, since he is unknowable, he can be no object: have it either way. The point is that one can talk about God only by admitting in advance he cannot possibly know what he is talking about.

Between the necessity of saying something and the impossibility of saying anything sensible there is only one way out: to have a quick say and then quit saying. I have long opined that a preacher should tell in the first sentence of the sermon what he understands by God, then use the word no more till next Sunday. My own advice I propose to follow, without making too many exceptions to the rule.

For a definition of God I am going back to one given me

when I was a boy of twelve, without the giver's intending the gift. I was directed to the oracle by what must now appear a scarcely noteworthy sequence of events.

There was an ordinance in town forbidding the riding of bicycles on the sidewalks, a law I was accustomed to violate without consequences. One morning, however, I had not only the hardihood to break the law but the hard luck to bump into our policeman in so doing. The latter gave me a steer toward the seat of law: I would have to go to the mayor, report my wrongdoing and pay whatever penalty he saw fit to impose; eleven o'clock was to be my day in court.

During the two hours of waiting I grew fully two decades. My mood pitapatted between the maturely adult attitudes of somber terror and sullen rebellion. In a trice I had become aware of myself as a lone individual set in the midst of an alien and an angry world. Let the day perish wherein I was born, let that day be darkness: let not God regard it from above, neither let the light shine upon it. Into the abyss of speculation I reached for the most rational idea, the solidest armor there: what play should I make? Should I beg mercy, meek and penitent? But, why can't a fellow ride on empty sidewalks? The injustice being wreaked on me might arouse the town to repeal such senseless laws. Did the policeman know my name? Maybe the thing to do was to take a chance he didn't, becoming wise through his ignorance.

Punctuality has ever been a built-in virtue I cannot avoid. When the appointed hour struck, I stood honor-stricken on the steps of the mayor's dwelling which was also his office. This official was old and venerable, the mayoralty having been a tribute the town had paid him upon his retirement from some distinguished service rendered in an ampler field: everybody called him Governor. He sat on the porch, his upper half behind the barrier of a newspaper, the only part of him showing being two long black-trousered legs which looked like sections of stovepipe. As I became audible, a bewhiskered jaw jutted augustly around the edge of the paper. Well, he grunted, he glowered, he growled, I didn't know which, giving me the corner of an eye.

I had to state my business. He crushed the paper in his lap while I made news of my criminal record. His countenance betokened a rapid descent through sundry stages of austerity, plumping finally in the very grave of gravity. Did I not know the law? he boomed. Still, ignorance is no excuse, no extenuation; the law presumes that every citizen is informed concerning its mandate; society can rest on no other basis than the majesty of the law; no one is ever too young to acknowledge it, no one is ever so young he is privileged to flout it: so on for a ponderous five didactic minutes.

I stood spellbound, practically persuaded I was hellbound. Then suddenly it happened. He jumped from the tall rocker, waving the paper fiercely, flinging it to the floor and flailing his arms. "Did you see that bee?" he cried madly, tearing off his tie, then his collar, one of that single-ply, stiffly starched style, old-fashioned even at that time. He frantically brushed his neck and unbuttoning his shirt front, flicked all the way down. "Did you see that bee?"

I had not seen it. But I reckoned it expedient to reply concernedly that I had heard it buzz.

"That bee," he recovered his poise. "I saw it, heard it, I felt it crawl down my neck. But where is the aforesaid bee now?" He combed his beard with his fingers. "Neither here nor there. That, I guess, was the bee that be-n't. The bee that be-n't, we will let it go at that."

Things were not through happening though. And I am about to claim my right to use that word, God, for the entitled once. God happened.

A sheepish grin seemed to shatter the granite of the old man's face. A strange incandescence broke through the tomb of his whiskers, zigzagging like a pulse of sparks through the wrinkles of his neck and forehead. The same strange presence illumined the porch, the same nimbus pervading the world as far as I could see it.

He put his hands on my shoulders. "My boy," he said, "I like you. I'm glad you came. What did you say your name was? Let us be friends. You're not big enough yet, but in a year or two, come around, I'll sit on the handlebars and we will take a ride down Main Street, right on the sidewalk. We'll write a new law for them. When you grow a bit, we'll show 'em. But till then, just be a little careful and ride in the road. Stop in whenever you go by."

The bee that be-n't: it never occurred to me that here perhaps was an image of God, never till Professor Tillich defined God as *Being-itself.* In trying to puzzle that one out, the old mayor's phrase popped back as distinctly better.

How shall God be conceived save as a notably potent nothing? God is no substance to be known by attaching attributes. God is no noun to be animated by adjectives. God is not an object open to scientific investigation, to be determined by the vestures of scientific theory. But God is the power that so transformed a situation that man and boy could meet face to face, communicating through a language that heart spoke to heart. And the spirit that empowers one to such a genuine

encounter lets him laugh a little over what he had been without it.

No amount of preaching or of planning could have accomplished what took place on that porch that morning. One
moment there is alienation, a man extolling the law and a
boy cringing before his dicta; the next moment the same
human beings are in the embrace of freedom and equality,
safe from the alarms of the law. These human beings were
identical in all assignable respects before conversion and
after conversion. The sudden conversion did not alter their
ages, their weights, their bank balances or church connec-
tions. But it did make a change, and I must differentiate their
b.c. and a.c. conditions somehow. This I shall do by designating the anterior couple as egos and the posterior pair persons.
God is what makes the difference between them.

Though ego and person have in common all traits that can
be catalogued, the person is real, while the isolated individual suffers from a deficiency of whatever reality I sensed that
morning as Presence. What is Presence? It is that which is so
appallingly absent when people get to talking about themselves and their objective concerns.

The shortest word in our dictionary is that one-letter number, *I*, and this same *I* has a disproportionately huge measure
of ambiguity. By *I* one can mean either his self or his ego.
Your *I* is utterly different when that *I* stands in the Presence
or in the darkness of its own solitude. In the former case, as
a true self, one can be nothing else than what one is aware of:
you are real when what you are aware of exists in complete
unity with yourself and in distinction just as complete. As a
self, you have no object apart from yourself which is not
a part of yourself. My existence is what makes your existence,

and yours makes mine. We cannot alienate each other without destroying our own reality and annulling ourselves into mere egos. My *I* and your *I*, patently these are not the same *I*'s before we are overshadowed by the *bee that be-n't* and afterward. Still we have no verbal way to express this, tremendous though the transformation be.

Our language could use a word that means both *you* and *I*. We have it, you say; there it is, that word, *we*.

But there are two *you-and-I's; you* and *I* before conversion and after conversion. *We* does not distinguish. As a rule and in the main, *we* means b.c. *We* refers to two *I*'s taken additively, your ego plus mine making a collection. *We* does not apply to people who have been stung to real consciousness by the *bee that be-n't*. *We* is a collective term for individuals meeting objectively in a sphere posited by their egos, in a sphere where all are playing roles determined by their positions in a predetermined order. *We* denominates two or more *I*'s forming an aggregate, each leaving the others untouched. You and I, however, if we exist as one, cannot be added by any process of enumeration to make a plurality.

The associations we form generally are not authentic; they consist merely of collections of individuals dumped together by accident or design, each constituent functioning according to the law of the dump. The entire cosmos may be conceived after this pattern: a multitude of material atoms in motion. Any group of separate units can make a team, no unit losing but rather accentuating its essential egotism in the teamwork. Individuals so teamed-up have ends in common. The union can be instituted by strictly physical agencies, such as residing under the same roof or getting caught in the same boat. Still the tie that binds may pass as spiritual with-

out affecting the character of the association. *We-ness*, togetherness, may consist in devotion to a stated purpose, perhaps a sacred one, like bringing in the Kingdom of God.
We, the people, may be *we*-ified to secure the blessings of
liberty for ourselves and our posterity, as the Constitution
preambles along. *We* may organize to recite a creed, to
celebrate a sacrament, and still find in the assembly solely
a collection of separate egos, whose motives however noble
are doomed to be pursued egotistically. Such *we's* are contrived by the consent of the belongers, and getting something out is a condition of staying in. Every individual in the
group is tagged with a sign marking his position in the setup:
a telephone number, private in Company C., a street address. No matter how minutely or intimately the *we*-system
is organized, there are no real *I's* in it at all. Its members
are automata, albeit intelligent ones. And when a scientist
determines laws for the behavior of human society, it is
wholly bootless to protest that men are free.

The egocentricity ascribable to the b.c. *I* is by no means
subdued by congregating divers *I's* into a *we*. The *we*, their
togetherness, may serve to magnify the egotism of its constituents. Nationalism, for example, puts a chip on every
patriot's shoulder, and the yokels on village streets get to
swaggering because their country boasts the biggest battle-
ships on far-off seas. The object of any *we* can only be to
aggrandize one another's *I's*. Egotism seldom declares that
a single ego—the declarer's own—exists; the most rapacious
egotist is rarely a solipsist. Egotists indeed are the most
sociable of people. But the society they create is impersonal,
its scene a stage where they can strut and show off. Egotists
can please one another, amuse one another, inform and

advantage one another, enhance and enslave one another. But they cannot produce real fellowship, the communion as distinguished from the community of *you* and *I*, which exists alone beneath the wing of the *bee that be-n't*. Within that fellowship you are the object of my love. But you are not the object of my verbs. I cannot think you, I cannot judge you, I cannot know you. I cannot compel you, and you are free even to withhold yourself from me. You must reveal yourself of your own accord and initiative if I am ever to become aware of you. You are a perpetual mystery and an incessant surprise. By all ordinary standards you are a miracle.

For *you* and *I* in this extraordinary sense there is no pronoun, *we* referring to our ordinary relations before conversion. But we do have a noun to indicate *you* and *I* in personal fellowship, in the full reality of our selfhood. That noun is God.

God is love. When you and I join together as real persons, mingling our existence, merging our spirits, congruent at our centers, that is the relation called love. God presides in our midst though he performs none of the functions of presider. God presides by being present. God is love, the love we have for each other when our love is God's love for each of us. Love never meets a need nor answers a purpose. Love is not altered by finding reasons for and against. Love judges not, not even the value of itself.

God is our name for *you-and-I*. This forbids any notion that God is an object apart from us or beyond us. God is the quality that qualifies us for mutual participation. God dwells in us; he is our dwelling place, when we live in the hive of the *bee that be-n't*.

The second incident I am to tell of befell years later.

Early one morning I was sitting in New York's Washington Square park, when I became conscious of a man on the opposite bench, so thoroughly conscious of him that I was conscious of nothing else. Why such a familiar sight should fairly have startled me, I did not ask. No event is so eventful as that mysterious X which marks the intersection of the surprising and the commonplace. A vague presentiment had become an abrupt and dreadful certainty: another man inhabited my world, a trespasser and an interloper. A man— the most frequently encountered element in New York's atmosphere I suddenly beheld as the remotest. A man lurked at that unbridgeable distance from me which stretches between the convict in the electric chair and the executioner who throws the switch. There he was, evidently doing a crossword puzzle, flitting through the mazes of ups and downs and acrosses, fitfully alive within the catacombs of death.

What anybody finds in puzzles has always been a puzzle to me, why one should stake his time and ease against the teases of a paper antagonist, winning at the most a victory fit only for the wastebasket. Perhaps it was because of my cultivated disdain for the dizzy drove of puzzle addicts that the man on the opposite bench became objectified into a whipping boy for the whole horde, while I proceeded to whip my mind into the same state of self-distortion that is distinctive of the puzzle fiend.

How infinitely improbable that this man should exist, what a puzzle it is, and what is he doing here? Is he aught besides the ghost-in-a-mechanism contraption I see him to be, slipping letters into slots as dutifully as a business machine? If he is more than that, or other than that, then I am not really think-

ing about him at all. In that event the object before my mind
is an idea of my own, and its objectivity is but an illusion.

Let's start all over: here we are face to face. Yet face to
face is precisely what we are not. In becoming aware of
him I find, in the same act of awareness, that I must play
unaware. Pretense must take the place of presence, pretense
alleging mutual absence. I cannot permit him to detect me
looking at him for he possesses the fearful capacity of talion:
he can give an eye for an eye, he can look at me. When
stranger faces stranger, a stare is a scare. So I must be handily
double-faced, shifting my gaze in avoidance of his, squirm-
ing for refuge behind what I think him to be. I dare not
evince any concern in him or invite a response from him.
Though free men presumably, we are both bound by the iron
law governing park benches and their occupants. That is a
rule of whatever game we may be playing.

If I yell across and ask the man his name, he will snarl
back that it is none of my business. Being busy with what
is none of your business is the attitude of contemplative detachment, of aesthetic enjoyment, of logical judgment. To
be busy with what is none of your business is to be objective,
the object being alienated to the limbo of nonexistence where
anything can enter save only yourself, that self being the
creator of all it surveys. The capture of objects within this
realm is called knowledge, knowing being the operation of
attaching concepts to the object—which is really no more
than a concept itself. You know a thing when you say something about it that puts it in its place; which place is the mind
of the knower.

But what essence can I conjure that will put that man in

his place? He seems defiantly unknowable, stubbornly insoluble in the acids of objectivity. Human being, my fellow
man: I'll call him this and let him go. How idiotic—there
he sits, chewing the end of his pencil. Being of the same race
and species is supposed to be a lofty moral concept, availing
to draw together what is otherwise separate; it is an objective
relation that renders us akin. Yet every grandiose ideal is
liable to function as a megaphone to amplify the ego uttering
it; just as the United Nations uptown only aggravates the
nationalism of the constituent nations.

Human being: people are hell, says Sartre. Human being,
that is exactly what I hate about that man. I cannot be objective about human beings, they won't let me. Theorists are
prone to proclaim that wars have causes and that by eliminat-
ing the causes war can be abolished. How neatly and objectively logical, and how asinine. No cause whatever need
be assigned to any war: that other human beings, our enemies,
do exist is cause sufficient. That man, opposite me on the
bench, nauseates me just by being there. Every man is alien
and loathsome to every other.

I felt myself resisting any move the man was making, almost angered when he uncrossed his legs as if to get up and
leave. Where might he be going? I must know. Knowledge
is power, knowledge is will. I flushed with the passion to
know. To know—man's insensate and sinister aspiration to
possess and to dominate. Knowledge is a species of possession. Whatever we know we render subservient to the rules
of our understanding. That we can rule over, overbear; that
we can domineer.

Flower in the crannied wall, could I but comprehend you,

what you are, root and all and all in all, I should know what God and man is. And knowing you, I might compel God and man to do my bidding.

Man on the park bench, I pluck you out of your cranny, I hold you under my thumb. I press hard with my fist. I squeeze you to the cement pavement with all I have to mash with. I trample upon you and spin round on my heel, till from your pulp shall ooze that issue of knowledge that embalms all things in the mausoleum of my mind.

Flower in the crannied wall, I pluck you out, then God becomes a cranny in my wall, an idea in the vault of my brain. I pluck you out, then time itself stalls into a static streak in the marble of eternity. Man on the park bench, man alive, you must play dead. In a suitably known world, nothing can move, nothing can happen.

Suppose now, poetry aside, I have that flower of Tennyson's yanked from its cranny, its roots dangling before my ogling gaze, the most I actually know is that it will wilt and wither. And as for the man on the bench, the facts I have amassed concerning him are such inconsequential items as that he does crossword puzzles and that his pants need pressing. Any object we create by our knowing falls short of our requirements. Whatever we judge, perforce we judge adversely; we judge it to be faulty. Whatever actually is, vies and jangles with the object we substitute for it—the real with the ideal of what ought to be. Judge not, we are admonished, for the sound and sufficient reason that to judge is to sentence ourselves to the hell of the ideally better. True, we may have the correct idea of what the good is. But no one can really be good who knows the good by definition. Love is never love that lays down modes and conditions for its own expression.

So, flower in the crannied wall, I am going to snatch a whiff and a glance, then leave you the way I found you. That way I know God as I will never know him if I pull you out and pack you to the laboratory.

And so, man across from me, let us escape to reality. Let us cease making God a disease by taking it easy with each other. Let us retreat from the outposts of our egos to the homelands of our selves.

I announced that these pages would recount an incident, but nothing has happened so far that might be considered even incidental. But something did happen, just then. I looked squarely and honestly at the man. His eyes met mine halfway in a sort of handshake. The man on the bench smiled.

There are divers kinds of smiles. There is the smirk: someone smiles at you to judge and to reprove or accuse you. Then there is the grin, one smiling at oneself in approval and admiration.

But the smile on that man's face was neither of these. He was not smiling at me, neither was he smiling at himself. He wasn't even smiling at the world. What happened rather was that the world smiled through him, the body being his but God's the spirit. Such a smile is more than an incident. That smile is a miracle. The conversion it effects is marvelous to witness and benign to share.

I could hear the shell of my ego cracking. The objective world I had been erecting came crashing down.

What is a smile, what's in it? Nothing statable, manifestly, nothing measurable. Objectively a smile can be explained as a facial configuration resulting from the contraction of certain muscles. But in reality a smile may create a new world, imposing a new dimension, that of luminosity, revealing a world with other persons in it.

Not a single question had been answered concerning the man on the opposite bench. The smile did not inform me of his name, his vocation, his religion or politics. No one's knowledge was expanded, nothing was proved. I knew no more than before, save that I did know the nugatoriness of knowing.

Patently a smile is indefinable. When sincere and spontaneous, a smile is devoid of purpose or utility, it is no symbol, it derives no significance from being a means to an end beyond itself. A smile is the reality itself, the presence that encompasses us, the ambience that renders us akin. That ambience is the environment wherein you love yourself by finding the other person to be lovely. The love of God, of oneself, and of one's neighbor, are one and the same love. Our own existence is enhanced and fulfilled in the existence of one another.

Where is God? The face of God is the smile on the face of the man on a bench in Washington Square park. The most ungodly of abodes is the so-called supernatural. God is the power that raises any natural ordinary event to an extraordinary degree of reality, exalting normal life to the pitch of the divine. Religion does not consist in thinking about spiritual matters while you fret and frown over your material lot. Religion consists in laughing while you work.

I watched my nameless friend cross the street, and when he was lost around the corner, a sudden impulse seized me to seize the newspaper he had stuffed between the slats of his seat.

That man, I promptly discovered, had not been doing a crossword puzzle at all. Instead he had been filling the vacant background of a display advertisement with random scribblings. Most of these were readily legible. Some of them I can reproduce from memory after many years.

Since then I have encountered the principle in philosophy of *coincidentia oppositorum*. The man's musings pertained to that theme. There were epigrams such as these: the sight most resembling the sunrise is the sunset . . . . the phenomenon likest birth is death . . . . no difference obtains between North Pole and South Pole though they stand at far ends of the earth . . . . of all human emotions the closest to love is hate . . . . work and play are variations of the same basic singsong. . . . .

And then a pair their author had cast into a rhymed couplet:

> Between heaven and hell there's but a scant mile.
> To tell God from the Devil there's only his smile.

Most philosophers (including some like me who scarcely are) esteem their thoughts entitled to preservation, indeed to immortality. The man on the bench, however, was willing to entrust his to the transiency of a discarded newspaper in the park and almost certain oblivion. Did not this in itself enact a meeting of opposites? And any man who really practices an ideally cherished principle is himself a rare occurrence. And meeting him is a memorable incident.

II

WHAT IS MAN, THAT HE IS MINDFUL OF HIMSELF?

KNOW THEN THYSELF. . . .

THERE WERE PARK-BENCH PHILOSOPHERS long before there were park benches.

The distinction goes to Socrates of having been the first man to make mindfulness of himself a full-time job. From his day to ours man has been the main problem on man's mind. The unexamined life has been deemed not worth living.

To know himself was the command of the oracle that gave Socrates his commission. This mandate rested on two assumptions: first, that self-knowledge was possible to attain and, second, that it would be beneficial if attained. Self-knowledge might not come easy; good things seldom do. Still, make the effort, and you will come by a confident mind by day and a peaceful mind when you close the day in sleep.

These assumptions have slipped through the centuries rarely being challenged and enjoy high prestige today. It has been observed of course that practitioners of self-knowledge, both buyers and sellers, do not always get along better than anybody else. Socrates had trouble with his wife. And a psychiatrist occasionally has to consult a fellow psychiatrist,

16

or may even end it all by suicide. But such debacles, it is said, merely show that no man's knowledge is perfect or adequate. He who has tried the hardest needs ever try a bit harder, and the best-read student of the subject must keep on the constant lookout for a better book. Self-knowledge like any science varies in value according to the techniques used and the skill of the technician.

To cast doubt upon these conclusions, or assumptions, is a major task of the present volume. We have been told by one we esteem as great as Socrates that taking thought about ourselves adds nothing to our stature. This apparent misunderstanding between Jesus and Socrates can be settled perhaps by understanding more clearly what is meant by the self. It is my contention that we cannot think about ourselves at all, either for better or for naught. The attempt to do so substitutes for the real self a figment projected by the thinking. The more resolutely we seek to know ourselves, the less reality those known selves contain. The pursuit of self-knowledge transforms the pursuer into a egotist. And the knower, this rational ego, is not the real person; which person is deformed and disfigured in the course of being reduced to a specimen for analysis to work on.

Any system of man's self-knowledge, therefore, resting as it does on a fallacy, is bound to terminate in disappointment and frustration if it promises results, that is, moral and dynamic effects. Socratics are logically tied to the principle that people will do what is good for them once they know it, but the unprincipled observers note that people fail miserably in this respect. How can pure reason become practical, Kant asked; how can you, the sodden impure, be suddenly transformed into a state of purity? In being known you are distorted into what you are thought to be, into what the doctor tells you you ought to be. Still, the prospective cure is scarcely a lure. Why must I pray God to make me good when I would rather be bad, whined the Sunday School lad, tapping depths of self-awareness unplumbed by his pastor. Genuine goodness, moreover, is not to be grasped by gasping out formulas of it. The really good person could not define goodness; certainly he would never try. No one in either pew or chancel honestly wants to be the sort the sermon eulogizes. To talk one's self part way into such unwanted glory constitutes the dishonesty called self-righteousness. We forget that hypocrisy may actually rank as a minor virtue; we are often better off for failing to practice what we preach.

Our *retreat to reality* implies both a place we are fleeing from and a place we are seeking to reach. We live on two levels: the real and the known. These planes, despite their interpenetrations and our oscillations between them, are distinct and incompatible. They are a world apart. Language provides no means of distinguishing them, for language pertains to a single level, that of the objective where objects can be named and determined, fixed in position and rendered amenable to laws. Only objects can be talked about, objects being themselves created by discourse.

Science cannot avoid contriving the hypothesis that to be unknown means not to be. Still science is entitled to speak only for itself. And when science denies nonobjective knowledge, science can only be laughed at for taking itself too solemnly.

In a field there are twenty sheep; one sheep jumps over the fence; how many sheep are left? the third-grade teacher asks. Bobbie ponders the situation, finally blurting out an emphatic, "None." "Bobbie, you know nothing about arithmetic," the schoolma'am explodes. "And you," Bobbie mumbles, "you don't know sheep."

There is a vast difference between knowing about sheep according to the symbols of mathematics, and knowing sheep according to the nature of the brutes themselves. Only objects can be dealt with in the schoolroom, which outside the window may appear utterly unreal. Bobbie came to a knowledge of that outside world not by counting himself out of it but by participation in it. He had taken nineteen quick leaps over the fence in the ovine stampede of following the leader. His head rang with excitement though his answer banged him to the foot of the class.

In a time like the present when an almost universal prejudice obtains in favor of science and the exclusively objective character of knowledge, it seems to be a strain on the term itself to speak of knowledge derived from immediate participation in the real world. The knower, our prejudice requires, must be detached from the thing known. The calculator never becomes what he calculates. In counting one holds one's self to be of no account—all of one's self save that pinched-off blister called the knower. Thus it is an obvious mistake to expect results except scientific knowledge from such rational operations, a mistake so obvious that most of us manage to make it facilely. Count your blessings, we exhort ourselves. Yet anybody with Bobbie's sheep sense could tell us that addition is no way to generate joy and gratitude. You never get warmhearted fiddling with cold figures. Misers are prudent men but seldom vital ones. Their gold may glow but their faces do not. To rate a blessing as a literal fact robs it of its beatific quality. The knower can be smothered by a multitude of objects and be empty himself. In becoming mindful of yourself you stand in peril of exhausting that mind into a vacuum.

Bobbie's knowledge did not jibe with that of the teacher. Between shepherd and pedagogue I do not propose assuming the role of compromiser nor an assumption of the rule to split the difference. I propose instead that we retain both characters intact as representatives of two levels of experience both of which we can identify in our own. When you are told to know yourself, which is being addressed: the rational entity that determines an objective realm, or the person who exists only in communion with other selves?

The former, it is true, can be known, and the known self composes the content of psychology. The known self conforms to the pattern the investigator lays down, resembling more closely a sheep which has been slaughtered and hung for storage in the cooler than a sheep grazing in the field. The known self must fit a standard; this does not require, however, that there be a single standard acknowledged by all knowers. Psychologies indeed are exceedingly diverse and discrepant, as numerous as the psychologists themselves. Any science must necessarily carry on in an objective world, but it is by no means necessary that objective worlds correspond. Thomas Aquinas and John Watson would concur in their insistence on objectivity, then squabble over what features the object must display. Psychology covers an amazing range of pecularities between such extremes as scholasticism and behaviorism.

The objective validity of no psychology can be impugned in the interest of any other, all being fashioned out of facts. When their truths clash, you pay your money and take your honey. All are equally true, all are for sale. You are free to have your pick, provided you admit this involves no real freedom and that your choice makes not a whit of difference in what you actually are. Your choice of course may make a difference if you are looking for a job teaching psychology; in which case you should embrace the brand that lands you the job. As long as any psychology removes you for its duration from the real world, you may as well get set solid in its fictitious world. All knowledge said to be objective is fictitious, and when anyone asserts emphatically that his view is objective, his real emphasis is on the *his*.

The theory you adopt to explain yourself has nothing to do with what you are. The real man has no assignable position in any textbook of psychology. He cannot be pinned down save by his own act. He cannot be vested to resemble the soul substance of metaphysicians, he declines to be dressed in any concept whatsoever. Still I have to denominate him somehow, and the something I shall call him is spirit. *Spirit* cannot be defined. The ways of *spirit* are unthinkable, surpassing man's understanding. *Spirit* is freedom, but this freedom is not the freedom honored in tomes of philosophy, not the freedom of patriot's dream nor that of the poet's scream. Freedom is spirit, which as the word indicates is as simple and natural as taking a deep breath.

The real man can be envisaged as a spiritual being, provided spiritual be not taken in its frequent sense of opposite to material. This neat antithesis, of spiritual and material, finds no confirmation in reality. It produces only confusion to hear materialists execrated as wicked men and idealists praised for saying nice things about God and the soul: the confusion being compounded when, out to borrow a dollar in some emergency, you find the materialist responsive to your appeal and the idealist's love devoted solely to abstractions of his own ego. In one's spiritual accounting such items as intellectual convictions and credal beliefs must be largely discounted. One can change his creed with less effect on his conduct than comes about through changing his shirt.

Know then thyself, presume not God to scan. . . .

Presumptuous it may be, the study of God. But the study of man, well, let us call that preposterous.

THE DUALITY OF MAN

If you are certain of a single thing about yourself, it is that of being an indivisible person. You cannot be hyphenated into body and soul. Your body is no mere instrument for the use of your mind. Your legs do not take you for a walk, you take the walk. Your body is you.

Yet if you know a second thing, it is that you are divided. One part of you does your thinking, the other part gets thought about. You can be severed in twain precisely along the line of the conventional hyphen. Such well-attested pairs of twins as body and soul, reason and emotion, essence and existence—they are your components just as they are mine. They are us, whenever we become mindful of ourselves. The conflict between higher and lower, between ideal and sensate, the flesh and the spirit—the story of that strife is our biography.

Is the cleft real or illusory? How can we pull ourselves together, really get going? Shall we fly heavenward to escape the split, to the sky with Plato? Or go with Walt Whitman to the dogs? To soar with the angels, or to lean over the barnyard fence in envy of the cows?

They do not sweat and whine about their condition . . .
They do not make me sick discussing their duty to God . . .
Not one is respectable or unhappy over the whole earth.

Animals possess the integrity and simplicity we lack; angels, presumably, possess them too. Animals are blissfully unmindful of themselves. They do not dote on self-knowledge. We keep pets chiefly for the vicarious satisfaction they afford us, enjoying their doing what we cannot do. We derive a specious exaltation from a dog's refusal to exalt himself. The dog abides by the precepts of Jesus, taking no thought for the morrow and letting the dead bury its dead. If he loses his collar, the sole property he might claim, that loss bothers his master more than it does him. The dog doesn't worry over tomorrow, he isn't wrung with remorse over yesterday. He cultivates no complexes, requires no psychiatric adjustment. He never whines to be entertained. Television has no charms for him. He doesn't fret in boredom. When existence has no excitement to offer, he stretches out for a snooze and conjures no bogies from the abyss of nothingness to torment an empty mind. Your dog never pores over the letter that failed to arrive, never extracts an hour's misery from answering a telephone that didn't ring. All of which is to say that the animal possesses as a free endowment the secret of living which you must wrest from an unwilling hand that isn't even there. Down on his level—or is it up?—all is present, here and now, where there is neither sin nor death, where there are no controversies with the past nor histrionics dictating to the future.

Don't waste your time, time that you do not have; be content with the present moment, the only moment there is; all things pass, what alone endures is the song acclaiming their passing: good advice, that of your dog. But you cannot take it. Trying to take it may inflate us with romantic longings to rummage for poems. But the effort eventually generates additional grief. Aping the simplicity of the ape just complicates the human predicament. And those who monkeyshine with an anticipated angelhood are making even more trouble for themselves.

To live totally in the present is undoubtedly the proper caper. But the present as the dog has it is not the same present available to man. Any living organism must maintain a permanent identity through a series of changes; life consists in just that. For the animal this requirement is met within the dimensions of space. Time, for the brute, is overcome by the actual negation of past and future, leaving every present moment clean-cut and unchallenged. But man has to take issue with time in a different field, to fight it out in his imagination. His permanence demands temporal continuity within his own consciousness. Past and future have a pseudo-existence in memory and anticipation. Man's present is painfully elastic. How much time constitutes the present? The present instant? The present day? The present year? The present life? It is hard to say, but harder not to say. Is death the end of existence, or a mere incident in it?

Thus time that man has only in his head adds up to more than he knows how to handle. Anxiety is the sign he is wasting it. But how can one profitably employ time that he cannot possibly have? To say honestly that he has no time to worry, that one world at a time is enough, that is the seal of man's redemption. Whatever we are planning tomorrow is disruptive of today, unless tomorrow is already here and now.

In being mindful of ourselves we straddle the present moment. We plant one foot in the past, the other in the future. Consequently we are nowhere at all, missing the spot where creation is being enacted. Certain individuals take a more or less settled station on one side or the other of the knife edge of reality. On this score a duality obtains between optimist and pessimist. Their antagonism stimulates such pride in both camps that virtually everybody wants to enlist in one camp or the other. Optimists and pessimists, however, have more in common than either cares to admit.

Optimists haunt the future where their treasure is. They endow time with magical potency to bring heaven to earth. Their consciousness is messianic, the ideal reigning supreme albeit the present mess scarcely warrants the prospect. Whatever is, the optimist accepts only under protest. Indignation is his characteristic response to any actual event. A perfectionist inside, he rejects everything that happens outside, for nothing happens up to his expectations. You must not be fooled by the optimist's good cheer and his apparent buoyancy. He is excruciatingly difficult to get along with. Gushingly agog over tomorrow, he finds in today only occasions for finding fault. Anybody's utopia is planted firmly on everybody else's nerves.

In the point of view of the pessimist, on the contrary, time goes around in circles. Wherever he chances to be, he has been there before and remembers he didn't like it. That an event occurred previously is sufficient reason that it cannot be occurring now. The pessimist wants nothing to happen, his theory being that everything possible has happened already. He scoffs at the sunrise: that is the same sun he saw setting a few hours ago. To thrill over a novelty is like congratulating the undertaker on the lifelike appearance of the corpse.

Feebly enlivened by a memory of the good old days, the sight of today depresses him into the apathy of the cynic. The last event to drip from time's spout is the bitterest to quaff.

Both optimist and pessimist put off living, the one putting it ahead, the other behind. They agree in fleeing from what is here and now, though they run in opposite directions.

What shall we call it when you hold your ground? To be there, all there? To be on the spot? To be yourself in a world that is itself? To ask of life no more than what you have because you are withholding nothing from it? What shall we call this attitude of tending to your own business? Surely it is entitled to a Latin name too: I will call it Existentialism, hoping that the term gives no offense. And let us note that such Existentialism is itself dual with the duality of the optimism-pessimism antithesis. Optimist and pessimist turn out to be not so opposite as they seemed at first glance. The difference between false views is always superficial relative to the difference between delusion and the real thing.

THE SEARCH FOR THE POLES

The wedge of self-knowledge splits us into hemispheres. These were discovered by ancient geographers of the mind and have been explored ever since. To these sections have been attached a variety of names. A favorite pair of such contrasting halves affirms a cleft between the inner and the outer life. Our inner pole is reputed to be excellent and lofty, the outer pole is accused of being debasing and defiling. To the thinker is ascribed a divine vocation; any volume labeled "meditations" is assumed to be religious. God himself, according to Aristotle, is eternally devoted to thinking it over. Contemplation alone invests man with the essence of deity, being the proper pursuit of a rational being. Workers, on the other hand, are concerned merely with the copies of ideas as these are blurred in things. Manual labor degrades the mind to the crass level of the body.

This is the classic cleavage of spiritual and material, a dualism so normal to our folklore that even those subscribe to it who are subordinated by it. The supposed nobility of the inner life and of its practitioners tends to elevate a class in society which without the supposition might seem but a dead weight. Yet so potent is snobbery in the policies of mankind that people who merely talk about values manage to make an ostensible value of themselves. But why does the outer languish under a curse save that the inner has put that curse upon it? And to what is the superiority of the inner due save to an occult bit of knowledge which the knowing faculty credits to itself?

Whatever the spiritual may consist of, there is no access to it except through the material. Wherever the supernatural be sought, the sole avenue to it lies in the natural world. The best way to keep one's mind alert and healthy is to get one's hands occasionally dirty. The manual worker who finds his condition abject and servile has made it so by imposing that judgment upon it. His outer world is twisted to conform to the inner estimation of it. Hatred is engendered in the ego; hatred of one's work shows considerable talent in the art of contemplation. The drudge is no less a thinker because he is allowing Plato to do his thinking for him. And the laboring man's self-disparagement is not to be relieved by sermons on the dignity of labor when it is evident that the preacher regards his vocation of preaching as much more dignified.

We are being constantly imprisoned by systems we ourselves have devised, becoming victims of egocentric incarceration. Materialism is the offspring of the mind and must be excogitated within before it can be riveted on from without. Every political tyranny embodies the purest idealism, and any ideology will debouch in despotism unless there is an opposing ideology to thwart it. The totalitarian state hatches out from a utopian egg formed in somebody's insides. The dictator is the mystic in action when circumstances permit him to act. Any outer world has been thought out first; thinking is no exclusively inner transaction. How can we be free in a world which we have fully armored to repel our thrusts; when we have encased the real world with the conceptual panoply known as the outer world? Spirit and matter, inner and outer, these are not true poles—rather they are alternate designations of the same icecap. The real world is never encountered as either spiritual or material; the real person plies neither an inner nor an outer life.

If we intend freedom to be real, we cannot seek it in withdrawal. There are no crevices between thought and deed where the spirit can germinate and flourish. Only hypocrisy takes root there, to thrive parasitically on genuine goodness. Sometimes people who are credited with an inner life get admired for being spiritual. We rate a man spiritual if he gabbles the sanctioned abstractions and looked plenty scared when uttering vocables deemed to be sacred. Anyone who parrots the creed passes for being pious. This is the fallacy Jesus lashed in his onslaught against the Pharisees. Enshrining the inner life inscribes a pat formula for idolatry and dogmatism both. Idolatry does not imply that the worshiper lacks an object for his adoration. An object he most certainly has. But that object is not real, it does not exist. It has been wrought

and graven in the mill of his own ethical and aesthetic idealism. Inner and outer are merely alternate names for nonexistence. However high the arrow of contemplation may fly, it
never strikes reality and is sure to descend with a deadening
thud.

Reality is no object of discourse. Science deals inevitably
with what is objective, but whatever is real cannot be scientifically known. The existent resists being pictured or symbolized; it refuses to be put on slides for subsequent projection on a screen. You must be there to get it. A report of
any event is secondhand, and in listening to it you are a poor
second yourself. Reality is never fit for print. The most I can
hope for, therefore, is to hint at the whole man by inspecting
him in his polarized state. To that end let us scrutinize another false face, the dualism between our private and our
public lives. We immediately recognize that each of us possesses these separate aspects: we are persons and impersonal
figures too. This disjunction does resound with an echo of
reality.

The private is generally, though wrongly, held synonymous
with the strictly personal. Into the category of the private
are clumped tatters as diverse as one's prejudices and one's
underwear. Your right to privacy entitles you to freedom to
worship God according to your scruples and to whatever you
do in the bathroom. The public grants you unbridled liberty
when you go to church and when you go to the toilet. We hotly
resent interference in either sanctum, both being barred to
outsiders.

Public and private, however, are elastic containers and
their rubber content is subject to wide fluctuations. Prevailing
custom tends to sweep practically everything, save what has

been specified above, into the public domain. Gone are the
good old ways, when the amount of your income could be
regarded as a personal matter. And the privacy of your castle
is now being plundered by invaders more stealthy than the
tax collector and more extortionate too—by such despoilers
as television. Civilization seems resolved on gadgeting us out
of our privacy and reducing us to public dependence. The
dignity of the free man consists in the freedom to be anything besides himself. We find ourselves enmeshed in activities where our status is that of an onlooker and our state
one of abject passivity. Newspapers and radio blare reports
on the cold war, narratives of ball games, of congressional
harangues. We are parked in situations where there is no
chance to participate. All we can do is to listen, maybe bet
on the outcome, and occasionally vote. We become entangled
in affairs we cannot share. Our interests are alienated in
areas beyond our reach. Our personal lives wither. We know
a myriad politicians and movie stars by name; but these
names are public property and that domain is peopled by
spooks.

Such territory is bound to be wasteland from the point of
view of spirit. Public affairs are places to work and to play,
and what happens there is none of our business. Cultural
activities are never our activity in any authentic sense. To
be on their scene requires a leap of the ego and its identification with a stated object. Yet who can deny that the ego
relishes the exercise. Man's own creations fascinate him and
so compel him that he is eager to sacrifice his self and to lie
prostrate before his minions. Our private lives meanwhile
so shrink and shrivel that they are restricted to the cubbyholes
referred to. Still protected as sacred are your rights to your

God and to your underwear, provided you do not show them. Etiquette forbids that you drag either out as a subject of polite conversation.

The absurdity we flounder in stems from our initial identification of the private and the personal. The personal in reality is at a polar remove from either the public or the private of ordinary convention. *Personal* really designates any situation, be it public or private, where you can be your self. Anywhere you really are, you must act as a person.

There is no spot under the sun where man cannot function in a free, spontaneous, self-authenticating capacity. In respect to such personal conduct, however, discourse is out of place, our stock of concepts being relevant only to the objective. The retreat to reality must come about without instructions from guide books, without the slogging of slogans and the fanfare of flags. Existence is never theoretical, it cannot be symbolized, it either is or it is not. In fulfilling the demand of existence you need not be stimulated by advertising, persuaded by argument, motivated by appeals. Your decision is your own. Your act is you. You merge with your world, which must have the quality of yourself. Nature does not repel you, nature is no unnatural antagonist to be dominated and diverted to your advantage. Nature is yourself.

One naturalizes one's self primarily in the physical body, that inalienable environment where the personal and the private become identical. No freedom is thinkable without physical freedom, all theories which locate freedom within the recesses of the inner life being due to the intoxication of sour grapes. Happiness is no mental state but a partnership affair where the cells of the body exult in osmosis and the blood rejoices in its pulse. Health, whether of soul or body, social or individual, should be envisaged as a condition of coexistence obtaining among personal entities who can fuse with one another and also stay distinct, whose mutual dependence is no wise incompatible with the independence of each. Health is family life where every member occupies the entire house though the other members fill the whole of it too, and no one can tell his own property from the belongings of his fellows, everyone dissolving in every other yet remaining insoluble as well, the family composed of persons completely together and just as completely apart.

Nothing exists in nature that cannot be construed in this wise as personal. We are inclined to limit the possibilities, however, by our own potentiality of discernment: to limit personal contacts to those we make with human beings. Even within the species, moreover, we tend to be stingy; we exclude the Russians, probably inasmuch as they are materialists. And we are grudging too in our dealings with the admittedly deserving, exhausting our love in paying them highly impersonal compliments: our fellow men do have immortal souls, each of which is infinitely precious in the sight of God. Everybody hypothetically is welcome in church, but we hug our coattails in alarm when a stranger slides into our pew.

Of course we love our neighbors; no one is so unneighborly as to deny it. But who is my neighbor? The answer must be the stark disjunction: anybody or nobody. The next man you accidentally meet is authentically your neighbor, else you have no neighbors whatsoever. Your neighbor is flesh and blood, here and now. To conceive of your neighbor impersonally fizzes into a futile homiletical effort to personify a conception.

That the mode of expressing the sentiment is a private matter does not restrict the range of your neighborhood: everybody belongs who comes within the range. But personal love, howsoever extensive, is polarically different from loving the public. The public is a ghostly region located in the mind of the lover. Such impersonal love is equivalent to the love of one's own self. Love as a public attitude quickly settles into the egotistic sediment of patriotism. And patriotism, when lovers get going, extinguishes every vestige of the private life. This beloved public may graciously leave you your private God; but if you are a male of draft age, the army will abolish the second of your inalienables and regulate your underwear. Patriots recite the line that it is sweet and noble to die for the country and they leave no doubt that they expect you to do it.

When the personal element in human life is ignored or overrun, no private right avails to withstand the voracity of the public maw. Public and private are by no means as opposite as we fancy, both being but varieties of the impersonal attitude. Certain impersonal objects are undeniably indispensable and likely valuable. What is equally and indispensably valuable is that these objects—these institutions—be taken for what they are and that no personal quality be imputed to them; let them be kept in the head and out of the heart. Whenever a nation, for example, plays the role of pseudo lover or pseudo beloved, its citizens are doomed to the pseudo reality of being soldiers.

You cannot meet a nation personally. The state is a public corporation. To attest your love of such an object is merely to affirm that it is your cherished idol. Though the state be objective enough, its character is that of an agreed-to fiction, and when an ample proportion of those concerned fail to agree, any particular state comes to an end. Howsoever puissant and useful it waxes, no state can claim moral or spiritual standing, and to profess to love it falsifies the nature of love and the reality of the professor.

Thus the religious spirit—a synonym for the personal—attaches no decisive significance to patriotism or to treason, its opposite. If we render unto God that which is due him, we wipe Caesar out of the atlas. Traitor and patriot wear the same prison uniforms though the stripes run in different directions; patriot and traitor differ only in the idols they acknowledge allegiance to. To the religious man all political sovereignties look alike; his kingdom is not of their world. God created men of one blood, in whose stream every nationalism congeals as an embolism. Whatever be its ideology and its opinion of itself, that ideal projects a collective egotism.

Though it be egotism that creates states and governments, only perfect egotism would propose doing away with them. Only the perfect egotist can go to the extreme of anarchism. To the rest of us no way appears possible to get along without political institutions, and without those areas of consensus that render government cheap and effective. So, for the present, I am glad I'm an American. I am glad that ours is the land of the free and of the subtlest submarines. Still, I am unable to distinguish this elation from the glee I used to have in college when we had a championship football team. And I delight in political fiascos, like the McCarthy rumpus, that reduce politics to the patently unlovely. Solely by recognizing human institutions to be faintly ridiculous can we fare intelligently with them. This is not subversion; no subversive is so malignant as the thoroughgoing rationalist who is resolved to cut and dry institutions from the dough of his own head. The most pernicious skeptic is the devout believer whose eternal verities have been excreted by his own cortex.

The state is one of many bridges we must pass over but on which we should not build our dwellings. Much shuttling is required by our cloven condition, for neither pole of any duality provides man with a fit habitation. Man is neither soul nor body. His is neither a public nor a private career. And his various halves can be united only by bringing them into tension with a whole that has never been rent. In the systole and diastole of its beat, not in the organ itself, shall be found the heart of faith and reality.

We are caught in the trap between what we are and what we think we are. The ambiguity of the self may become clear, albeit hardly clarified, as we take off on a polar expedition to the region of play. *Optimi corruptio pessima:* let me soften in advance the scorn I expose play to by admitting that human activity when most consummately real can be envisaged as playing with God. 1092323

PLAYING THE GAME

Duality is our dish; it is called schizophrenia when it gets cracked. The integration promised by self-knowledge results in no state of health; one may lose his mind in becoming unduly mindful of it. The spirit must be continually changing to maintain its changeless identity. The consecration of one's mind to an ideal good merely stiffens one into an ideal corpse to fit an ideal coffin . . . all of which is to say that man is a playful creature. If only he would play God's game instead of the devil's, the latter being the prototype of the countless games man has devised for himself. When man adopted the career of law-giver, he fell into the devil's hand, a card in the devil's deal.

Human culture is a composite of games. All these are cut from the same pattern, that of the ego-object relation. Although games vary in every assignable particular, one bulking in amplitude, another rating as elegant and refined, they exhibit skeletally the same features and fixtures. They all lack spiritual quality, their egotism smothering the personal reality within us.

Still this spiritual core remains an ineradicable pole of our being. Men do not wholly cease being persons in belonging to opposing squads in a football game, in bearing to one another such impersonal relations as buyer and seller, professor and pupil, communist and capitalist, red or white. The moral voice retains the right to protest whenever the antagonism staged by these rivalries does violence to the man. But the point deserves more pointed emphasis than it receives that this spiritual insight never infuses the game itself. No game can be rendered spiritual by any trick of ethics. That men are unrenounceably brothers is no ethical ideal. Brotherhood is the prick of existence itself, felt in spiritual intuition. Love of one's neighbor cannot be deduced from the data of any possible game.

From their common matrix in reality every game extracts its joiners, choosing up sides and pitting contending teams, distinguishing them by the colors of their uniforms and the noises they emit in shouting. Ground must be staked off, the field of play determined by assumptions accepted by all the players. An objective order is acknowledged by each subject engaged. This order is known, it is published as the rules of the game. To express in action the system of ideas previously thought out makes what is called fair play. If a player adheres to the prescriptions of the textbook, even at the cost of losing his pocketbook, he is said to be a good sport. Such rigid idealism is equivalent to a sense of honor. This sense we fondly acclaim. But let us note: honor is no spiritual treasure. What is honored is merely the universality which every ego asserts as pertaining to its own ideals.

Play indubitably is governed by standards. But to invest these standards with a moral character, thus injecting a spiritual quality into play, results only in the introduction of confusion. The Sermon on the Mount presumably has something to do with spiritual living. But how could its precepts be practiced in any game: in a bridge tournament, an advertising conference, the Battle of the Bulge? Just broaching the idea, if you blew serious about it, would get you booted out.

The rational mind reels out the rules. The will, however, has a rule of its own, and it is the will that keeps the whirl going. The body, whose energy flows through the lines reason lays down, is blatantly and brazenly self-assertive: any physical object preempts the space it occupies. The preamble of every rule book, therefore, declares the purpose of the game is to win: to grab and to hoard without shame or apology. In play both soul and body get their way with the soul in the driver's seat. The flesh is damned if it asserts an autonomy of its own in appetite and passion, gluttony and fornication being heinous sins. But when the body serves as a docile instrument of the nobler member, anything goes. Greed, insolence, ruthlessness are permitted and cheered, provided they redound to the glory of the ego. The body is applauded as it throws its weight around, as long as it throws it in the right direction.

Play schemes we spawn in endless profusion. From these we extract the satisfaction spiritual living seems to withhold. A measure of satisfaction these subterfuges do confer. They permit a kind of knowledge that in real life eludes us. We create objective spheres to correspond to the decrees of the ego. A difficulty may arise in enlisting others to agree to the specifications. To secure their adherence and company—togetherness in the usual sense—we must find them like-minded or persuade them to voluntary assent. To gain cooperation, self-interest must be appealed to. When reason lags in collecting a crowd and maintaining a consensus, ideas have to be backed by force. In time of war no government bothers about the consent of the governed; it drafts whomsoever it wants for its team.

The rules of the game, accepted as objective, operate mechanically. Every player must learn what they require by reading a book or by consulting an authority. The science expert, the military commander, the baseball umpire, all rule out any insinuation of spirit, for spirit is wayward and unpredictable. Knowledge is exalted into the supreme virtue. Such an impulse as to forgive a transgressor proves disruptive to the game and, being obnoxious, it must be ruled out. Only amateurs and children take back moves. Objective fixity panders to the egotistic craving for certainty and precision. The play proceeds smoothly till a gang just as rational as our own announces it has contrived rules that are better. Whose game be superior can be decided only by fighting it out. Thus war is both the top game and the bottom assumption of every other.

Any game defines winning in specific terms: the long end of the score, dictation of peace pacts, money in the bank, marks on a report card. Acquisition of these tokens becomes a tinsel of triumph, a symbol of mastery all players must acknowledge as such.

But for the spiritual self there is no wealth in totting up such pelf. The spirit fixes no goal which assigns it a fixed purpose. Religion may envision a Kingdom of God as an ultimate outlook, yet the prospect remains vague and fluid, and the destination of any man who knows exactly where he is going cannot be heaven. The ways of God are inscrutable and it is presumptuous of mortals to chart his course. We can speak of good and evil only by confessing we do not know what we mean. In our ignorance of God's requirements it behooves us to impose no arbitrary requirements of our own on one another. Real faith is never engendered by adhering faithfully to the requirements of any game. We do not make mammon into a true God by being honest in our service of him. And to repudiate any game ever thought of, or the rules that determine rectitude within its sphere, is not in itself spiritually wicked or abhorrent.

The spirit obviously is not of this world. In this world we shall pay tribute to every established order, not perhaps that of strict obedience, but the tribute at any rate of disobedience according to even stricter canons. Stealing second base, for example, is subject to more stringent regulations and scrutiny than a player's taking it on an honest two-bagger. A rule must always govern the modes of breaking rules. Those West Point cadets caught cribbing a few years ago, the worst they did was to slip through examinations on a slide not previously greased by convention. They may have merited the kicking-out they got; that was for the authorities to say. But whether they deserved the opprobrium, that is for the spirit to say.

Very likely their faces should have burned red; still, should their reputations have been blackened? Now that the smudge has worn off, perhaps we can review the episode for hindsight enlightenment.

Despite several changes of calendars West Point probably hasn't changed. Any academic institution displays man's duality operating in high gear. An annual fray deploys between the graders and the graded. Each side accepts the configuration of symbols, the conflict being waged over marks. Straight A's are coveted, treasured by the player who draws a hand of trumps, envied by the dub who shows a bust. The term examinations which the jackpot depends on deploy into an Armageddon. In this battle of wits, bluffing is an accredited rule of the game. The professors are adept at the ruse, remaining aloof, almost supernal beings; oracles of erudition, their being consists in being known. The examination hall can no more be regarded a spiritual environment than can an international arms conference. Nobody is really there.

Every student knows he must not cheat, and everybody knows the casuistry that defines cheating. But I recall from my own student days a generous friend whose name I have forgot though it is enrolled in heaven. He failed to get the right idea, and being bright and well-informed used to pass crutches from cell to cell for the benefit of the lame and halt. Wholly bereft of honor, he felt a kinship with his fellow mortals menaced by dominions and powers, and yielded to the urge. I esteemed him then, and still do, morally superior to the grimly grinning grinds, those toplofty egotists who carried on the combat according to the rules.

Teacher and pupil of course might meet on a different plane. The scholastic game might be abolished—why not, for it is devitalizing and boring to all concerned. This academic play, which issues imperceptibly into work, might be abandoned. A relationship of coexistence might ensue, a personal bond uniting master and disciple. This would render the ritual of written examinations both superfluous and ridiculous. The prospect, however, seems so remote I regret having suggested it. To encumber a college campus with such freaks would negate its very purpose. Everybody associated with it would be unfitted for the practical pursuits of that world into whose ways education is an initiation.

Why not instead, when the *status quo* palls, effect a minor change in the rules, revising thereby the code of honor?

It has ever been considered honorable to cram the textbook into one's head the night before the crucial test: why not restrict the cramming to only such questions as the student has ascertained beforehand were going to be asked? Is the cribber not more sensible in his preparations than the crammer, his idea more expedient? It saves both midnight oil and one's self the trouble of loading up with needless information.

But this tack, you protest, entails cunning. What of that? We will simply acknowledge cunning as a rule of the game and award the prizes according to that criterion. The craftiest fellow packs them off instead of the most scholarly. But there is the trifle of honor, you insist. But what is this sense of honor, save the will to universalize one's rule? The sense of honor is a purely formal principle, without content when it is pure. You can fill it as you opt. Let's not be so shackled by our dogmas that we suffer the fate of die-hards in what is a supple and slippery world. Cunning is but the growing tip of mechanization anyhow. It yields readily to the induration of the parent stalk. Witness the ease wherewith in bridge the art of finesse got objectified into a science. The alter-egos of the cribbers will soon catch up with them. Next term the professors will be tapping out phony lists of questions and letting them be stolen as regular routine. You have to run faster than an ordinary thief to keep ahead in any game. The ego promptly fits a stylish jacket on its new-born infant, rendering it an accredited member of polite society. This ego appears to be perfectly stable and permanent, among its gifts being our idea of eternity itself. Yet this ego actually is extremely fickle and perfidious. Any man can completely revamp his code of honor overnight and be true to himself the next morning.

Cunning is what should count. The army training camp should heed this appeal. Virtue for the soldier consists in the knowledge of how to outsmart. An officer who sneaks through by cribbing will likely win more for us in the Orient than the intellectual stalwart strutting along with honor outmoded and a rusty creed intact. Cheaters alone may prove a match for the Russians, whose heads are not ground down with excess baggage. In war, General MacArthur has remarked, there is no substitute for victory. Rational superiority doesn't tally unless it can be totted up in chips. The excuse does not count that the foe fights unfairly and flouts the fripperies of civilization. There is no absolutely correct way of accomplishing mass slaughter. No objective order is so stable as we think when we are basking in our own. No spiritual quality attaches to the old rule book nor to the new edition: so why should we boggle over trifles of decorum? Duplicity is a basic ingredient of every game. To win is the basic purpose. To deny this is to aggravate the delusion by doubling it in hypocrisy. The denial, besides, inscribes a pat formula for losing the fight.

Duplicity and pretense sink deep into the roots of every sort of play. Self-deception stalks the knowing subject when he predicates the permanence of his objective world. Pretending that one's chosen constellation of symbols controls the situation is a blunder besetting every Pharisee, the pretense blinding him to what is actually going on and badging him with his distinctive complacency.

To revert to the West Point scandal: why were the authorities so shocked to discover the cheating? The culprits were athletes, and it is generally known that football stars do not shine in the classroom with the same luster as glamorizes them on the gridiron. That these luminaries receive concessions in one coin for benefits they confer in another can scarcely be called a secret, nor that these concessions are scholastic as well as pecuniary. Why did army officers profess not to know what they could have learned on any street corner? Total ignorance of what goes on constitutes the peculiar knowledge of the Pharisee, his assumption being that things behave as he believes.

To put in a good word for the much-maligned cadets: they did no personal harm, their act was nowise immoral. And they were planning an objective service. Swiping the marks was but a means of sweeping the Navy off the field. What does it matter, relative to this end, if eleven lieutenants slip into the Army without knowing that the chemical formula for water is H_2O? Hannibal and Attila and Napoleon didn't know it either. Why pretend to be virtuous in denouncing a fiction no one else is remonstrating against? Such sclerosis of the intellect bodes gloom for us in the next World War. Every game involves pretense, but to pretend that you are not pretending, that is the infinite regress of self-righteous complacency.

Play is where we go when we ride the dualism of mind and body. Play displays the knower in action. This knower is an egotist, resolved on universalizing his objective view. As long as he does nothing about it, never hinting that it is more than a matter of taste, other knowers can rattle off the *de gustibus non est disputandum.* But let an overt action drag the body, if only the tongue, upon the scene, the case is different and disputes do arise. In the physical realm of space-time there just isn't room for a multitude of individuals each of whom has the idea of being the whole thing. Man, having become mindful of himself, finds his mind full of collisions with other minds, which if somatically enacted, will promptly extinguish him body and soul. These must be rendered otiose and harmless, unreal; play is the recipe for releasing a host of egotistic wills, having garbed each in pseudo-idealistic fakements. The body is allowed to perform the part of a beast, but always of a trained beast, often of a delicately restrained beast, but never of a natural beast. Ego snarls a threat at other egos; they crash through the jungle, roaring to their hearts' surfeit; yet all the while these brutes have been tamed, muzzled, and leashed. On the playground the cages can be opened, and egos by virtue of their being organized can be permitted to gore one another without bloody consequences. Their wills behave docilely within an objective ring under the whiplash of law.

Whatever is done in play is done in pretense. Nobody really intends anything. One can imprison his foes, knock them out of action, drag their carcasses from the arena, while spectators howl their glee and vows of vengeance. That it is all in fun gives the savant the right to mimic a savage. It's merely a show, there is no shedding of blood, and the next inning the dead are miraculously restored to life and glut their appetite for carnage. The lion can fiercely bare his teeth, but with safety to the lamb, for his real teeth have been replaced by a set of plates that do not bite. An objective condition declares that victory must remain symbolic. Nothing genuine is won or lost, and a big time is enjoyed by all. Good sportsmanship simply demands that each fictitious beast assent to the fiction. The winner is forbidden to gloat over what is really a sham conquest and the loser to harbor a grudge over a bogus defeat. But play is as confiscatory upon the emotions as the federal income tax. Nobody save the sternest ascetic is apt to pay the extortion in full. The noblest of us secretly dislikes the upstart who consistently drubs him at bridge.

War puts on a full-scale exhibition of this characteristic pretense. What indeed is war but the sport of kings? True, many of the pawns undergo no visible resurrection. But seldom is anybody of actual importance lost, and the casualty totals fall short of the motor toll on the highways during peace. Besides, we will not speak of the dead as being slain; they are just put out of action, like pins on a bowling alley. Their names remain sacred in our annals; gaily we decorate their graves. What more glorious than to vindicate the honor of a sovereign people? Than to die propagating a deathless ideology? You wonder why the miltiary who swallow this should have coughed and choked over a few boys cheating in a classroom quiz.

OPERATION TIGHTROPE

The spirit of man cannot be domesticated within the haunts just described. There is no moral way of juggling such apparatus. Play is neither good nor evil from the viewpoint of spirit. The real self languishes outside the fence, a distinct pole in continual tension with the artifact deployed inside. Occasionally this self may slither across the tightrope to set the situation aright. The real man does not perish despite the toxic doses he must gulp. The real world cannot be obliterated, eschatology always referring to the world of play.

Interference seems called for whenever the real person hears players fretting over freedom. The sole freedom any player can avow lies in altering the rules he is compelled to play by. Such a change may result in a fresh system of determinism but hardly in the negation of determinism itself. Every game as its initial postulate annuls the act of a free person in making decisions of his own. It abrogates the person himself, supplanting him with the soul-body mechanism. The knower must make the will behave according to law in order that the body can be known. If the body violates the rules laid down, that does not show that the will is free but only that it is wicked. Thus the soldier forfeits his birthright as an existential being. He is debased into an incorrigible dogmatist by his oath to defend the Constitution. Thereafter he justifies what his conscience might condemn by the pretext that he has acted under orders. His sole duty is to his team.

This resignation from reality has its advantages, which precisely is the reason men play. People do not honestly want to be free, what they want is to rant about freedom. True freedom burdens one with responsibility. A free man is accountable for his deeds. His acts are himself. But the soldier finds it convenient to be no more guilty of murder than is the gun he fired. Gun and firer are to be regarded as equally mechanical, propelled by an outside force. Neither intended to shoot. In play nobody intends anything. The airmen who dropped bombs on Hiroshima did not intend blowing up thousands of Japanese. Their sortie was done in sport. That was somebody's good idea to terminate the war, and the big idea of war is to win. Every player performs automatically, the smoother the performance the more proficient the player. He is answerable to no moral accusation, he has no cause for regret, he is incapable of sin. But he is incapable of freedom too. The tragedy of mankind lies in too many of its members having abjured the right ever to intend anything at all.

All play organizations portray the same features as the totalitarian state, whatever their compass and importance. The scientific principle of the Uniformity of Nature was well known before it became a metaphysics. A bridge foursome exhibits an identically rigid format and cherishes it with similar solemnity. One unable or unwilling to master the rules of bidding, for instance, is unacceptable as either partner or opponent; the dub has no portion with those who know. The official baseball guide has many times the thickness of the Book of Leviticus. And let any player blaspheme the least jot or tittle of those scriptures, he suffers the anathemas of any heretic. Devoid of a sense of honor, he can expect no mercy from the honorable.

Every performance on the field, at the card table, or the laboratory, serves merely to illustrate the static pattern of the game. This object the players have concocted and therefore know. But its actual embodiments they are powerless to control. Hence any ideology, be it Marxian communism or an amateur prize fight, precipitates a bureacracy as its contribution to culture. Hedged in by a manifold of ordinances, the game must exclude the hazards of chance. Whenever a real contingency is descried through a hole in the blanket, the authorities hastily spin a new rule to plug the gap. The player who has wriggled into it will likely be tossed out because of the discomfiture he has inflicted upon the powers that be. For a rational event to be decided by chance is derogated as a fluke, and to win by a fluke is less dignified than losing. The loser indeed bloats in self-righteousness; with the eternal verities on his side, he soars into the stratosphere. The defeated candidate solemnly asserts he had rather be right than be president. The real man on the sideline gets baffled by the magic that converts a prig into a paragon.

Spiritual man on the tightrope may take a more downright view and express it more drastically than merely to note how sham the freedom extolled in play actually is. Sensing there is no genuine freedom in pottering with the rules, he may propose shattering its objective frame entire, battering it to bits as an obbligato to the retreat to reality. This is a perilous escapade, however. All men desire to know, everyone knows that. And the invader from the spiritual realm is sure to impress as a rank skeptic and an enemy of the human race. A skeptic he is, his warning being that every objective structure prized by man is a swindle and a snare. The fruit of the Tree of Eden exudes a poisonous juice, suitable only for use as an embalming fluid.

We used to play a game, called, after the cry it set up, "Button, Button, Who's Got the Button." The player who was *it* scurried about in the center of a ring, contriving to halt the movement of a rubber disc as it whisked through a maze of shuttling hands, all grasping the cord whereon the coveted object circulated, the idea being to tap the fist that concealed it. Some youngster, after an hour or so, was sure to decide his time was being wasted. He was sure to discover himself trapped in failing to trap the button. Snatching and snarling the string, he would shout in exultation: "Who wants the button anyhow?" Nobody really did. We were all pretending, we were all bluffing one another. That shock invariably broke up the game, for any game is inherently fragile. We then undertook the serious business of cake and ice cream.

Who can tell, the H-bomb or its more dreadful successor may prove of inestimably greater significance than nuclear physicists ever fancied. It may bring to an end the very game it was designed to promote. What does any nation want with the button if, when the fury is spent, no nation remains to redeem it in cake and ice cream? Symbols cease to be authentic if what they symbolize isn't there. Yet finding this out will be a painful experience. Only children do the trick with ease and grace. Getting back home winds an arduous course when you have forgotten where you came from.

A CONCLUSION THE WIND BLEW AWAY

No civilized society extends its welcome to the spoilsport. He appears to despoil the very foundations society rests on.

Long ago there was brought to Jesus an evildoer caught in the act. The Law of Moses decreed that a woman taken in adultery should be stoned, and the Scribes and the Pharisees were there to see that justice was done. Society could not endure with such a transgressor romping in it. What did Jesus say?

Now, Jesus was an exceedingly acute observer. His was a fiercely flaming passion for spiritual reality. Confronted with the question, Jesus stooped down and wrote with his finger in the sand.

The headmen pressed for a judgment. Audibly he did render a verdict. That was recorded: "He that is without sin among you, let him cast the first stone." Then Jesus bent over and wrote in the sand again. He was not drawing pictures. No Jew ever did that.

So far as we are told, this was the only thing Jesus ever wrote. Nobody thought to look what it was. The Scribes and Pharisees did not care. They would not care today. His words the wind blew back into the earth whence they had come.

What did Jesus write? It was nothing the professors of self-knowledge could add to their tomes. It was not written by a man who was mindful of himself.

III

WHAT CAN WE KNOW?

ALL MEN BY NATURE desire to know, Aristotle declared—
which is to say that shepherds want to know the way pedagogues know. When a philosopher speaks of knowledge, he
means objective knowledge.

Knowledge of one's self, for example, must conform to
the standard object created by that knowledge. As known, you
are determined by that object's being defined, just as your
reputation in town is determined by what people say about
you. Being a member of a community, you are the creation
of the community's busybodies. The concept of man fabricates
the container every man must fit into. This concept is the
product of philosophic gossip. Man as an objective entity is
what the tattlers have told off.

Of these none has been so gravely listened to as Plato.
Plato sought a clue to the nature of man in the constitution
of the state. The individual citizen was to be conceived as
a minified republic, the state as a magnified man where alone
the individual could discover and realize himself. Thus
Plato's anthropology was a reflection cast by his politics; he
squinted at man as at an image seen in a mirror.

Cassirer, a recent reporter of what man can know about himself, needs a mirror of greater dimensions than Plato's. He depicts man as an image shaped by his entire culture. "In language, in religion, in art, in science," he writes, "man can do no more that to build up his own universe—a symbolic universe that enables him to understand and interpret, to articulate and organize, to synthesize and universalize his human experience. . . . Human culture taken as a whole may be described as a process of man's progressive self-liberation. Language, art, religion, science, are various phases in this process. In all of them man discovers and proves a new power—the power to build up a world of his own, an 'ideal' world." *

The arts and the sciences, in this view, make the crib the child that is *you* is cradled in, wherein you are to grow into a living embodiment of that culture itself. I do not quote Cassirer because he has said anything original and startling, but because he has expressed a prevailing notion in a clear and emphatic manner. Cassirer means you, and if you do not like what he thinks of you, my advice is to look no further for a more agreeable concept: decide instead that no such object can be adequate, no objective knowledge will do.

The acquisition of knowledge is tricky business, especially the knowledge of knowledge itself. Every knower is a distinct and discrete individual. His baby is his own. But the crib he swaddles his infant in must serve equally the offspring of countless other knowers. Each knower's task would be immeasurably lightened, were he the only one on earth. Then he could know exactly as he wanted to know, without other

* *An Essay on Man* by Ernst Cassirer. Doubleday Anchor Books, Doubleday and Company, Inc., Garden City, N. Y., pp. 278 and 286.

knowers' interference. Knowing is a private, solitary enterprise. Still, knowing purports to achieve absolute universality,
just as if the universe were not bustling with obstreperous
others, each a producer, with parental affection for the children of his own ideas.

Whenever you affirm, *I know so-and-so to be true*, you
intend your assertion to be true for everybody. Your knowing
organ is not satisfied with the sound of its own pipes. Your
voice is ready to summon arms to enforce its edicts, rational
arguments first, then if these fail to persuade, a more telling
force. Knowing pertains to the head. Retracting a mind-made-
up involves loss of face. One can yield the certitude of what
he sees without such a sacrifice. Seeing is not believing,
despite the proverb. Your face does not get lost in the mask
of a blush when you frankly admit that the stick slanting
beneath the surface of the pond is not really bent, though you
saw it so. But to change your mind requires an act of
capitulation less nimbly and humbly accomplished. It is hard
to crawl out of a hole you have dug for yourself.

So-and-so's being true composes an objective world. To
alter what has been ordained objective destroys the object
and attacks the knower who has made it his sanctuary. Your
known edifice is the one and only, its objectivity certain and
voracious. Upon its universal validity you insist, to it you
are committed. Why these extremes of unique individuality
and encompassing universality happen to meet in the human
ego, that is an ultimate problem, the radical source of man's
tragic predicament; that is the devil of it. That they do
makes every man potentially a soldier. Their congruence
leads in academic speculation to the view that this ego possesses a transcendental character. On lower levels it is respon-

sible for our collective woes. Luckily we are likely to be rescued from the crisis by the weakness of the flesh and its reluctance to leap into the pit at the vaultings of the knower. The least amiable of us is still better than he knows, the body shrinking from the task of proving that the mind is right. *So what*, the soma quacks at the psyche's wild geese.

Objective knowledge can be formulated and transmitted only through verbal statements or other symbolic means: these are what it consists in. But where do the symbols come from, that coalesce into objects?

Traced to their native lair, all concepts are found to dwell in what Plato called the realm of ideas, what Santayana calls the realm of essence: that vast celestial dictionary where all the words ever thought of are contained, and more unthought of. Into this thicket of infinite possibility the knowing subject goes gunning. The quest for knowledge entails a game of pursuit and capture, the object being the quarry and the subject the hunter. When a trap is sprung or a shot reaches its mark, the chaser exulting cries, "I know"; his capture is brought to earth and possessed in this very ejaculation. Thereupon the prey is wound about with sufficient predicates to insure a specimen of rational explanation and valid knowing. Thereby objectification takes place and the subject rejoices in his mastery. He is owner and keeper of what he has caught.

Such a triumph is accompanied by a sense of self-liberation which Cassirer extols. But this might seem to be mere self-indulgence inasmuch as the entire transaction has occurred within the hunter's own mind: notwithstanding the realm of essence being universal and accessible to everybody, a free-for-all. Does the object not issue solely from the subject's ideas and the relations he fixes among them? And from his expectation that the captive will stay fixed? Other knowers applauding the exploit do not modify the character of the object, but rather augment the number of selves being indulged.

Kant, whose disciple Cassirer was, declared that we know phenomena alone, that is, whatever fits the traps we have sprung. Phenomena—the Kantian term for objects—consist of the symbolic constructs we interpose between ourselves and reality. Our knowledge of these appearances, systematized in a science, can be certified as objective only by reality itself remaining unknown, reality being Kant's thing-in-itself. But the real world, precisely, is what we want to know about. The hunter, unless he is an idle sportsman, is out after food. All he gets is game, interesting to stuff into a topic for table conversation but nothing to nourish the body. Thus knowledge, according to Kant, is unreal, fundamentally a diversion: the transfer of ideas across the hyphen linking subject and object, accompanied by the assertion of *I know*. The really intended target of knowledge remains tantalizingly elusive, a mysterious X, the thing-in-itself. Knowledge deals with shadows, whose outlines are projected from ourselves, ectoplasm congealing only in absence of light.

Since knowledge is phenomenal, its symbols never penetrating to the real thing, objectivity grows more impressive as its contents become more abstract and make slighter pretensions of contact with existence: in mathematics, for example. Mathematical truth is the height all truth aspires to. Everybody save downright incorrigibles acquiesces in its elementary principles; few egotists seek attention on the grounds that two plus two equal five, and there never has been a global war to test the multiplication table. This con-currence generates utility, and utility is the sternest criterion of truth. The mathematical sciences prove eminently useful. They enable us to manipulate Nature to our convenience, technology being so convenient that we overlook the enigma of how it comes to pass.

THE SEARCH FOR KNOWLEDGE

Can the hunter make of itself the hunted, the searcher search for itself? What happens when the knowing subject is stood on its head and made the object of the knowing process?

Turned upside down, the subject vanishes in the somersault. The subject is not to be caught in the trap, for the subject is the trap. David Hume could detect in the subject no stable and statable entity whatever. When the beam of attention is focused upon it, the subject dissipates into a stream of possibilities with no actuality emerging from the torrent to be hooked and landed. Self-knowledge—taking the subject for an object—plunges the taker into an act of epistemological suicide, the gun blowing the gunner out of his wits.

What if the self be conceived as something more substantial than the knower, the real self or the person? Can this whole of mind and body be made an object of a part? The answer is that this has been done divers times and oft. This is what the psychologies are about.

Psychology, however, suffers the character of all scientific knowledge. The object floats apart from the subject; the object is what the subject has snared and subdued. The self is netted in somebody's idea of the self. The self thus becomes what a person ought to be, what he is condemned to be, by involvement in the idea of his nature. Stripped nude to sit as a philosopher's model, the real self is reduced to a thought. A fugitive in the studio, the self seeks refuge in the abode of the subconscious, which but asserts the impossibility of the conscious knowledge of one's self. Within the confines of the subconscious the banished self languishes uneasily, occasionally upsetting the easel and causing the human being to appear nonrational to his executioner and plaguing every rationalizer with the same anxiety he proposes to lenify in his patient.

Any symbolic structure designed to nail the real self down and to render him amenable to manipulation constitutes a psychology. Sundry psychologies are always being packaged for popular favor and acceptance, merchandise that is soon shopworn and cut-priced. Every psychology aims to hitch to the star of universality. That few of them even get off the ground is due to a double difficulty: the element in man that represents reason, the subject, cannot be objectified at all, and the real self assumes with equal grace any form imposed upon him. Thus man-as-he-knows-himself shows a bewildering variety of shapes and sizes. He has been depicted as a noble figure and a depraved one; he has been execrated as a mass of perdition and worshiped as the number-one divinity within his own temple. Calvinists declare him powerless to make up his own mind, New Thought boasts he can make up God's. Every textbook man seems somewhere else when you look for him on the street.

But real man is here and now. Man is energy, man is power. Power is what makes things happen, power makes the world go round. Power is but our way of saying the world does so. In the objectification of the dynamic forces of Nature reason strikes a snag. Power looms as a surd. There is no symbol of it except the unknowable X. There is nothing we can say about power besides denouncing it as demonic: power corrupts and so forth. Its effects we can measure, but for power itself there is no accounting. This dynamic within the self we call the will, more occultly the libido. This will is necessarily evil.

Accordingly everything in man below the neck must be excogitated into a foreign invader, hostile to his soul. Goodness pertains to the head. Kant held that an act cannot be good if you desire to do it. To defend the standards hoisted by reason you engage in relentless civil war. The will and its cohorts—impulses and emotions—need perpetual shackling and shaking out, or enlightenment as the current phrase prefers it. To grant this ancient foe a fling is the tactics of the Freudians. But this is merely a ruse of battle, the same strategy with a minor shift. The flesh still bears the brand of an alien; the flesh contends against a higher authority. The ego may be flexible in its judging, sometimes appearing as indulgent and even fraternizing with an admitted adversary. The subject may welcome any object in its camp. But what the subject cannot do is to adopt the object as a free and equal member of a personal self. Humpty Dumpty cannot be put together again by another Humpty Dumpty even though the latter has a Ph.D. in psychology. The subject-object dichotomy is not to be transformed into a real person by releasing the rabble at one of the poles.

Any objective view of man, be it Calvinistic or Freudian, debases him into a congeries of instincts and tendencies. Whether he succumbs to their motivation or staves it off, is of slight real significance. These forces, the psychologist maintains, can be maneuvered through education so that an individual may behave the way he ought, which means the way the educator deems expedient, that being the way a select company of his peers regards proper.

In this enterprise psychology merely hit the trail blazed by the more natural sciences. Physical Nature had already been brought to terms by a battery of push buttons. Science perforce conceives all of Nature as a maelstrom of matter in whose toils we are caught and from which the knowing subject is estranged. The knower regards Nature from an altitude ranging from disdain to dread. Though theoretically the objective attitude is impassive, the knower faces Nature with disquiet, with a terror due to the nothingness of the ego itself. This bogey which psychologists endeavor to conjure away is precisely the anxiety the ego conjures up. Rationalization encounters an impasse in the flux: vanity of vanities, all is perishable, Nature is change. Release from her clutches is the purpose of philosophy and the liberation it jubilates over.

Asceticism, therefore, is implicit in the venture of knowledge. Action must be avoided for in action the body necessarily takes part. A dogged thinker is left eventually with a single action possible, that of thumbing his nose at the smelly mess. To get out of it, however, he will toe the mark and play submissive to his fate. Finally the Stoics discerned how extremes can meet: the gestures of thumb and toe are one and the same. The wise man makes peace with his antagonist through yielding to the inexorable. He wrings from outer catastrophe the consolation of an inner victory. His banners flutter through a vacuum. Magically he saves his soul. He regales himself with Bertrand Russell's *A Free Man's Worship*, then seeks further solace in mathematics. His is a crown for which the Universe has furnished neither gold nor gems. Freedom lies in being free of everything save one's ego, and that ego reigns supreme and exultant.

Nature-knowledge of this traditional Stoic type underwent a kind of Freudian revolution some centuries before Freud. This revolution was settled by the treaty we now call science. Having overtly smeared Nature as the enemy, may man not covertly woo her back into a shaky alliance? Why cannot the material world, though weighed and duly flayed, actually be used? Why not turn that despised domain into an instrument to serve the interests of those bodily culprits that keep sneaking back into the subject, upsetting its repose? Man had long opined that in his flight from the material realm he was entitled to pack along snippets which had been isolated, sprayed with the perfumes of contemplation and rendered aseptic in works of art and sacraments. Consecration to celestial ends performed a work of magic. Such sacred objects became symbols and carriers of value, receptacles of the ideal. Why should monks be so tight-fisted and stiff-necked with their prizes? Why not pass the good word around? Why not embalm the whole works?

Plato and Hobbes had dubbed the natural world bad; Locke and Rousseau started calling it good. What an era of difference an adjective made! All that was needed to exhibit Nature beneficent was to let out the belt and to stretch the harness of symbols which girdled her loins; to extend the compass of objectification and invent new clamps to render Nature amenable to formulation. The real world and the material world were soon being thought identical, though "material" was no more than a concept of man's mind.

Knowledge is power, knowledge is utility. Knowledge gets

devoted to butchering its victim and dressing the carcass to suit the customers' tastes. Why not?—philosophy for centuries had adjudged Nature unworthy to associate with; we are damned anyhow, so why not have fun on our descent to the bad place? Certainly science has put on a gala performance. The game still waxes exciting. The fearful asceticism latent in the carnival is muted by its superficial hilarity. The asceticism becomes dimly audible, however, to those on the receiving end of aerial bombs. Ascetic the escapade inevitably is. Men are never so resolved on punishing themselves as when they are bent on the gratification of desire, if desire be divorced from the self. The severest cruelty we can inflict on ourselves lies in the abnegation of what we are.

It is a baffling phenomenon that man's search for knowledge has eventuated in a craze and clamor for everything besides knowledge. The uproar that is civilization hawks only the fruits of the Tree, the useful and the pleasurable. The explanation is quite simple.

All men do not desire to know, despite the excellence of the dictum. Most men find this desire fleeting and feeble. The ascetic pledge it entails is too austere for them to sign. Self-knowledge requires self-mutilation, self-castration. The subject must be kept pure, but the powers threatening it with invasion are not to be whisked away by denigrating them as impure. And even if the knower succeeds in threshing itself clean of taint, what is left? So divested, this knower runs head-on into a contradiction. The drive for knowledge, turned upon the subject, plunges the knower into the limbo of non-existence and rams him into the sink of skepticism. Man cannot know himself, for there is nothing to do the knowing. There is no substantial subject whatsoever. Denuded of objective furnishings, the subject dissolves into an apparition, merely the reflector of images it has cast.

The mystics, grasping the nettle of nothingness, affirm that the subject is capable of such infinite expansion as to contain in a single gulp the totality of being, becoming identical with the ideal object it extrudes. The subject can swell to assimilate this objective absolute when it be taken as a whole. In this case subject and object become indistinguishable, the consciousness of possessing lapsing into consciousness of being. This contention may be valid enough, as long as the object is conceived in terms of the utmost generality, the limits of the realm of possibility grasped as the necessities of thought. Then the object secures a formal fit with the generator that has brought it forth. Ideas, like property, are objects we possess. But any form of property, including ideas, may possess us, establishing an identity of the thinker and his thoughts. Consciousness and what one is conscious of may fuse into that condition of unity prized as the mystic consciousness. The mystic is truly possessed when his possession is the Absolute itself.

But such ballooning of the inner man is bound to deal harshly with his outer counterpart. The cruelty is scarcely to be mitigated by the excuse that it is self-inflicted. The dynamic factors of human nature are nonobjective; they cannot be articulated with the rational subject whatever its objective system. Thus the mystic must take constant pains to suppress his feelings and will. His abode is exclusively his mind; he nullifies every vestige of bodily existence, even time and space. He loiters in eternity. The bystander, however, observes that the mystic's hulk, despite the mauling it receives, persists in hanging around. The ordinary man therefore is

content to let his subject squat comfortably and settle somewhere between infinity and zero, to plump between Hume
and the Hindus, satisfied alike not to know nothing and not
to aspire to knowing everything. Most of us shy away from
making knowing a full-time job. We are apt to settle for
just sufficient knowledge to make sense of our games and to
make ourselves respectable. We manage to be normal—that
is, to resemble one another. There are patent drawbacks to
the dive into mysticism. The philosopher must eat, his stomach
sustains a tenuous contact with reality. He has a trencher
stake in existence and is put on the spot three times a day.

Besides, we remain persons howsoever nebulous our reality
becomes. There is another kind of knowledge that corrects
the cognition dependent on concepts. The spirit has valid experiences of knowing; this nonobjective knowledge we may
deny, yet we realize positively the lack of it in the scourge
of nothingness. We wander through our palace of symbols,
feeling destitute and homeless. Something is wrong: man's
nature has been violated and rumbles in a wreck. Modern
man may miss the point when told he has been deperson-
alized; still, that point is stabbing poignantly at his heart.

He elbows through a concourse but stumbles on no community. He rattles in the crowd, a solitary atom endowed with
inalienable rights, but those rights evaporate into ghostly
figments when he essays more than to think about them. Each
of his fellow men is said to be likewise unique and a precious
jewel in the coffer of an infinite mind, but in the aggregate
those jewels make a mess that stinks. He listens to advice
aplenty on how to pursue his highest self-interest, yet his
mentors seem to be doing a better job on that head than he
can do. Love soothes his ear—a lyric vocable that word, love

—but what a disappointment when it implies the aping of Hollywood. Modern man's hopes are pricked by the mention of home; then his own home dispels the sentiment. His heart is warmed by the sound, God, until God gets demoted into a conservator of values or the author of the Constitution. Promises of security entice him from the doldrums, but the breeze dies when security proves to be merely the promise he will not starve in his old age. Modern man—this ordinary fellow, you and I—resigns in confusion: where shall he seek knowledge of himself and of his quandary? Can he seek security if insecurity be inherent in the very act of seeking? May he not find what he is looking for by abandoning the quest?

Let this modern man retreat to exactly where he is. If he isn't there already, let him go home. A child lives there too. The clatter of tiny feet may be heard ticking up the stairs, through the door. "Mommie, Mommie," cries the child, gasping in fright, of what modern man knows full well. "Here I am, what do you want?" Mother replies, "Nuthin', I just wanted to be sure you were there." Down the little person toddles, a glad step at a time, back to the yard, at peace with the world again.

Though his specific self-knowledge is scant, the child senses a reality that surpasses understanding. Woe unto him through whom offenses against this come; it were better for him that a millstone were hanged about his neck and he be cast into the sea, than that he should offend one of these little ones. This offense is committed in any offensive of self-knowledge.

THE OBJECTIVE WORLD

The autonomous and atomistic subject takes its stand apart from existence, apart from the body that implicates man in time and space. Whatever the subject is cognizant of constitutes its object, and any configuration of these an objective order. Such symbolic structures the ego can spawn without number, each guaranteed adequate for the interpretation of being.

Any object gleaned from the field of possibility and groomed as knowledge may shuttle from the objective side of the fence across into the subject. Here it becomes assimilated, henceforth to rank as a necessary postulate of thought and to be thought with instead of about. Thus the subject gets equipped with such tools as axioms, categories, self-evident truths, creeds. Thus are eyes evolved through which the subject can survey new lands to be explored and exploited. A flood of sensations continually breaks upon it, apparently from without; the subject need not be helpless under such incursions. Through its ideas and the orientation they afford, the storms can be subdued and the winds rendered law-abiding and put to turning mills. We can screen ourselves from the impact of existence by imposing upon it an objective configuration.

Concepts without intuitions are empty, intuitions without concepts are blind, said Kant. True. No intuition can stay blind and continue to be sensed, and a wholly empty concept is incapable of being thought of. Certainly there are countless concepts no human mind has ever entertained, and just as likely we have subtle intuitions we neglect because no knower has seized upon them and given them names. Probably we miss much that fails to fit into the objective world we have figured out which serves to protect us from misfits.

Knowing consists in fitting the given into the systems we give. When you perceive that the grass is green, you enlighten the impression, and designating the grass as the source of the color marks further progress in enlightenment. The idea of green, of course, can be applied not only to that particular patch but to the leaves of the tree as well. It is a universal, and as such it exhibits relations to other universals. These relations need not be invoked by impressions from without but may be induced by thought itself: green is not red, for example. This difference is not entirely dependent on sense for its detection: it can be defined in terms of vibrations in a medium you never sense at all. Green soon gets fixed in meaning. It graduates into an object and an instrument of knowledge itself. A concept once settled upon is free to go on the search of further data to fill it, settling them peremptorily.

Some concepts find little trouble in asserting their prerogatives in the objective world. They seem natural-born to rule, and the flow of events is soon brimming their cups. Such concepts as green, tree, chair, appear so objectively reliable that children operate with them handily. These are called by Northrop * concepts by intuition. The availability of others, Northrop's concepts by postulation, seems more remote and adventitious. The objectivity of these must be accredited by other concepts, accruing secondhand from their status in the system within which they are domesticated. Such an idea as wave-vibration-in-the-ether would be one such, inasmuch as no knower can be expected ever to have seen the object

* See *The Logic of the Sciences and the Humanities* by F. S. C. Northrop. The Macmillan Company, New York, 1947, Chapter V.

of his discourse. Still a knower born blind might depose that the ether yielded the only reasonable notion of green. The hitching of concepts and intuitions to make knowledge is probably a less trim and prim affair than Northrop makes it. Offhand it would seem that green is a concept whose objectivity is attested past doubting, and that such a concept as the Holy Trinity must be held longer under the spout for filling. Still, a color-blind bishop might hold otherwise.

Objective knowledge is based on concepts; it is symbolic. Yet something more is required than the utterance of the vocables themselves. To be admitted into the select cognitive set a concept must be intended as cognitive, objectivity being acquired in a sacrament of noetic baptism. A concept cannot function as a simple sign, like a dog's yelp. The object of which one is conscious must be consciously superior to any random inkling of it. The idle greeting of sensa as they drift by, in the spirit of companionship, falls short of knowledge and fails to transform the source of such experience into what is known. Cultivated listeners pay slight and only scornful attention to such twaddle. Plato distinguished two sorts of knowledge: one kind he dubbed opinion, the loose popular chatter referred to, which differed little from the jabber of monkeys. Such talk was unworthy of the ears of a philosopher whose drums were attuned to rational language alone.

But, one might ask, how can opinion and rational knowledge be told apart, except that the magical formula, *I know,* has been pronounced over the latter? This sleight-of-mind wields a mighty stick. When you know and know that you know, your idea is transmogrified into a credible object. It is yours and nobody else's. You are going places with it. You are captain of your cruise, no longer wafted by winds of popular opinion. You plume yourself on your knowledge; you're justified in fighting for it, entitled to be snobbish about it. But—the other fellow can elevate his opinions by the same twist of the head.

This *I know* you pronounce so glibly certifies a concept as standard equipment in the subject itself. It makes a quasi-mystic of the knower. Symbols are thereby transferred from the objective side of the dyad to the subjective. So appropriated by the knower, ideas prosper as beliefs, world-views, causes, standards by which all else is judged and to which reality must conform or suffer rejection and calumny.

That is the devil of it: concepts which on one occasion are objects of conscious cognition are whisked on the magic carpet of knowing to the inwards of the subject. Here they direct attention further afield, becoming unconscious methods of construing whatever else is wished. Ideas are smelted into weapons of evaluation. Objective knowledge ceases to be an end striven for and becomes the instrument through which reality is interpreted, and distorted, to serve the rapacious ego. Loci of utility are staked out in Nature, by a single subject or by a gang of subjects. Spheres of objectification are plotted, oases in Nature's desert, clearings in her chaos, fairylands of culture. Civilization comes about through the subject's amalgamation with clusters of ideas, priorly extracted from the labyrinth of knowledge, the amalgam becoming an arsenal of tools. Such an idea-bloated subject struts as a realist. He can be certain he sees things as they are for he sees only what he has eyes to see. Truth consists in protruding his ego flat as a yardstick whereon everyone else is laid out and measured.

This pseudo mystic might resent being called a metaphy-

sician, hardly knowing what was meant. He does not know
how the cosmos is to be explained by that system of atomism,
determinism, matter, and energy which those who do know
have riveted upon it. The ordinary materialist would barely
snag a passing mark in even a Russian high school; still he
is quick to envisage the universe in materialistic terms.
Scientism is a lens he has bought ready made; the spectacles
fit so neatly on his nose he has forgot what things looked like
without them. Hence he can be relied on to overlook or to
explain away what fails to jibe with his determinations. Such
incompatibles he will charge to error or to superstition. He
is the judge of what's what.

The normal American can scarcely be stretched into a
social philosopher, his sole concern with society being to
wangle from it all he can get. He does not know the economic
sphere as Adam Smith knew it, or Karl Marx—indeed, he
has never read a line of either. But he does know for sure
that one was right and the other was wrong. Disciples need
not study their masters and know for themselves. All they
need is to get the proper authority lodged in their brains,
and the ideology will machine the process of sorting their
fellows into sheep and goats.

In this wise, corpora of objective knowledge are transformed into criteria of judgment. Invariably judgment is
predicated upon knowledge, as any judge is prompt to inform
you. All judgments being equally objective, conflict among
them leaves no recourse but to fight it out. Whether this mode
of administering judgment be lenient or ferocious, depends
on many factors. Within each of us there lingers a trace of
the real person who is averse to judging at all. This personal
self extrudes as a surd in any regimented society, impressing

stalwart citizens as a menace and better off in jail. So among
those who do judge the temper of judgment varies according
to the tension between the judging subject and those nonobjective forces of his nature originally at odds with what
he has made himself. These powers boil and churn within
him. Their energy is ready to be directed to any end, their
voltage fluctuating from man to man, and within the individual himself on how deeply he is moved.

One point is certain: whatever be the conglomeration of
ideas gumming the subject, that man is an egotist. Though his
cherished ideology be that of human brotherhood, he will
express this egotistically. You may heartily endorse his
doctrine of love. But you hardly want him to begin loving
you, especially if you happen to be on the suspicious side of
his favorite curtain.

Every egotist knows. When a high head of steam gets piped
into his subjective center, he bulges into a bag of convictions.
He rages valorous and volcanic in the prosecution of causes.
If your pets frolic amiably with his, you applaud his con-
scientiousness. Togetherness becomes a synonym of rectitude.
His egotism redounds to your own. You may join his team,
squelching a pressure which tomorrow may squirt in envy
and split the alliance.

It is indisputable that people can be classified on the basis
of beliefs that activate their egos. It is incontestable, too,
that a sanguinary struggle goes on without cease for the
possession of men's souls, and that this struggle makes what
historians write about. What may not appear so plain is that
this uproar blows only from a brainstorm. It is of no real
consequence and is utterly devoid of cosmic relevance. The

stature of man is unaffected by inflating the bladder of his ego.

There is a species of conversion that substitutes one objective configuration for another within the sanctum of the subject. This is merely swapping idols. This type of conversion is superficial though we mobilize the army and navy to bring it to pass. Its superficiality is independent of whether the ideas involved pertain to theology, economics, astronomy, or ichthyology—it is conceivable that a nation might go to war to confirm its theory on the right way to catalogue fish. People so converted are the same mechanisms they were before. A lever has been shifted; they recite a different creed. The washed brain belongs to the same man, even if the laundering is done in our own tub. A communist can get converted to a Catholic, the single perceptible change being his line of talk. The dogmatic fascist makes an equally obnoxious democrat though his harangues be copied from another book. For man really to be born again implies more drastic cleansing than a brain bath.

Every objective world lacks something, which is what the knower himself lacks who institutes it. Ineluctably an intellectual contraption, any objective whatever lacks existence. The conceptual realm of contemporary physics, for example, consists of a four-dimensional continuum that is not to be perceived nor even imagined. It is so thoroughly ideal that it can be manipulated only through mathematical sorceries. But is any objective not similarly remote, the constructs of theoretical sciences being but more patently so? The object of every subject is necessarily ideal, just as the ideal is undeniably objective from the cognitive point of view.

It is undeniable too that objectivity, whatever its scope, isolates and alienates the knower. There can also be no doubt that the subject-object constellation generates an estrangement from the spiritual person, from the real self. The knower-known artificer comes to birth on the bed of man's egocentricity; it makes man self-centered. Real man is not so at all, real man seeking and welcoming another, the Thou, to exist in communion with himself. True, the ego sets about to meet half-willingly a need it cannot wholly eradicate, gathering togetherness, founding organizations, each to fulfill a purpose. But that other self is never to be fabricated out of clay, and the statuary proves frustrating to its sculptor.

No object of his own devising can adequately contain what man contains within himself. This we seem to realize in our stealthy expectation that whatever is objective must somehow hurt. We are prepared to suffer for our ideals. We look for an element of the objectionable in everything objective. When you are solemnly asked if you want to know the truth, you brace yourself for a shock: more than likely it is cancer. The teeth of the saw of knowledge cut against the grain. To pant for an ideal, if that ideal be authentic, resembles a dog's baying for the moon: the object is unattainable. The God modern man worships bypasses man's outstretched hands and lets him have it in the neck. Thus the freedom the subject boasts of in its flight into nothingness turns into determinism and brute necessity. The ego succumbs to the servitude of its own creations.

Whatever be certified objective is certain to wound and to lacerate. That is how we know it is truly objective. The trek of knowledge cuts an ascetic trail, though the half-mystified need not follow the whole way into the monastery. Being strictly objective puffs the pride of the pure scientist and conscientious journalist. That one's emotions do wry one's judgment is inescapable. But these emotions are inescapable too. Man cannot flee his finite situation. When his will is exiled from the scene, that will comes skulking back, a hungry beast. Whenever the objective self-asserter howls about the facts, get set for a load of dirt. Hatred is the distinctive emotion of intellectual man. *Woe unto him that striveth with his Maker.**

"The reading from the vantage of a distant star of the capital letters of our earthly life," wrote Nietzsche, "would perchance lead to the conclusion that the earth was the especially ascetic planet, a den of discontented, arrogant, and repulsive creatures, who never get rid of a deep disgust of themselves, of the world, of all life, and did themselves as much hurt as possible out of the pleasure in hurting— presumably their one and only pleasure. . . . These two phenomona, science and the ascetic ideal, both rest on the same basis, the basis of the same over-appreciation of truth, and consequently they are necessarily allies. A certain impoverishment of life is the presupposition of the latter as of the former—add, frigidity of the emotions, slackening of the tempo, the substitution of dialectic for instinct, seriousness impressed on mien and gesture. . . . Almost everything that we call 'higher culture' is based upon the spiritualizing and intensifying of cruelty. The seeker of knowledge operates as an artist and glorifier of cruelty, in what he compels his spirit to perceive against its own inclination, and often enough against the wishes of his heart:—he forces it to say Nay, where he would like to affirm, love and adore. . . .

* Isaiah 45:9.

In every desire for knowledge there is a drop of cruelty.
. . . There is the not unscrupulous readiness of the spirit
to deceive other spirits and dissemble before them—the
constant pressing and straining of a creating, shaping, change-
able power: the spirit enjoys therein its craftiness and its
variety of disguises, it enjoys also its feeling of security
therein." *

GETTING ON IN THE WORLD

"In the beginning," said Anaxagoras, "all things were
mixed together; then came the understanding and created
order."

That aboriginal state of affairs, however, persists even
though ordered to desist. Cosmetics reach only the skin and
so does order. The chaos may be swept outside the door of
man's tidy objective world. Still there it is, the disgusting
thing-in-itself, slush he must slop through whenever he leaves
the house. And leave he must as often as he ventures upon
action.

That men are moved by their emotions has always wailed
the despair of world-designers. Yet what else is there to move
them, what's to move the order-creator himself if not his
emotions? By what other means is he to make effective the
dominance he claims for the understanding? Ideas are never
dynamic in themselves. They must be propelled by the
muscles of the thorax even to get out of the head. Ideas must
be put across. A path must be shoveled for them through the
mud and mire. Whenever you intone, *I know,* you have

* Friedrich Nietzsche, *The Genealogy of Morals,* pp. 121 and 167, and *Beyond
Good and Evil,* pp. 156, 158, and 159. Modern Library, Random House, Inc.,
New York.

indentured yourself to the business end of a spade. You are committed to demonstrating how right you are. That means work, for the primeval matrix wherein power is spontaneous has been alienated in the act of knowing. Power never penetrates to an objective order. Your conception may exceed in truth, beauty, and goodness any previously conceived, but rolling it around in your own mind will get you no further than rolling off a log. You have to apply to Nature for help, to corral and inveigle her to play your game. Your power lies in deflecting natural forces according to the lines you know.

Ideally it is a shame that you have to act, it's a scandal that the existential world manifests a temporal character. To yield to the infamy without voicing a protest disgraces a thinker. To do a good thing without knowing it is a good thing transgresses the principles of ethics. Virtue is knowledge; virtue must be unnatural, the virtuosity of an idea. Plato despised the creative talents of the poets, bundling them with soothsayers, on the ground that their insights were not consciously gained. They may have hit the nail on the head but they used the wrong hammer. Myths to be entertainable must be deliberately recognized as myths, like Plato's famous own. Knowledge is the best of everything—but whose knowledge? Socrates endeavored to mitigate the palpable egotism of his program by admitting that he knew nothing, knowing only that he did not know. His condemnation of acting on instinct he softened by not acting at all, thus elevating the idler into a paragon of rectitude. His guardian voice never urged him on but consistently dissuaded him from attempting anything, admonishing him to take it out in talking.

The mandate of reason remains invulnerable: stick to your

principles though this means being stuck in the mud; never do wrong. This mandate has persisted as the prime excellence of every Pharisee: goodness consists in the shunning of evil. The examined life turns into an empty one. Vitality shrinks with the ascendancy of the head. One is doomed to the grooves of an objective order. The sole action approved is the noble one of going around in circles. Organic and psychic power vary inversely. The ego craves certainty and security; the nearest it can approach this condition is for nothing to happen.

To declare the ideal to be real does confer on man a consciousness of independence and a sense of superiority. It liberates the mind from the whirlpool of the unintelligible, through ignoring the waters that cover the earth. Our ideas forge useful tools for controlling events. But our knowledge, however useful, remains restricted to symbols, and when knowledge aspires to reach reality, it expires in magic. What we really want gets volatilized in a vague devotion to progress within an otiose realm of values where we can never possibly be. What we really are vanishes in the vanity of becoming conscious of it. Self-consciousness tears us to pieces. It must be got rid of and our riven parts seamed together. Cultural activities are designed to do just this. The individual is enabled to submerge his ego, to dissolve it in a solvent that is not itself. Amusements afford a way of losing one's self. We are entertained by entering for the nonce into what is not ourselves. Solitary cell-dwellers conspire to quarry from their walls materials for a circus where all may watch a gladiatorial combat or a TV show. The egotist must locate other egotists to alleviate his loneliness. He must unblock his will, shriveling in inanition and numb from boredom, by making it tributary to a mighty stream.

The tighter the knots we have tied ourselves in, the tougher the collectivity we total up. One object for all subjects, one purpose single and indivisible, a correct ideology with the edges of individuality snipped off, an objective universe of not-to-be-questioned validity—that is a spendid definition of totalitarianism.

But people who seek refuge from their private miseries in ganging up must have another gang opposing them to knock down. How else can truth be ratified? It is grand to get together but this means getting an adversary on the run; how can grandeur be exhibited but in winning? To rescue yourself from nihilism, you have to annihilate somebody else.

A dire alternative compels us to choose between extinction through boredom and coming to a semblance of life in extinguishing our enemies. Clearly then the ideal of universal peace should be abolished, for its achievement might well abolish us. Those bombs may prove equally fatal whether they fall on us or we drop them on the Russians. In the latter event, by wiping out our foe we annul our own purpose in living by bringing it to fruition. Our will dies of starvation when there is no hostile will to feed on. What indeed shall it profit a nation if it gain the whole world and lose its own soul?

A dismal prospect? Yes, were there not an alternative to the alternatives mentioned. We are free any time as spiritual beings to choose reality. But if we want to get on in the real world, we have to get out of the counterfeits.

MAN AS SPIRIT

To be spirit is to be what you really are. In relation to the subject-object setup, spirit must be envisaged as the polar opposite. Spirit is no thinker, although spirit does think. Spiritual knowledge is not scientific; still it is valid. Spirit's world is nonobjective, yet that world exists. Spirit merges into unity the emotional and volitional factors of man's nature, distinguished from reason by reason. Spirit is simply the person, in the existential situation, in a definite here and now. And the person is revealed only by his participation in that situation.

Spirit can be known solely in association and communion with others like himself. The spiritual, however, is never to be identified with any possible collectivism, the spiritual community entailing no fusion of members. No matter how intimate the contact, togetherness obtains among entities that are real in themselves. If love be romanticized into a mystic or monistic identity of lovers, that love is egocentric, the romantic's love of himself. True love implies the coexistence of those concerned, being a one among many.

Spirit cannot be spotted as an object in any objective order the ego generates. Thus spirit has properly been banished from laboratories of science where he would only annoy as an intruder. No more can spirit be overtaken in such impersonal spheres as business and politics. It merely befuddles us to regard economic and political relations as moral ones.

Spirit is not to be opposed to the material, egotistical being the correct antithesis of spiritual. Spirit should never be sicked on the body to start a dog fight. This has become the favorite sport of saints. Says Gandhi, "We are only part human, the lower part of us is still animal. Only the conquest of our lower instincts can slay the animal in us"—rather sanguinary, such snorting of slaughter, scarcely worthy of a saint. The spirit, however, is no animal hater, no animal baiter. Spirit does not despise the flesh nor vie with it. The spirit is body, bodiless it could not exist. Whatever truly is, is spiritual. On the other hand, the pure spirit extolled by philosophers and mystics, which is incorporeal and immaterial, means the knowing subject—a ghostly concept whose counterpart is matter, its objective twin.

The query is as foolish as any answer must be false whether spiritual states correspond to objective specifications or are merely subjective. Spirit doesn't correspond to anything; spirit is reality itself. Spirit cannot be reflected in symbols. Spiritual knowledge is derived neither by tinkering with things nor from the shuffling of ideas. To know spiritually does not mean being rational, but it does not require being irrational. Spiritual man may rate high on any ethical scales, yet to adhere to standards of textbook morals is never his motive nor purpose. He does not try to be good, he doesn't preach what he knows the good is. Evil he would never define as ignorance. The sin he bewails is the failure to act freely and fully, to be wholly there at the right time. Spirit is spontaneity, integrity, ease, and health. Spirit is uncaused, unimpelled. Spirit is lawless, being itself the highest law. If a scholarly generation asks of it a sign, spirit might retort by resorting to a paradox: it is better to be wholeheartedly evil than halfheartedly good.

Spirit is freedom. Yet freedom does not imply free will in either the psychological or legal sense. Spirit is freedom, but not through stipulating a distinction between right and wrong and a subsequent deliberate choice. Man is spirit only when he need not choose among alternatives, when he need not paw and ponder over objective courses. Freedom is a notion the free man barely entertains. The individual, on the contrary, who strives to free himself from life's entanglements, attains ironically slavery to his own apparatus of escape, glutting himself into the emaciation of the ascetic.

Still, spiritual behavior never degenerates into the erratic or arbitrary. Spiritual man cannot go it alone. He is stationed in a family; he exists in the midst of a fellowship. He does not fear differing from others and expects his neighbors to be different from him. Diversity is the natural state of spiritual people. Yet differences never range into the outlandish, for all men dwell on the same land together.

The spiritual man is distrustful of contraptions which, ostensibly designed to bring men together, tend instead to keep them apart. He is for direct action, for transactions from face to face. He has no thoughts that flowers can express as effectively as he can himself. He loathes the telephone. With a little effort he can get to any bell the postman rings. Whatever is spiritual is not to be conveyed in a greeting card, the spiritual assenting to no token of itself. The genuinely personal may not be symbolized by any whim of paper. A symbol is a surrogate for someone who isn't there, and being there is precisely the being of spirit. Spirit is vitality, and vitality is feeling. And feeling is an omnipresence that pervades the entire organism and spills over into the situation spirit enlivens. Spirit is an immanence that encompasses the tissues and cells and makes man the unity he is.

The subject, of course, will have none of this. The subject

projects the emotions into somatic counterparts designated as causes. Thus anger gets shunted into the big toe which arouses it when tramped on, or into the adrenal glands, as you prefer. But inasmuch as the subject is a discrete individual, when the passions converge in action, they must express the egotism of the will. This will, being necessary to subdue the body, looms itself as a monster to be manacled. The culminating principle of rational ethics, accordingly, is never to act as the impulses impel. Desires are alien to the higher self. Philosophy as Plato taught entails a gradual death. Knowledge widens the rift between soul and body. While the ideals of the soul are refined and ennobled, the body seems less willing to rise to its vocation of implementing them. Augmenting self-knowledge aggravates self-contempt.

Deliverance from the impasse is so simple that the wise and prudent can be counted on to miss it. To be real, the self must be immersed in reality. Spiritual man requires a spiritual world to live in. Being personal implies having other persons around. Getting away from yourself means getting along with somebody else. We know ourselves in being known. Self-realization is a cooperative task, in the main the other fellow's job.

Spiritual knowledge receives scant attention where knowledge is mindfully pursued. Everybody, however, seasons living with a pinch of it, except perhaps—paradoxically— mystics and other adepts. Spiritual knowledge has a name though that name has suffered corruption: the name is faith. Faith is ordinarily conceived as a sentimental substitute for science; faith is a flimsy hypothesis that tough science may spurn outright or cotton to in *noblesse oblige*, according to caprice. Faith is believing what you know isn't so. But real

faith is no inferior knowledge of any objective world whatsoever. Faith is authentic knowledge of the spiritual world,
of a world where love is the power that moves mountains.
Faith and love figure in philosophy books as poetic symbols
of what does not exist. But faith and love in the book of life
are not symbols at all. They are existence itself.

Knowledge of existence therefore is nonobjective. *To know,*
in this nonobjective sense, instead of predicating estrangement and isolation, reverts to its antique Biblical usage for
a meaning: to know is to be in contact with, to know is the
relation between man and woman in the act of procreation.
Such knowledge is creative. Whoever is known knows the
knower and each, reciprocally known, makes the other what
he is.

From the standpoint of objective knowledge, spirit proclaims the end of the world. Spirit is eschatological, spirit
is catastrophic. Spirit is a spoilsport, smashing the game.
Spirit is an earthquake, shaking all knowers on its surface
into a proper knowledge of themselves. Spirit makes all
things new by stripping off the frippery superimposed upon
reality. Spirit is presence, destroying whatsoever is not here
and now. Spirit fires the ashes of the past in the gases of the
future and the present is the burst of flame. Spirit is an
eternal presence, eternity compressed to a point. The self
of every man is no minute fragment of the universe; the self
is the universe itself in miniature.

EXISTENCE

Getting to the bottom of the human situation depends on
striking a basic term in which to couch it, one that does not
abruptly split into ambiguity. Consciousness is often said to

be such: consciousness cannot be defined. But consciousness forks in divergent meanings. Consciousness is at once the state of being conscious and what one is conscious of. The latter prong fishes for an object; the preposition "of" casts about for something to harpoon. By object, by anything objective, is signified the object of the preposition when we know ourselves to be "conscious of." Being conscious, however, is quite different, being a unified state. A primordial rift has severed consciousness in twain and precipitated an alien element outside its drift. The stream of consciousness has banks to flow between, objects in the landscape to be distinguished from its waters, which results in knowledge through self-consciousness terminating in suicide by drowning.

More fundamental than consciousness is what we have been referring to as existence. Existence implies neither idea nor thing, neither subject nor object. No wedge can crack it. The experience of existence and whatever exists cannot be dissociated; they are one and inseparable. In the moment of existence there is no distinction between the exister's internal state and the external event denominated the existent. Existence is immediate, ineffable. When past, the corpse may be dissected, but the living present must be left intact. Existence cannot even be affirmed, existence being no predicate. To become conscious of existence is already to have converted it into an object, a symbol to work over or to play with. But this is to review the remains of what no longer exists.

Existence can be no more than a name for the unnamable. Existence marks one's contact with the world at the point where "one" and "world" are not to be demarked. In existence sight and insight are merged. Reality cannot be questioned, for reality would have to be the questioner. Existence is conscious, but spirit is conscious of no object beyond himself. The knower does not exist since in existence he participates in what he knows.

It must not be inferred, however, that in existence consciousness devours its world, sweeping it into the maw of metaphysical monism. Existence owes no such sacrifice to the Moloch of the intellect. Existence does not condemn the universe to parade as a troupe of puppets to the tune of idealism. The existent person, quite to the contrary, discovers other persons to be as authentic, as free to be themselves as he is to be himself.

Existence may sound like a consummation devoutly to be striven for. But it cannot be striven for; it comes to pass through a cessation of all striving. How are we to become aware of and to establish communion with the reality lurking behind the objects we think and talk about? What is the mysterious *thing-in-itself*, the unknowable in the crannied wall which we vainly try to make knowable in science and philosophy?

We reach under the table, only to encounter swarms of molecules and electrons. We examine its top, but our findings reduce to sense data—sounds when we tap, resistance when we press. Out of such crude stuff, we are told, our world is constructed. Whatever there be more fundamental and intrinsic, that is bound to give us the slip. Sensation marks the closest approach we can make to reality, the object sensed being the end of the road. From that point on it is a guessing game, with measuring devices and assorted theories to guide us to guess aright. If only we had some sense whereby we could intuit the ultimate mites of matter bumping one another in space, then speculation might crystallize into certainty.

In the beginning everything was chaos, then came the under-standing and pummeled the mess into order. The infant's mind, said William James, is a buzzing confusion. Out of the buzz and maze of sense data the mind institutes culture and an environment fit for habitation.

It is a long time since we were babies, and it's hard to say just what our original experience was. My word for it is as good as anybody's, and that word is to the effect that in the beginning we do not have commerce with the world through sense data at all. These objective fixtures of empirical psychology are strict fictions. Sense data are objects, what we are conscious of when consciousness attains a goal outside itself. But the infant is not engaged in receiving impressions to be stamped and classified in the pigeonholes of the psychologist's desk.

What does the few-months-old child actually see when his mother enters the nursery? Is he occupied appropriating sense data, splotches of color, a vitreous object poised against a moving background, the approaching formation emitting sounds from an aperature near the top? On behalf of the child I beg to say that this is a faulty rendition of his mental operations. What the baby really sees is his mother coming to feed him, he sees the smile on her face and the tenderness in her heart, he sees her looking at him and her intention to satisfy his hunger. And this child, when he is six years old, though he has seen that mother's eyes thousands of times, would have to stop and think if asked whether they were brown or blue. And he would be more liable to get the color tags askew than to err on some quirk of his mother's tempera-ment, on which score there can be no sensory impressions whatever.

Despite all the empirical psychology ever invented, we continue to see things as they exist, not as they are objectively delineated. We pierce beneath the facts of sense. What people are speaks so loud that we cannot hear what psychologists say is all we do hear. The body and its organs become artificial abstractions when they signify other than a medium for the transaction of spiritual business. Existentially we meet one another by overlooking the false faces of perception. We know a friend is glad to see us before we notice his hand extended in greeting, and if we do not respond to the feeling we may fail to see the hand. I can tell whether a man I know is lying or speaking the truth though I do not know how I know and could give no rule of inference. A woman uses rouge, not to make her cheeks red, but to make her person vivid; and every woman should know that when people see the cosmetic, the hand has been clumsy that put it on. Yes, despite all empirical psychology, nobody except the psychologist's masterpiece ever built his mind out of the bricks of sense data.

Still, we must grant that existential knowing may properly be called primitive. It provides no adequate way of getting on in civilized society. Science, organized business, anything that is organized, want facts and figures, details and data— all manufactured products, for which existence furnishes only the raw materials and very raw ones at that. Nobody considers cultural enterprises high-handed by reason of their having been tossed off so nimbly from the mind's finger tips. Still, the penalty for preferring a symbolic world to the real world is to become a tinkling cymbal one's self.

Science is inevitable, that is evident—man being by nature desirous of knowledge. But let us serve our sentence, similarly inevitable, as a respectable tragedy, not as a farcical massacre. Nature must be cleansed of supernatural taints, true enough. Man can secure his freedom only by freeing his world of all traces of himself: science has so decreed. Existential intercourse with reality may be termed childlike. But to dismiss such experience as a bogey stalking the dignified corridors of the intellect, that is to be childish. We hear sad lamentations over man's failure to attain maturity. The reason may be his abandonment of so much he knew before he grew so erudite. If the scientist had actually been born into the sphere he has learned to dominate, his career in dominating it would scarcely be deemed worthwhile. If we did not know other selves as well as our own, and know them even before we know ourselves, our wanderings in the wilderness of egotism would be too desolate to be borne.

Few men by doctrine and none by conviction are solipsists. We believe in the existence of our fellow men. But in saying this we are not using the word, existence, in its proper sense. We are using it as a predicate. What we believe in, strictly speaking, is their objectivity. This we can demonstrate, by the argument from analogy: a visible body behaves as you would behave under the same circumstances, therefore it must be animated by what animates you. This argument may be given an ethical twist: you have an obligation to regard others as spiritual objects, likely deserving your favor, certainly instrumental to your convenience and well-being. That other people are objects apart from us is just the way we like them; that makes them amenable to our pushing around, and push we will, we'll even push them into heaven. We tell of loving our fellows, provided it be understood that love is the direction of our own wills toward the acquisition of an object whose possession will bring us happiness. Those desires can be refined to the stage where the beloved will be treated with consideration, maybe with tenderness. We may even extract a taste of happiness from the care we lavish, if our tongue is sufficiently delicate.

But such bliss does not mean you exist with the person who is the source of it. You may merely have enlarged your objective world to include him, you may have created a value within yourself, rather than having discovered a mutual value with another. No imputation of personality to an object is equivalent to personal intercourse. The former attitude lacks spontaneity and inevitability. It is subject to theory, it is provisional; it can be canceled and normally is, when that individual threatens interests of the imputer's own. Such ego-handed-out love makes hypocrites of us. Though we entertain the highest sentiment for the brotherhood of man, we pass nonchalantly by on the other side when we glimpse a brother lying in the ditch. By brother we never meant him, never anyone in particular, in time and space. Actually all we ever intended was to make a pious noise.

Existence is personal; existence is nonobjective. A person can no more be reduced to a mind than to a body. Metaphysical personalism, in filling the sky with objects cut according to its ideas, only populates the world with spooks. Mystical pantheism achieves no identification of the self and Nature, rather the identification of the subject with its own emanations. Existence must be shared. We exist by virtue of our participation in one another. No inference nor ratiocination on the part of the recipient can ever take the place of the giver's own revelation of himself. Existence means entering the life of the other, loving him in and through the matrix that sustains us both. God can be loved only in and through his created world. The natural world which keeps lovers apart is at the same time the supernatural bond that holds them together. But no object of knowledge can possibly be an object to be loved.

Nonobjective knowledge must await the free self-disclosure of the person who is known. To the range of such revelation no limit can be set. Knock and it shall be opened: a door may fling open anywhere under the sun, or in the sun itself as St. Francis testified. A hospitable spirit welcomes a multitude of strangers within his gates. No creature is an alien, every one a friend, and the confusion of tongues is quickly quelled when the heart translates. The most rigid Cartesian may find his dog more than a mechanically operated object; his parched and arid soul may even drop a tear in watching the felling of a tree. A house can speak if we keep silence in its presence and are not too aggressive putting it to use. Love of one's native land may sink deeper than an objective pretext for going to war to defend it; beneath its soil still dwell the souls of the departed. Its ground contains what no chemical analysis could detect, and the fact that it is natural does not rule out its being spiritual too. Wherever spirit meets spirit that place is holy though the altar be made of flesh and blood, even of stone. But no existent event can occur within the wastes of an individual's mind where he spends himself on symbols, albeit he calls these symbols objects, one of which he may worship as God.

Existence is value. To create and to preserve its reality is man's true good. To deepen and to propagate receptivity to it is his highest purpose, a purpose that can be prosecuted only if there be no objective purpose to do so. This is but to rephrase the commandments to love God with heart and soul and mind, and to love one's neighbor as one's self.

According to Cassirer, "Man can do no more than to build up his own universe—a symbolic universe that enables him to understand his human experience. Man discovers and proves a new power—the power to build up a world of his own, an 'ideal' world." Thus man achieves freedom and "self-liberation."

Accordingly, all we actually mean by an objective view, all we intend by appealing to the facts, is to constrain others to accept our particular array of symbols. The true, the beautiful, and the good are objective enough. But the sole criteria of objectivity is the fist, or the club, of a particularly potent subject.

In Cassirer's *An Essay on Man,* there are vague allusions all the way through to "things," a cloud bank that somehow undergirds and overarches the objective structures. Of this nebula Cassirer professes to know nothing. It can be fitfully touched and tapped for the data of sense. But in attempting to pry beneath its shimmer man just gets burnt. Our symbols ultimately signify only the unknown and unknowable. We exhaust our powers in culture; we can know ourselves solely as a reflection in a mirror we have polished. There is no penetration behind its silver sheen. Unless something is there, the cause of sensation, reality mocks us in mystery. We beat upon it as upon the walls of a prison, but the only response is a thickening of the gloom. Horrors! it may all be the work of the devil.

Thus man is objectified as being engaged in a game, let's say of handball. The game is as enduring as his career on the planet, a game reputed to be no less glamorous and glorious because it is known to be merely a game. Man swats his ideas against the barriers that encage the players and provide a background for the show. With the walls he makes no contact; all he knows is the inferential conclusion that something is there. From the way his balls bounce he can render plausible sundry myths and theories, sufficiently reliable to contribute to the gaiety and the continuance of the game. On occasions he discovers that the walls themselves can be planed and smoothed through technology to make the balls bound in livelier fashion. But the reality that encloses his culture is impervious and imperious. It is alien, brutal, tyrannical. Even the bodies we need and use to keep the sport going seem to belong to the environment rather than to the soul that makes them caper at its behest. Man's freedom finally resolves into making the rules for the game he plays.

Though Cassirer would not like the word, I cannot forbear suggesting that man seems to be pursuing values that might be called super-natural, or at least extra-natural. I do not like the words either. I would say instead that such values are spurious and deceptive, that whosoever is taken in thereby is very much out in the cold. If man be doomed to find his heaven within himself, man indeed is in a hell of a fix.

Two boys were playing at racquets, what we will conventionally call a real game in a real court. The ball bounded frantically among the brick enclosures, batted back and forth by the racquets of the players. The contest became punctuated with wrangles over the score, with disputes as to whether the rules were being kept or violated. To an onlooker the fray seemed violently real, the combatants terribly in earnest. Suddenly one of the players threw his racquet in a frenzied effort to place a shot. It slipped from his grasp and struck the coping of the back wall. There it dislodged a brick. The brick crashed to the pavement and landed midway between the contorted bodies of the athletes. Suddenly too the boys broke up the game. That little world dribbled to extinction. Aren't we lucky, said one of the boys. A miracle that it didn't hit us, said the other. Each boy, clasping his racquet under one arm, wrapped his free arm around the other's shoulder. They left the court, embracing each other, in silent greeting to a new reality revealed in the fall of a brick.

IV

MAN THE PLAYER

CLARIFICATION OF TERMS used in consistent yet perhaps peculiar senses is never amiss. There are two which are basic in this discussion: *spirit* and *play*.

Spirit first. By spiritual man I mean man made in the image of God; what according to Genesis resulted from God's breathing the breath of life into that which he had formed from the dust of the ground. Spirit, in my use of the word, is not identical with the spirit of metaphysical idealists, the latter spirit being *ego* in my dictionary.

Spirit and the spiritual cannot be explicitly defined. The terms must be kept as plastic and sensitive as what they apply to. No lexicographer can legislate them down. Whatever is spiritual must be experienced to be known. There are two ways of knowing: one is dependent on the subject-object setup, the other is the spiritual way. The latter is not to be objectified for purposes of discourse, nor is the capacity for it to be transmitted in any manual of instructions. The quest of self-knowledge reduces spiritual matters to rules. While spiritual man may conform to such rules, to do so is never his motive. He may obey the Ten Commandments, but not because the finger of Moses once chiseled them on stone. The spiritual man agrees with nearly everyone else to let two plus two equal four, but if he met that character in Dostoevsky's Underworld who preferred two plus two equaling five, his attitude to the eccentric would be amusement, not rage.

The word *moral* might be accepted as a synonym for spiritual, if moral did not bear the opprobrium of meaning customary and conventional. Moral signifies deportment that coheres with the mores of the group. Most Americans believe they are being moral if they pay their bills and abstain from fornication. Such behavior is adjudged moral whether the judges so behave or not. By spiritual I do not mean this. But if I grope for another synonym and hitch on the term *religious,* I am confounded by these same people considering themselves religious if they go to church and abstain from fornication. This is not being spiritual according to my understanding, nor being religious either; religious should mean spiritual. I shall settle with semantics by trimming *moral* and *religious* to fit the spiritual, leaving you to discard the snippings.

No act is to be deemed moral just because it is customary and proper. Still no act is to be denied a moral quality by reason of its being so. What could be more commonplace than extending a cup of water to a thirsty traveler? Yet this can be a highly moral, and spiritual, transaction. To behave morally is to act spontaneously, freely, without purpose or deliberation, to impinge as a total self upon a personal situation. Moral response is possible only when the environment is perceived as moral, too—when it is personal. Moral conduct is inevitably personal and religious.

The exact content of what is done is immaterial. Spiritual quality is to be recognized by no objective test. The spiritual person never aspires to be unique and original, he does not shy away from the normal or even from the trivial lest he be rated banal and unimaginative. He never stands on his head to produce an effect nor toes the mark to produce another. His art is nonobjective. But theorists of things aesthetic who like this term should note that an act, be it a painting or crossing the street, is necessarily objective if it is designed to express distinct individuality, even though the resulting object is comprehensible to its creator alone. Straining after originality rams one into the wall of objectivity. The genuinely nonobjective comes to pass through sheer inspiration; it is revealed. The nonobjective, however, is not to be confused with the bizarre. The bizarre indeed is seldom satisfactory even as an object, for it loads on the subject that has fashioned it the onus of putting it across on other subjects, and these are reluctant to see it that way.

The actual content of a spiritual act, rendered objective in telling about it afterward, is rarely startling. The moral man acts nonobjectively by being personal rather than individual. He strives for no effect; he has nothing to sell; he is motivated by neither hope of conquest nor fear of consequences. He is simply the integrated being psychologists are forever scrabbling for, and he is so precisely because he does not aspire to be integrated. He has not got that way by poring over self-improvement guidebooks. His techniques are dissolved in his touch. His spirit permeates his hands and feet. The spiritual man is just being himself, without suspecting what a subtle feat that is and how much money other folks are spending for the know-how.

Now for *play:* I must make my use of this word clear. Much activity frequently called play I exclude; I bar in advance the random caperings of children and animals. Play primarily is no juvenile pursuit, although children play too and soon learn under adult tutelage so to organize their doings as to bring them within the scope of my definition. This definition negates at once the notion that play is frivolous. That man laughs while he plays is no indication that he is not sober and somber about it. Man is the only laughing and the only playing animal; he is being distinctively human in both these exhibitions of himself. Play is the larger category, including much that is done in dead earnest. Professors, judges, the whole tribe of scribes and Pharisees, are addicted to play. Nor can play be scorned as the opposite of the sacred. Considerable play is carried on in a manner commonly regarded as pious, there being no distinct line demarking play and ritual. Play engrosses the entire content of cultural activity, everything that Cassirer treats of.

There are sundry theories of play, psychological perhaps, that connect the phenomenon with instinct and the biological roots of human nature. Thus play is explained as due to surplus energy, play serves the function of discipline, it makes preparation for the workaday world. With such explications I have no concern; I regard them all as play themselves. The play proclivity of man does not relate him to his phylogenetic forebears, it dissociates him from them. Man the player is a unique species.

Here is my definition: by play is to be understood a system of organized activity, pursued in accordance with a statable pattern of ideas, which all participants comprehend objectively, to which they give assent and support, and which they have assimilated into their knowing subjects to guide their activities and to judge the results. Players know what they are doing, at least to the extent that they can acquire further knowledge. Whatever activity falls within this description I call play, or what is strangely similar to it: work. Play and work, though usually looked on as opposites, differ in only minor respects.

PLAY IS FORMAL

To say that play is formal but repeats my definition of it. In play the movements of the body are determined by objects in the mind, the effort being to make the movement identical with the idea.

Once on a tour of New York's lower East Side I paused to observe clusters of elderly men intent on a game I had never watched before. Wooden balls of two sizes were being rolled in a railed-in alley. The purpose of the joust seemed to be to strike the small ball with the large one. Though the form was probably not complex, I was not able to figure it out, I was baffled in reducing the proceedings to rational order. I stood outside the know. The foreign tongue jabbered by the players seemed in keeping with the event. Spectators I appealed to for enlightenment dismissed me with haughty shrugs. The pastime struck me as a waste of time, the stiff decorum of the participants adding a cadaverous smell to what failed to make sense. The entire affair was as eminently proper as a formal tea party one might find on Park Avenue uptown; at once I glimpsed the latter's nature too. Why should free-born human beings spend an afternoon chasing balls they themselves have set in motion? The poet who boasted nothing human was alien to him could never have witnessed a game whose rules he was ignorant of.

An aura of the occult enswathes every field of play, to be immediately dissipated by initiation through learning its rationale. Once one has mastered the rules of the game, mystery vanishes and its essential character becomes the essence of one's self. The ideology becomes identical with the knower; then he can judge the contest and crown the winner. Inside the framework one can inhale a breath of freedom, knowledge being transformed into virtue and happiness. That framework has made the game and confers its benefits.

Bowling is no indiscriminate slaughter, no mere toppling pins over by hurling weights at them without knowing why. The bowler does not care about knocking down sticks of wood, just to kick them as they lie prone and gasping. He has no grudge against the pins whatever. Even a fanatic left alone in a phalanx of alleys would scarcely heave a shot, unless he contrived some motive, say that of practice. A moron or a monkey could be trained to fire the artillery, accomplishing perhaps more effective decimation than a champion bowler without being eligible for even an amateur league. No—in the game the massacre must take place in a specified manner. It must answer a purpose, just as a massacre must in war. It has to be formal. Divers dogmas, that of the foul line, for instance, need be rigidly respected. Players alternate in regular order, the score is tallied on a certain type of pad, the computations are made in approved arithmetic. The contestants must accept *a priori* a convention asserting what winning consists in. It sounds very complicated, and if you had to solve the enigma for yourself, you might bemuse yourself for an evening over a relatively simple ideology. Imagine doping out a game of chess, or being let down in a Buddhist temple without a book of rules.

Play sans the rational overhead ceases to be play. The formalities make the fun. Any departure from, or infringements of, established principles is intolerable, signifying the end of the world. The individual who refuses to be bound puts himself beyond the pale, incidentally weakening the society that expels him. The laws rely for their enforcement solely upon the consent of the governed, their power residing in the wills of the players. The rules are manifestly reasonable, since only on the basis of their acceptance can the affair proceed. Any overt doubt on this head impresses as perverse, likely sinister. Skepticism ranks as the deadliest of sins. Even children eject from their circle the heretic that doesn't want to play, little persecutors doing the job in a big way. The assumption justifying the punishment is that the wrongdoer wrongs himself most of all; he lacks self-knowledge, in flagrant defiance of his own highest interest; he isn't selfish enough. During the Middle Ages heretics were burned out of the church's love for them, their execution lessening the sins they would have to atone for by lessening their time to sin.

Players are notoriously averse to going deeper into the rules' validity than a stentorian assertion of their truth. Actually there are no further depths to go into. A rule is a rule: why should the batter be retired after three futile strikes? Why not give him four? People who play baseball have agreed that three shall it be. Asking questions marks you a suspicious character, a subversive deserving investigation. Still, skepticism adds spice to any game, an antiseptic that resists boredom. There are losers as well as winners, and the will to win is more pressing than respect for the amenities.

Will and reason are locked in perpetual civil war and tug within every player. Hence any form of play that tends to be permanent extrudes as part of its apparatus an official organ to mollify internal agitation and to quash skepticism in the bud. The game must have an umpire, a supreme court, a faculty, a priesthood at the peak of its organization. These bureaucracies serve the double function of coercing dissenters and of altering the rules so as to retain the loyalty of all members of the institution. Flexibility need not destroy order; indeed, a measure of it must obtain lest order smother to death. A sensitive government grants appeal as a right, and sometimes maneuvers reforms before its subjects launch active rebellion. Play can sport its formal jacket without any particular set of forms being absolutely static. All that is required is that the process whereby change is regulated be regular itself.

Barring those who betake themselves to mysticism, the reason of men must compromise with the mutability of a relative world. He who wins today may be on the losing end tomorrow, and it behooves the successful to be tolerant. The flux of Nature on whose surface our ideal constructions float accepts all systems only fitfully and with repugnance. Precisely because Nature repulses us, we shift the venue to a field of play. Play, like art—a species of it—represents man's endeavor to improve on Nature. This effort ordinarily we restrict to selected segments, subduing Nature piecemeal. But a really ambitious player may aspire to impose on her a universal system of his own devising, conquering the universe at one swoop and rendering reasonable every possible happening. Such an omnivorous formula would negate in advance any alternative to it and alterations within it, thus enticing as the mystics' paradise. So to master his environment, to regulate all living, to play without the bother of staking off a playground—in short, to be God—this is the ideal of the perfect game that haunts man's imagination and inflames his ambition. But this supreme quest conceals a supreme threat to mankind. The consummation spells the attainment of infallibility and with it of omnipotence. To the rules promulgated by such a knower no exception could be taken. Spiritual living would be annihilated. All behavior being ideally determined, the difference would be merely verbal whether in this Platonic republic men were said to be dead or alive.

Long strides have been taken toward formalizing Nature into this status of the inanimate. But until man yields completely to the role of player, tension will persist between this aspect of himself and the spirit. Most of our activities are carried on within the confines of formal orders. To that extent our deeds are nonmoral. Occasionally we do crawl out of the frame-ups and deal with one another personally. You and your next-door neighbor may settle a squabble over the boundary line, neither of you can say how, save that it was done in the spirit of neighborliness. But if you go to law over the dispute, you will have to know how, you are involved in a game whose rules are abstruse. You had best get an expert to play your hand. The law is formal. Its purpose is not to make neighbors love one another but to preserve social regularity. *Fiat justitia, ruat mundus*, proclaims the inscription on the façade of the courthouse.

That legend may publish a lofty idea, that justice be done

though the world be destroyed. But no grandiloquence speaks to the spirit. The spirit sees no sense in such nonsense. The spirit is immutably mundane. Freedom depends on keeping the world alive and life creative. A real man never gloats over the spectacle of formal dicta scowling through uninhabitable space. Play is formal, but in being so is its sole reward.

PLAY FORMS ARE AUTONOMOUS

This is but to acquiesce in the familiar slogan of art for art's sake. With any game's contention that extraneous considerations cannot be lugged into its domain, no exception can be taken. The gist of play is the freedom to define ends, make rules, fix bounds and standards. So long as players do not make nuisances of themselves, the public must keep hands off, even paying to get in to watch. No art is right or wrong beyond the limits it has set for itself. To demand that fiction writers teach textbook ethics, for example, is naïve and befuddling. What are textbook writers for?

Clashes on such scores are occurring constantly within the total arena of play. But they are of scant concern to spiritually minded outsiders. Every rumpus over morals in art is stirred up by moralists who want their rules to rule in places that are none of their business. Each system makes a law unto itself, though there need be no unanimity among the lawmakers. Objective truths can no more make war on one another than can armies of tin soldiers; the clamor for unanimity comes about through each subject involved seeking to universalize its own will.

Play activities as autonomous orders vie and compete for prestige in public estimation and for cash. Every bureacracy aims to extend the range of its bureau; any 'ocracy is vora-cious. Big business is the game each business tends to grow into. But obesity brings degeneration with it. If everybody must play, nobody plays; he works at it instead. If we were all compelled to adopt baseball as a daily exercise, that game would sink to the status of the commuters' train: morning and evening sacrifices to the Moloch of toil and routine. Sufficient freedom has to be allowed for the individual to join in or to stay out, else the illusion of freedom would be lost.

Whenever any game waxes too greedy, it encounters the hostility of similarly organized groups, for time and money are stringently limited in this finite world. Each play form's autonomy implies no right to preempt the entire fund of hu-man energy, and when any trespasser hogs the preserves of others, it is liable to get socked into altruism. To live and let live is the paramount principle of democracy.

Thus, the rampageous stock market of the '20s disrupted other rackets when clerks and elevator boys got to speculat-ing in shares, especially when they got speedily fleeced and had no wool left for other shearers. Tighter enclosures had to be built around Wall Street to keep petty gamblers out. If the World Series lasted all winter instead of a week in October, that classic would become an issue for the states-men in Washington, and it would likely get taxed into a reasonable condition of servitude. War made a better game in bygone centuries than it makes today, when it was waged by professional soldiers without sucking in entire popula-tions. Too rapacious a show ceases to be a show and becomes identical with fate. If a game is to retain its autonomy, it must pay polite respect to competitors and to the cardinal virtue of self-restraint. Players, outside the army, are forbidden to coerce the bodies of those who refuse their invitation to join and have to rely on the wiles of advertising to convert the erring. Physical force is to be concentrated in the central political body, whose function is to keep rivalry among subordinate organizations at a relatively harmless pitch.

This self-restraint goes by the name of tolerance. But tolerance does not exclude stealthy extensions of monopoly. If all play orders are autonomous, how can any claim intrinsic superiority to the others? Why symbolic logic is to rate nobler than tossing horseshoes, Shakespeare than a movie script, the Old Masters than Greenwich Village—the adjudication of these whys remains a bit obscure. Aesthetic values accordingly are dependent on advertising for their clarification. The entertainment emerges best which customers will pay the most for, in time and lucre. There can be no appeal from box-office receipts, best-seller lists, auction gallery prices, from what the experts say. The caliper such gradations are established by is snobbery, on which subject more will be said in a moment.

To be autonomous every game must occupy its specific time and place. It stakes off its private preserve, erects a fence around it, isolates itself from the time and space of Nature. Every game, like a picture, needs be framed; it must be sheltered by its charter. Our land is dotted with such retreats: college campuses, legislative halls, temples, card tables, stages. Each sport is hallowed, consecrated to a special service; each renders a performance valuable in itself, augmenting its value in its irrelevance to others. All float through the firmament like meteoroids, each a miniature universe, having sprung into being from the fiat of its creator by the magic of a godling.

Raw materials, of course, must be quarried from Nature, though some of man's play worlds such as mathematics come virtually *ex nihilo*. The materials as they are dug from the mine are crude and have to be refined into suitable apparatus. Nature does not produce the perfect sphere required for bowling. Her offerings have to be milled and smoothed. However, the amount of stuff which man employs in his play life may be astonishingly meager, play manifesting a decidedly ascetic cast. The mathematician, angling for a single equation to gulp the world at a single swallow, asks only an armchair and a pencil. Players can seldom be reproached for materialism if bulk of materials be the basis of the charge. Chess addicts deem themselves superior to bowlers since their game is more intellectual and proficient operators can even dispense with the board, play blindfolded, and keep track of the moves in their heads. Though baseball in its commercial ramifications adds up to quite a heft, the materials utilized on the diamond are scanty. A tiny leather wad that one could slip in his pocket supplies the *pièce de résistance* for the afternoon gluttony of thousands of spectators, and a moving van might cart off all the equipment possessed by a major league. The less the material element is required for its prosecution, the greater is the degree of autonomy a game can claim and the more specious as an escape mechanism it becomes.

A game, however, does require time. This time is a time of its own. The game may be suspended and annulled for the nonce by calling time-out, a rule which holds for war as for football. The duration of any game is limited. It can be repeated, occasions without number, any idea embracing a manifold of particular cases; in which respect a game differs drastically from real life where an event can occur but once. Uniqueness indeed is no idea any system of idealism can make room for: ideally nothing happens, nothing exists; ideal time is fictitious. Yet this time span varies widely according to the game. If the compass be long, relative to an individual's fourscore years, a delusion may arise that the specific form of play constitutes a permanent fixture in the universe, destined to preside over human affairs forever. Such a pattern may be regarded as a revelation of God, supplanting in esteem the cosmic flux. The rules of that game may get codified in sacred scriptures, the dogmas of the institution that expounds the written word may be venerated as divine. And the recalcitrant who declines to be bound thereby may be cast out of the community which has identified existence with its own culture.

Still, any formal mode of behavior, howsoever immense its scope and duration, proves vulnerable and transitory. It loses its grip, relaxes its grasp, turns up its toes. Its time runs out. Historians recount the rise and fall of civilizations. Any civilization shares the ephemerality of a half-hour of quoits. Its span is limited to its own time and space. It possesses no spiritual significance. At its demise every culture leaves the world as if it had never been. The clock strikes, or the lightning. The pins of history are reset on a parallel alley. The game must go on, with different players and with different rules.

The reason for these debacles is as plain as it is hidden. Any activity of man that claims autonomy for itself severs itself from its source, and this source alone is self-sustaining and self-renewing. The roots of the spirit survive underground though the blossoms wither into dust. This radical attachment man senses at his moral core. His conscience protests when business cries for freedom from political control, when the church shouts the same slogan, when church and state both are exhorted to let science pursue its course untrammeled. Everybody rushes hell-bent for truth and liberty, everybody demands the right to define these ideals as self-interest may dictate. Everybody assumes that all things work together for good. But nobody notes the proviso: to them that love God, to those who live in the real world where everything is together.

The bodies of men cannot range as autonomously as their egos. Practical conflicts supervene to spoil our various sports. Objective truths object to one another when human wills invigorate their embodiments. The same people belong to both church and state, making it impossible for the sway of either to be uncontested. Physicists should be aware of the murderous uses their toys are put to; if someday their contraptions fall on their own heads, they may realize research is never pure. The bodies of men yield to no such neat fractionation as their minds. Thus no enterprise makes good its boast of antonomy, unless it be a book that no one has read except the author. A struggle for power ensues that we call history, each aspirant checking his rivals, to the inestimable benefit of the rest of us. No play regime achieves the monopoly that motivates it. And amid the chinks and crannies of the mosaic, which is always being cracked afresh, the spirit pokes through and may thrive.

Moral man meanwhile has his doubts. He is as skeptical

of all cultural programs as each of these is of its competitors.
The clamor of art for art's sake sounds as silly as it sounds
obvious. The spiritual world allows no such splintering. Any
declaration of independence is a declaration of irrelevance.
Whatever befalls a real person hits him as a whole. What
else does the term *person* mean?

No purpose can be unreined for its own sweet sake, for
the diversion of the gallop. The real person never strives
to be diverted from reality. Neither art nor science can be
granted the luxury of launching out on its own. Not even religion, though it promises to save the soul and to fizz up the
ecstasy of mystic rapture, is to be sought for the sublimity
it confers. The truly religious person will have nothing to
do with religion if it means such a fractional antic. Its good
is only a goody, its God a mere plaything. No image nor
symbol can usurp the throne of the Living God. Play may
be as autonomous as it prides itself on being, but the spirit
courts no distraction from the real.

PLAY CREATES A COMMUNITY

Its autonomous character does not imply that a game is
a solitary performance. You cannot make money or even
fun playing with yourself. Among the notable features of
play is the desire to win. Play involves rivalry, play is a contest. This makes it social, whether it be sociable or not. The
togetherness of play, however, is distinctive. God sets his
people in families perhaps, but the play ensemble scarcely
belongs to the domestic type.

All its community requires is an aggregation holding in
common the formal order, each member expecting to secure
thereby a measure of self-expression. Our environments are

minutely cross-hatched with such organizations; we may belong to a score of these communities, barely aware that we belong to any. They cut athwart one another's established lines in bewildering fashion. The president of the corporation may exchange pleasantries with an office boy on the fiasco of the Red Sox. But a tender word or two marks the terminus of their companionship. The underling should not strain the tie by hinting for a raise; though tears drip into a single pool, minds run on separate tracks. The diamond tragedy forges no bond to sustain a weight beyond a passing chat. No one is deeply concerned about a baseball team, howsoever dire its plight.

A game beds strangers side by side. The Communist Party in America comprises an otherwise nondescript assembly of doctrinaire reformers and disgruntled losers, the former motivated by nebulous goodwill, the latter by the will to wring revenge out of the winners' necks. The members of a lodge or a church are hardly on speaking terms outside the regular speaking place. They come in contact only tangentially, like charged pith balls suspended on threads, then rebound from one another's vicinity. Corporations are organized for specific tasks stated in their charters, the peddling of books or hair dyes, and the constituent egos have no mutual relations beyond meshing their egos as cogs in the wheels. To ascertain what team mates have in common, you must inquire the purpose of the team. Anything of a personal nature grinds in the gears like grit. Sometimes the law of the sovereign state must be summoned to do a job of oiling, it being illegal for example to ask an applicant for admission what his religion is. Office and factory staffs spend the major part of the time together without even wondering whether a fellow worker might be more than the animated bag across the desk. Play abstracts only that fragment of a person which serves the immediate end, and any residue left from the distillation slags into superfluous waste. Political commentators dread mention of what they call personalities, assuming that whatever is personal the player should be ashamed of. Nobody sees anything amiss in a notorious Hollywood adulteress doing the role of the Virgin Mary. And not long ago a top-loft idealist was being touted for a world peace prize though he had just been divorced from his wife.

To be relieved of their barren aspect, play groups strive to embellish their doings with rituals. Priests swank in colored chasubles. Vestments engender an *esprit de corps* within and impress those without with an esoteric éclat. The sorceries of advertising convert the crassest commercial outfit into an oozer of glamor. Brand names are endowed with magical potencies. Any toilet paper maker that can afford a public relations bureau can soon be basking in oriental splendor. Sports pages are couched in an occult jargon that only the elite find intelligible: *Ted Homers, One On*—what could that mean, even to a Ph.D. if he doesn't belong to the elect? Physicians snootily scrawl their prescriptions in Latin, and lawyers too baffle their customers with scraps of Caesar's language, though none of these could decipher a line of Caesar himself. Philosophers ply a vocabulary that nobody else is expected to understand and are inclined to sneer at their own ideas if these be expressed in lucid prose. Theology has long been a specialty, the specialization having consisted in making a god out of a glossary.

Not dead, Just sleeping, proclaimed an epitaph in the

cemetery. He is fooling nobody but himself, chuckled the spoilsport, who saw no sense in that bluff.

Of course play is fun. That is generates zip and adds tang to an otherwise tasteless fare, no one can gainsay. It's its zest that we want. Vitality we dolefully lack, so we turn to play as an egress from drudgery and tedium. We get bored, we lose contact with reality, we aren't there, we are wasting our time. We dangle on a loose end and a game makes a lifesaver to grab hold of. That any creature enmeshed in a universe as vast and varied as our own should be wearied by it all, that poses a problem which might assuage boredom in figuring out the answer.

Play offers relief from work, the condition our normal occupations bore into. Its magic key unlocks our prison, we leap out, stretch our wings, poised for the flight. A high degree of animation is induced by arts and sports. The voltage gets steep. Fans stand all night in order to sit in the bleachers next day for the crucial series, and others stand far longer in the trenches to vindicate the tenets of democracy. To beat up fanaticism requires no undue pounding on the drums. Fanaticism feels good. The resistance of insulating barriers is shattered, sparks snap and crackle, the scene is brilliant. Play is fun.

The moral objection to the fireworks is not that the display fails to glow and glitter. The objection is that the blaze dies down as suddenly as it is kindled, leaving the sky even darker than before. Nothing actually happened. Emotions settle out, and only cinders remain to mark the spot where you never

really were. Play is sterile and to regard it re-creation sprouts
a fallacy. Its pyrotechnics but shimmer on the surface. Beneath the appliqué of excitement boredom hardens into a
permanent state and fatigue becomes chronic. Nature declines
to imitate art, and art is impotent to imitate Nature. The rift
between them yawns so wide that in his acrobatics to bridge
the span, man finds himself somersaulting between play and
work.

The duration of the play event is discontinuous with the
time of existence. At the fall of the curtain the show is over;
by the time the movie patron has located his hat and pushed
his way through the jam, he has ceased to snicker at the capers
of the screen comedians. Earth seems populated by obnoxious
fat people blocking every exit. The subway train which trans-
ports the milling throng home from the ball game sewers
away the ardor steamed up there, drains it off as waste. The
hour's ride over, erstwhile rooters are ribbing their wives
because the steak is tough. The effete capitalist is not in-
spired by the opera to deal more romantically with his employees next morning. He is tireder than ever, his head yodels
for an aspirin. His egotism has been aggravated; why cannot
his office be reduced to the polite decorum of the Metropoli-
tan, to as pat a formula as the program handed him in the
theater? The zest engendered in play proves to be nontrans-
ferable, the evening's fun incompatible with the next morning's hang-over.

And what of war? War is the jolliest game ever invented,
the prime builder of morale, the dispeller of the gloom of
any depression. War restores fast waning social cohesion,
it arouses devotion to duty, fidelity to the common cause.
War refurbishes the ideals tarnishing in the philosopher's

shop, and their antique luster shines again. War is fun, especially if you can have it at home. War is fun, that is why we have it. That the fun fails to last is not so funny; war becomes a problem. The aftermath reveals nothing genuinely creative has got done. We stop deriving satisfaction out of the enemy's cities having been bombed and burned, we no longer gloat over his losses in dead and dollars. Then we discover the home front has been ravished too. Citizens are petulant and pugnacious, some of them downright subversive. The democracy we fought to impose on others is beset with perils in its native haunts. The totalitarianism we assaulted overseas hovers overhead.

Any game, war preeminently, does induce for its duration a buzz of activity. It stimulates ardor, it ignites visions. A game feels good while it lasts, but it cannot outlast its formal termination. Is activity, moreover, necessarily good in itself? A cancer marks the spot where physiological activity is high. The cancer's growth is rampant, but the metabolism of its tissue has forfeited its relation to the body as a whole. Its time span belongs to itself alone, the cancer is autonomous. Its scene is a histological playground. As the independent cells of the cancer go it alone, augmenting their number and rioting in their frolic, the body wanes in health and vigor. The value of fun depends on one's point of view.

What about religion? Everybody knows how readily churchgoing degenerates into a self-centered performance. Listening to the reading of Scriptures setting forth precepts of love and to sermons expounding them do not avail to make hearers more loving and lovable. Nobody really expects results beyond the church door, and preachers might be more careful what they preached if they intended anything beyond diverting the congregation. An impressionable lady may be swept along by the sentiment of the occasion to pass a hymnal to a stranger, but she would not for a flicker think of inviting him home for dinner, and meeting him on the curb outside she could scarcely recall ever having seen the face. Ecclesiastical good will should be kept free from contamination. The fun of play is the stretching of a rubber band, the player snapping back into apathy once the pull is released. Its exhilaration has no relevance beyond itself. It never spills over the banks of its fixed channel.

To imagine that play exerts moral effects vitiates most theories of education. Play is not necessarily toxic to the moral life, but it cannot be regarded as a tonic. Existential living is fun in itself, and the life of the spirit is never dependent on artificial respiration. Tension obtains within the moral sphere too, but the polarity between man and the universe is no mere internal relation within oneself. The dimensions of the spirit are of cosmic proportions; its powers consequently are genuinely transforming and creative, wholly different from the fitful and transient stimulation derived from play.

THE ENEMIES OF PLAY

Play being autonomous must be self-authenticating. Every form of it, however, tends to stale and to play out. The zeal of the participants flags, the game drags. This is liable to occur when frustration is encountered, when one finds himself on the losing side or otherwise rebuffed. Once a chess enthusiast, I find my interest in that sport tapering off, having found that the outcome is predestinated. The afternoon bridge party gets off to a hilarious start, only to deflate with the amassing of points, and after the distribution of prizes the women grumble their way home, growling opinions of luck. The excitement lags in politics between elections, there being no jobs in sight. You spend an evening jabbing at Kant, then decide metaphysics would be better omitted.

During periods of lethargy we may continue to play. But extraneous motives must be resorted to to keep us going. You persist at Kant to chalk credit in the course. I find compensation for checkmates in my opponent's highballs. The ladies reap elation in being licked by a fashionable set. Still, when any game has to be bolstered by ancillary and ulterior motivations, its play value has undergone dilution. The formal order itself has ceased to be convincing. The intrusion of calculated motives converts the play into work. The objective circus must stretch its tent to include the value of utility.

Any round of motions you go through for the sake of your health, to reduce your weight, to train your mind, or to save your soul, frowns into the dour visage of legalism and acquires its petrifying touch. If you go to the movies to be a good fellow, to be loyal to the crowd, you are wobbling on the line that divides play from work. Betting on the upshot of a contest spoils the sport and makes a business of it. When patriotism has to be manufactured by deliberate propaganda as a bulwark against alien enslavement, when religion is commended as a means to social cohesion and an alternative to the police force, the nation and the church show signs of internal dismemberment; they have ceased to be autonomous and self-validating. A need is descried to accentuate the selfish interests of the constituent units. If people demur at playing the game, they will have to get to work on the same project.

That all is vanity and all things pass, burdens the lament of every player. This burden, precisely, was responsible for the game initially. The same office that creates the play world presides over its obsequies. The same boredom heralds its birth and chants the funeral dirge, boredom being the blight of detachment from one's environment and the self-imposed isolation of man's ego. What play eventually succumbs to is the overformalization of itself. The rules of the game stifle the very game they are designed to set up. Free enterprise becomes shackled to a mechanism, movement is determined, and results can be computed in advance. The underdog has no chance for an overthrow, the dice are loaded, the cards are stacked. What's the use?—self-knowledge kills the self.

Mass unemployment constitutes just such a crisis in the economic sphere, for example. When millions are out of work, the condition is too prevalent for any victim to attribute his plight to sheer misfortune or to hope for a reversal of luck. Luck never offers an explanation, being instead the assumption that no explanations are called for. Fate is something else; fate is the certainty that explanation renders the event inevitable. And to the inevitable, man's proper response is ennui and a yawn. The ideas controlling society stiffen into dead letters when their object expires. No one can pitch in a game against fate. Boredom signalizes at once the origin of the social order and its disintegration. War destroys in the end the very government it had created. Every ideological construct eventuates in stalemate. The inner contest that kept the wheels spinning is settled by everybody getting tired of their witless revolvings.

Thus the religious wars of modern Europe were terminated by all sides losing interest in religion and relegating the issue to the individual's private caprice. Ecclesiastical objects were adjudged equally good; judges could take their pick. The individual was liberated to worship the God of his free choice, the understanding being God didn't matter. A new game promptly preempted the spotlight of history, that of nationalism. This shows already glaring symptoms of senility and exudes the stench of death. The strife among political entities will surely be composed, as that among churches has been, though likely not before millions more have perished in the cause. The arteries of patriotism will harden, nationalism will be gradually volatilized into a state of consciousness, and the individual will have a brand new freedom to revel in: he can select his favorite country as he now selects his church. Indeed, this is his right today if he is willing to drag his body along. So does boredom celebrate the requiem of every game.

Play, moreover, harbors another enemy within its bosom. This is skepticism. The skeptic foments insurgence more acutely than does the player who is merely bored. The skeptic is more fearful to cope with, though he is less dangerous in the long run. Vehement in his onslaught against the dogmas the institution rests on, the skeptic agitates rumblings that shake the bureaucracy squatting on its peak.

The powers lolling there seldom object seriously to people who sag and yearn for a cessation of turmoil; repose they fervently long for too. Any organization extends courtesy and tolerance toward its members who weary of what is going on. The somnolent hand of a bridge foursome may be dealt a shot of gin, or the *status quo* may be suspended till he is revived

by a round of gossip. Yet the buffoon who exposes his bust
in a fit of dejection must be banished from the sanctuary;
he smashes the game, spoiling somebody's rock crusher. Similarly, a capitalistic oligarchy deals graciously with spinsters
living on dividends, though they take no part in the affairs
that earn them and are distraught by mention of industrial
problems. But let an agnostic broach doubt about the system
that supports such excrescences, the reaction of that system
will be the expulsion of the offender. Any society is sensitive
to skeptical assaults, teaching that skepticism is the deadly
sin.

Still this foe may turn out to be actually an ally and a
friend. Franklin Roosevelt rendered valiant service to the
system he was no less valiantly accused of aiming to destroy,
while the pious dogmatist, Hoover, would probably have
wrecked it. The skeptic may succeed in manipulating a change
of rules and a consequent renewal of vitality. By some simple
device, like declaring deuces wild or cheating at examinations
or reshuffling the cards for a New Deal, the skeptic may re-
vive the corpse awaiting burial.

Whenever the spiritual person impinges upon a field of
play, he bursts on the scene as a skeptic too. There are two
distinct types of skepticism which are usually undifferen-
tiated. There is the skeptic who advocates a change of rules,
and the skeptic who rules out the game eschatologically.
Skepticism is the response of the real person toward any
regimen that purports to be absolute and define the purpose
of living. Such a claim spiritual man must denounce as pre-
tentious. Why call me good, why call yourself good? There
is but one good and that is God.

THE COERCION OF PLAYERS

What can be done about the bored and skeptical, the enemies of society who do not want to play and refuse assent to the rules of the game? How can the organization bring the rebel or the traitor to attend to the mandates of reason and to acknowledge the objectivity of its values? How can society enlighten the individual with a knowledge of himself?

Plainly two sorts of coercion are available, corresponding to the two halves of the soul-body dichotomy. In accord with the dualism the entire play life rests on, admonition and punishment may assume either ideal or physical forms. The church excommunicates and curses, but it breaks no bones and sheds no blood. The state tackles the problem at the other end.

The power wielded by any decree of excommunication I denominate *snobbery*. To be snubbed is to be ejected from the playground by the hoist of an upturned nose, by the lift of an eyebrow. Snobbery makes the most useful cudgel society has in its arsenal. Snobbery will reduce to immediate subjection all rebels except the few genuinely in earnest. Philosophers have universally ignored snobbery, being so adroit in its employment. Snobbery makes their world go round; it is appealed to, for example, when ideas are said to be weapons, the assumption being that the author's ideas are the artillery referred to.

Snobbery may be defined as making ideal relations effective in actual practice. The snob causes an objective order to function dynamically, with no dynamite being set off. Apparently will-less himself, he manages to get his will done by nuance or innuendo. The trick works best when the snob is conceded to have at his disposal a fund of power he could exert if pushed. The circle he operates in must tightly cohere; the subjects of snobbery must be tight themselves, tight in the vulgar sense of being drugged and drunk by their own ideas. Snobbery faces you with an accomplished fact; its touch is the delicate one of the last straw but still mighty enough to threaten your loss of face. Everybody else can see how blind you must be. If you do not appreciate Picasso, you belong in Philistia where there are no art galleries at all, you hardly belong with us. Your pride is invoked to club you to terms. Your own head brings you to heel. Your sense of honor alone keeps you from the honesty of complete capitulation.

Snobbery succeeds where it does succeed. No weapon is more convenient to use, but snobbery is dangerous to resort to. The backfire can be devastating. When it fails, unless there be physical power to back up the glassy stare and the glittering crown, a tempest may be unleashed in which the snob loses more than face: witness any proletarian revolt against an effete and supine nobility. The best people have to be acknowledged the best for them to occupy the best seats. The snob may be ensconced on soft cushions, but he had better not be too soft himself. And who are the best people? How do they get that superlative way?

Theoretically any idea whatsoever can be objectified into a basis for snobbery. Any idea can be ringed into a circus where performers jump through hoops at the crack of the whip. Snobbery operates equally well whether its objective designates illustrious ancestry, blue blood, red blood, good manners, bad manners, having nose and ears punched to hold ornaments, medals to pin on the breast, degrees to sign after one's name: any ideal superiority works, but only as long as those subject to its power cherish it as an ideal themselves. The victims must be conditioned to want to be like the snob as a condition for the snob to make them do as he wants.

Impute to reason whatever power you please, reason must be alert to grasp extrinsic power too. This transition from idea to matter can take place with amazing celerity. Any honor system, which is another name for snobbery, plumes itself on its faith in the inherent potency exerted by the idea of honor. Virtue is its own reward, vice its own penalty. To stew in the juice of one's iniquity is declared objectively to be atonement enough. Still, the authorities must be sure their ideas are functioning while their nobility is being acclaimed. So they are apt to pound them in with their kicking toe, as happened at West Point. The physical expulsion of malefactors, obviously, flouts the principle of the honor system, being a crasser violation of it than such a minor infraction as cribbing. But when honorable men find no virtue in the head, the sole place it may be sought is the foot. The alternative to snobbery is brute force, moral influence having been ruled out *a priori* by the rule exalting honor. The pen is mightier than the sword, provided your opponent has only a sword and you have a shotgun up your sleeve to reenforce the pen when that instrument falters.

Physical might, including the overt threat to use it, looms as the ultimate method play groups must depend on to rid themselves of protesters. This brutality assumes a wide array of patterns. The intransigent may be shown the door, he may be put on a black list, discharged from his job, thrown in jail, he may be nailed to the cross. What happens varies with the fashions that prevail, and depends on how severely the rebel has rocked the established boat. The healthier and more vital the organization, the greater its leniency and tolerance. Going concerns are inclined to trust the restraints of snobbery. Those stalled in their ruts show no such faith in the objectivity of their values. Skepticism dishes out a luxury that only a youthful and vigorous state can risk nibbling at. A crusty decrepit democracy must list subversives and watch them warily.

And I may add, a bit parenthetically at this point, any institution with real insight into its own nature would have for the skeptic in its midst a single answer: a laugh that would love him back into the fold.

There is a power which resides in neither the magic of snobbery nor the logic of a kick. That is the power of love. Spiritual power also is a power to compel. It is incorrect to say that the spiritual man wields no force, as idealistic snobs do say, who assert that power is inherently wicked and always to be renounced and execrated. But moral power differs alike from the egotistic brand I call snobbery and its materialistic pendant. Relative to these moral power is mysterious. It is not to be summoned through effort of the will, it is not reducible to any formula, it cannot be acquired by any possible know-how. Still the man of faith generates faith, he overcomes evil with good. The real person inspires confidence though he does not fix the form obedience shall take. If he imparts any lesson at all, it is the lesson never to imitate. Father and son differ in all assignable respects of taste and temperament, yet they are joined by an unbreakable bond of affection, perfectly one and just as perfectly two.

Spiritual power defies delineation in philosophic categories. Still, did not spirit hold our world together somehow, there would be no place for men to play in. If the arts and sciences were actually dealing with existence, they would soon disappear along with everything else. Thought invariably goes right past what keeps it going.

THE GENESIS OF PLAY

How came man to be the playing animal? If play be a hoax he falls for, who put the hex on him? Can man exculpate himself by pleading the pitfall was a put-up job?

Now we confront the ultimate conflict in human nature. Play exhibits the dualism between subject and object, the mating of the opposites knowledge springs from. The play world is the objective world man has created for himself, his own construct of symbols.

Every game precipitates a contest. Strife is the lot of the player. Conflict can be traced to the enduring dualism between man's ego and object, between the I and the not-I. Discovering an insuperable disharmony within himself, the individual finds himself in an environment that is hostile and repugnant. In getting away from that reality he succeeds only in fabricating a substitute he fain would get away from too.

Animals are not pestered by the dilemma. Their original integration with Nature is never disrupted. They do not play. Human culture stacks up as a ruse to regain the primitive Eden, expulsion from which dispatched man on the long trek back. Play amounts to no more than putting in the time till he stumbles on his starting place. It is surely a false start to play at being a cow, in Whitman's idiom. But implicit in the poet's envy is man's fury to destroy what he has made of himself. This passion annuls peace pacts before they are signed—the passion to turn upon and ravage the objects of his own handiwork, a passion that secthes forever beneath the complexion of civilization. If man has no cause to die for, life does not merit the metabolism to sustain it. Without a game to the death, life is not worth the candle.

What happened in that aboriginal garden to have called forth the curse? Legend has ascribed the fall to the noxious pulp of a forbidden apple. My own conjecture is more prosaic: the trouble started by *Homo sapiens* lying awake at night. Man is an animal afflicted with insomnia.

Sleep is the natural solvent of individuality. In sleep living creatures find relief from loneliness and rejoin the whole of things. The dog tired of the chase, the cat of her nocturnal escapades—these creatures ask no whys and wherefores. Oxen galled by the sight of harness and stable close their eyes and close off their minds, and are absorbed in the cosmic process whose manifestations they are. Whatever betides, their world remains unriven and therefore good. Man, a unique species, reacts with defiance. His wakefulness lingers after the need for it has passed, leaving him to reflect upon the transiency of this very need. Thereby man short-circuits himself from the universe and takes a stand outside. His consciousness of himself and of the organic process that enmeshes him become antagonistic. Boredom initiates a struggle to be sullenly and relentlessly waged. Civilization, its arts and sciences, express that rebellion in its active aspect, man's resolution to bypass reality and storm directly the gates of heaven.

The subject-object consciousness, whose feature is the detachment of the object from the subject, begins in memory. All contemplation is concerned with the past and deals in has-beens. Concepts are ejected as afterbirth from the womb of existence. Consequently one cannot know one's self, for while one is thinking and speaking, what one is slips into the bygone. Self-knowledge but grasps a series of extinct selves. Symbols are distilled from real things, the residue that remains after existence has perished. Concepts generalize and classify: we remember what experiences have in common. The idea of the rose flares out after real roses have withered; the idea survives their passing, an idea of the dead. That this ideal rose cannot be smelled and touched is what constitutes our detachment from it. We cannot do anything about it, we are bound to miss the point. The thought of the rose lingers as an object; this object sticks, it is static, superior to the weather, outside the time of Nature, in an order that negates time. Objective knowledge is confined to this realm of being. From the viewpoint of existence objective knowledge means entombment in eternity.

To be awake is to be conscious. Consciousness is a relation; consciousness cannot be conscious of itself. A dog is certainly conscious when gnawing a bone. But suppose consciousness persists after the bone is gone; the subject searches for an object through the haze of insomnia. Cannot this subject attach itself to the bone that once was and exists no more, to an object of its own conjuration? That image becomes forthwith an object in the strict sense. But the subject-object system is

quite different from the gnawer-gnawed unit the existent
animal is integrated into when actually eating. The ideal bone
alienates the thinker from his native environment, and in this
very feat of projection the ego is born. The ego is that element
of the creature that sustains a relation to the ideal realm.
In existence the whole self must be involved. Polarity obtains
here, too, but within unity. But the subject-object consciousness that constitutes man's inner-outer life is instantly entangled in a dualism with existence. The imaginary object is
thoroughly self-subsistent, and so is the ego that contemplates
it. Indeed, Platonists declare this system to be the true reality.
Yet the relation of this realm to the flux of Nature poses a
problem as disconcerting as it is obscure.

Any dog knows without being told that it cannot get along
on the image or the essence of a bone, in which respect the dog
may be wiser than the master. In many ways the ideal bone
is better. The ego takes keen delight in rolling the object
through the mind and examining its properties. But existence
cannot be one of these. The ideal bone cannot be chewed and
swallowed, it can be connected with the chewing-swallowing
organism only magically. Existence the ego can never produce by incantation. The ego can create the entire realm of
play but never anything real.

So man, the self-conscious potentate, finds himself mangled
between the mandibles of a riven world. The ideal is superior
to the real. There is more meat on its bone, one doesn't have
to bestir one's self to procure it, one may merely close one's
eyes. The trouble arises from the prospect of starving with
a cupboard full of ideal bones. The teeth-stomach mechanism,
which resents being put off with good ideas and Platonic
dainties, looms before the thinker as a foreign and un-

thinkable segment of himself. Man was driven from his Eden in driving in upon himself. The ego discovers an object in the body, which in being known is projected beyond the knower. The body, the material world, swing into man's ken as objects of Nature, "mind precipitated" in Emerson's phrase. But a precipitated world is a fallen world. Man tramples it down in the same heave whereby he rises above it. The fruit of the Tree of Knowledge is delicious but toxic. Humanity henceforth is doomed to eke out a career in a hostile environment. Having achieved solitary grandeur, man is harassed by anxiety and a grander starvation than ever threatened the brute.

All men desire to know, to figure out this anomalous predicament and to make the knower master of the known. Knowledge relates the ego to its objects in the only manner possible, requiring the known to be grasped in symbolic form. The intellect can make contact with existence solely by the tentacles it protrudes. These symbols the thinker deems real, existence being denigrated to mere appearance. These objects must stay put. Nature, in which the body is intricated, may acquiesce out of politeness, but seldom for long. Instinct fitfully interrupts, upsetting the game boards and negating the essences the ego hallows.

The ego longs for heaven where it can bask in eternity. It frets and fusses, straining at the leash that binds it to earth. Still this ego, save in the case of the mystic, cannot ignore existence in utter snobbery. The worst it can do is to make faces, to hurl bad names, such as illusion, fate, matter, and mechanism; its own body it vilifies as flesh, instinct, passion, and will. Such pejoratives are soon serving a further purpose: they become standards the subject construes events by. Ideas assimilated into the subject for ends of interpretation merge into magic. The line between magic and science can never be wholly erased. Thus it is commonly believed today that inventing a name for a disease makes half a cure, and that outfitting plush offices for cancer foundations marks a long stride forward in research.

Magic builds the road that science plods. Science unifies events as they are remembered, reduces them to laws, which laws are shifted to the future for purposes of prediction. The essences in terms of which laws are stated are infinite in their ramifications. Certain ideas are sifted out of the maze of possibility as relevant to existence. These may fit so trimly that all thinkers are constrained to think in such tokens, and an objective system seems blessed with the holy water of consensus. Yet there is no necessity to adhere to this unanimity. Any innovator is free to advertise a game of his own and sell to clients wherever he can find them. Philosophy, science, theology, all raise their structures on a common foundation, that of knowledge; all are objective in the same sense. But from the ground up their buildings differ in architecture, and inside the temples differ even more, in the jewels that adorn them and the rituals they inspire, each idol spitting contempt at its rivals. Snobbery chants the familiar refrain that each has the facts in its treasure chest; the word *fact* being an abracadabra in every book.

All constructions of thought, however, are bound to respect the elementary requirement of knowledge, that of causal determination. The knower has to get the thing known under his thumb, cut and dry it, hang it up on the peg of his mind. No law can make room for an event that is unique and beyond explanation. The idea of the mechanical subjugates existence and brings it to the terms of thought. When the correspondence of essence and existence is complete, then Nature can go about her appointed task of moving in conformity with the logic of an unmoved mover; then the universe may be judged acceptable, being the counterpart of one's idea of what a universe ought to be.

Occasionally public announcement is made that this pinnacle has been scaled. Some years ago Sir James Jeans proclaimed that the cosmos, definitely, resembled a great thought more than a huge machine. Theologians applauded the dictum with glee: that big idea could be none other than the God who was their professional monopoly. The grandstands resounded as if a home run had been hit. It was an exciting incident, but that was all. For there is actually no difference between envisaging the universe as a thought and as a machine. Logic and machinery are the same to the ego. Thought yearns for a suitable object. The desideratum of pure thought is a perfect machine, as Spinoza, the clearest of the thinkers, clearly saw. Indeed, the sole reason for the universe ever having been regarded as a machine is that someone was thinking about it.

PLAY AND THE WILL

No war horse troops so monotonously through treatises on human nature as the will. Is the will free or determined? Good or evil? How can its possessor contrive to control it? Like some fractious beast, the will must be gentled.

This concept of training the will gives a plain picture of what the will is: the will is that collective force which the ego alienates into the body. The will does not represent what man genuinely wants as a person. Spiritual man has no will in the sense of a dynamic detachable from his self. The will, for the ego, is what man is conscious of wanting when he is conscious of himself. The will is the goal of his psychological game. Thus the will is necessarily tainted with egotism, corrupted by the very dualism that has split man within himself and made one part the object for the other.

Each ego constitutes an individual soul, a discrete psychic substance, entitled by its metaphysical status to certain inalienable rights. Each ego dwells as solitary as a monk in his cell or an angel in the sky. One can agree and compact with other egos, but only through mutual consent and on a rationally comprehended basis. The relations among egos are contractual and purposeful, precisely those which institute a region of play.

Any play-work ensemble, be it a hockey team, a steel corporation, a church, or state, can be defined as a rational concretion, organized for amusement or utility, for the benefit of its individual components, a system therefore of concerted egotism. The specific content of its purposes matters not a whit. A gospel of love can provide the basis of a militant cult or a sanguinary crusade. Any ideology whatever will furnish sufficient incentive for war, if motives are mechanically maneuvered to that end. Within the memory of many now living, soldiers marched into battle shouting the inane slogan of war-to-end-war.

Believing such aggregations to be spiritual weaves the grand illusion of mankind. Persons may discover one another, howsoever impersonal their contact—there can be no law forbidding this. But the team as such is designed to eliminate every personal element. A baseball club remains intact though its units be traded to the enemy camp. A player belongs to the outfit whose uniform he wears, as a slave belonged to

the owner whose brand he bore. Desertion of one's gang is
no offense; it is highly commended if the act of treason be
accompanied by a raise in pay. The baseball magnates shuffle
players about in the fashion of a garage mechanic rummaging
a tool kit for a nut to fit the bolt. Customers like their game
that way. It satisfies a craving for the mechanization of all
human relations and the debasement of man.

Spiritual man enjoys no such freedom to determine his
cosmic obligations. Adages of proverbial wisdom such as
caveat emptor, eternal vigilance is the price of liberty—and
of solvency too, get the other guy before he gets you, do
not apply to moral persons. These gems of observation do
tell us what to expect of players. The rank individualism they
display players call freedom, especially those who turn it to
their profit. Where there's a will, there's a way; but skill in
screwing one's body through a jammed and jangling crowd,
success in getting one's impersonal way, does not finally solve
the problem of the will. A will that has leaped so agilely the
hurdles of space is still beset by time. The body is infested
by a multiplicity of desires, quarreling among themselves,
pulling in diverse directions, each clamoring to be the will
that makes up the mind. How can the will be trained so that
you can get along with yourself after you have got the better
of others?

Where there is a will, there is a job. Shall one coddle the
body, lapping up as much pleasure as can be gorged through
gratifying every impulse in turn? Or shall one despise such
pleasure on the ground that its source is carnal and beneath
his dignity? Hedonism and asceticism disagree on this point.
But they do agree on abstracting the ego from the flesh and
on recognizing this dualism as the basis of their answers.

Little of consequence, therefore, is involved in the alternative. Either horn of the dilemma punctures the spiritual life. Libertine and flagellant are equally logical, though their logic stems from different premises. Sensualism and monasticism flower from a common stalk. No choice more significant than the flip of a coin divides the lecher from the monk. The same vanity bedecks itself in the silk of the epicure and the filth of the cynic. Seraglio and cloister are equally favorite abodes of the devil; both remove their inmates from the moral affairs of mankind, and neither retreat permits the spiritual way of living.

Most people plump for some version of the ascetic life, for at least a mild degree of stoicism. The will must be disciplined and held in check by the charioteer of reason. This leads to the compromise of play. The ego wants to win, but in winning the will has to be put off by assigning it ends that are symbolic and false to its animal nature. Can one not play at winning? Is it not enough to know that you have won? Does not knowledge of superiority suffice? The booty you amass can be devoted to educational foundations, the spread of culture, and gaudy good causes. You never wanted the filthy stuff anyway. What we all primarily crave is the recognition of our ego's rights, and given that, we are ready to give up material winnings. So we will play that we're not actually in the jungle. The defeated candidate wires congratulations. A man may be down but he is never out. Live and let live. Be a good sport. Everybody agrees to pretend that, win or lose, he does not want what in fact he did want very much. The slickest liar zooms to the top. Nothing really happens in play. In making his ego paramount, man sterilizes his will. The will is trained to play dead.

This annulment of the will currently passes for sublimation. Sublimation is supposed to have a formula for integrating that split and sundered being that is yourself. But the civil war between mind and body ends in the uneasy truce of anxiety. Asceticism, heroically embraced and resolutely persisted in, may culminate in victory over the flesh, though it is a Pyrrhic victory and the ego emasculates itself in achieving it. Supreme on one level, its influence has dwindled on the lower level to zero. The ego wastes away pottering with symbols; there is nothing for it to do.

Halfway measures, however, avail only to mete out confusion. Observe the quagmire play has made of sex. Sex is machined into a gadget for psychologists to tinker with; sex is a piece of apparatus to be wrenched from the car, a sort of carburetor wherein the libido of the body is impregnated with the vaporings of the soul. Spiritually, sex is not to be detached from the person himself. Morally, sex begets that person's strongest attachments, and out of sex spring his deepest joys, the bonds that unite husband and wife, parent and child. Monogamy makes a satisfactory mode of living, a natural way, perhaps the only truly exciting way.

The sexual life morally expressed shows merely certain motions in common with the subject-object counterfeit known as romantic love. In the game of romance husband and wife, far from being partners in a single enterprise, are plunged into combat, sharing the feature alone of being of the opposite gender. In its pristine form of courtly love, romanticism made little of this, entailing a total abjuration of sex as a physical function. Love being otherworldly and ascetic was twisted into an egotistic flight from the body. The knight of old sought no carnal intercourse with the lady of his dreams.

She was too chaste and celestial to be defiled by his touch. A whiff of her handkerchief sufficed to sate his gonads. Then he was content to vanish forever, to die in bliss and to pursue the chase of the infinite in the realm of essence. The love-death of grand opera, despite its dilution to the insipidity of the popular song, trills the same theme, adapted now to the absorptive power of the masses who can neither aesthetically nor financially afford the Met.

Few carry the game to the extreme of Tristan and Isolde. Yet every other college girl will solemnly assure you she wouldn't marry the best man on earth. To tie one's self to any existential situation means a sacrifice of the perfect ideal. This bromide by no means implies that the young lady is resolved on being either a nun or an old maid. But you can infer from it that her husband is going to find her mighty hard to get along with. She may sing, give me all of you; but all she has to offer is her ego.

The debacle of using sex as an organ of mystic rapture and a net to snare the divine is evident on all sides. The egotism a radio crooner incenses shows up in the divorce courts. Exalting sex into a plaything of the mind impairs it as a physical function. Love has been so celebrated in story and song that it fizzles into disappointment when attempted in bed. The body fails to keep pace with the soaring of the ego. People read and talk incessantly about sexual love, then when it comes to performance they turn out homosexuals or celibates, wholly unsatisfactory as mates.

Their ideals are aesthetic, and the aesthetic consciousness has no real concern with the existence of what it contemplates. Prattle over sex, however profuse and obscene, has no real connection with sex itself. The gourmand cannot enjoy a full meal the way a truck driver enjoys it. The throngs now clogging the divorce mills are obviously not glutted with sex. Instead they are bent on rejecting authentic opportunities. A factor from a sphere outside is foiling and frustrating the drive of the flesh. Fabricating sex into a toy of the mind plays one out of sexual experience. Any distraught divorcee still under the illusion that another partner will fill the bill sighs a warning against the game of romantic love. The effect of play is to paralyze the will.

THE POLARITY OF MAN

Man is a composite creature. He has been split down the middle or, better, across the neck into higher and lower sections. Scribbling new labels for, and descriptions of, these elements of human nature makes the chief attraction of philosophy.

Incontrovertibly such duality exists. From it art and science trace their origins, from it work and play derive. Nothing is gained by denouncing this cleavage as regrettable and adorning it as the dogma of Original Sin. No reforms can be expected from exhorting man to repair the breach and to secure integration within himself. Self-knowledge pursues a will-o'-the-wisp. No tricks of psychology avail to this end. There is no royal know-how to maturity of mind, and any mind is immature that seeks it in a how-to-do-it book. The rift is as irreparable as it is tragic.

Still, pessimism need not present a motion to adjourn. This dualism is not ultimate. The ego-body couple constitutes itself but one pole of man's being. Man is more complicated than the scientists of his nature think. The other pole, usually left out in the cold, is the spiritual person. The universe, moreover, wherein man lives, is not to be identified with the construct the subject makes of Nature: that mechanical contexture of fate and determinism, the objective structure of science and philosophy. The cosmos inevitably possesses the same character as man himself, whether this quality be personal or impersonal.

It is futile to reprobate man the player and to execrate his play. Man is going to keep on graving his idols, despite the ravings of the prophets. We cannot fare without civilization. The capture of paradise, whether this is envisaged as a return to Eden or an advance into Utopia, charts a vain campaign. Man must make shift in a state of tension. The most we can hope is to get the poles straight between which tension must obtain to be productive.

The spiritual pole is not to be ignored. It must remain intact, albeit everything about it remains untold and un- tellable. Man has to resign himself to ultimate skepticism. To elucidate the spirit means to repudiate it. To know God ob- jectively is to kill God. To have religion is to renounce a religious way of life. The intellect is forbidden to press existence beneath its thumb, for existence hardens under impalement and stiffens into nothingness, and existence can be formulated only when it no longer exists. Moral behavior, reduced to rules, degenerates into stilted piety, righteousness into self-righteousness, good into evil. The spirit instead keeps himself alert and vibrant. Each occasion is a universe in itself. Not even life is to be reverenced; in degrading life into an object of awe and worship, we cease to be vital our- selves.

A program of self-knowledge is free to determine its pur- poses and to manipulate objects into means to those ends. It

is free to decree laws to govern players and to punish trans-
gressors. Spiritual existence, however, offers no such entice-
ments and privileges. Man is not free to join the universe.
He is in, inextricably, by virtue of his birth. In play the ego-
body figment is free to be bound. In the moral universe man
is bound to be free.

As a spiritual person man indulges in no conceits that he
has begotten himself. He is no self-made creature, whose
religion consists in adoring his creator. God is not a pseu-
donym for his ego. A real person never denies, nor forgets,
that others presided at his birth, and that after a few brief
flashes he will sink into the grave to flash no more. During
the interval his powers are rigidly circumscribed. No aug-
mentation of them accrues from a knowledge of them. Despite
his embellishments the basic activities available to man add
up to no impressive list: sowing and reaping, building his
shelter and spinning his raiment, singing and dancing, marry-
ing and procreating. Man's is a humble career and it behooves
him to walk humbly in it. His true freedom lies in welcoming
the common lot and in reaping freedom from whatever garden
necessity may sow. Whatever shall be revealed concerning
his creator and the meaning of creation is revealed in his
dealings with the created world and his fellow creatures. In
spiritual living alone man must descry both the source of
his freedom and how to express it. Freedom in the sense of
doing as he pleases is as far from the comprehension of the
real person as it is from his choice.

It is hard for man to give up his soul; it is even harder for
him to admit there is no other way to save it. Man writhes
under the chastisement of being told that his confections of
culture are but snow upon the desert's face. But to realize just

this is the condition of their endurance and improvement. It sounds like atheism to say that to find God we must abandon all belief in the idea of God. Still, the spiritual pole of existence has to be kept free of rubbish and preserved unadorned, whatever be the price to human pride.

The universe is full of a number of things. And if we would but consent to be so many more, we might be as merry as kings. And just to be merry, now and then, would do us good, more good than those who know all about us will ever know. Instead of playing being gods ourselves, why can we not, once in a while, play with the Living God?

V

STRIFE OF OPPOSITES

TO BE OR NOT TO BE: Hamlet was stabbed by the very fork whose prongs he had polished. Man cannot choose merely to review the choices before him. Even suicide calls for positive action. Man is body as well as mind, will as well as reason. Decision he cannot shirk by curling up in the cupola of an interrogation point.

The career of no entity in the cosmos takes the placid form of having its own way. The inertia of every body subjects it to gravitation. The rest of the universe combines to fix the path of any moving body. The shortest path is not to be deduced from the principles of logic. This course is dependent on pressures within the environment. Nothing exists in the vacuum of its own individuality. Existence implies acting and being acted on, pushing and getting pushed about. Nature is a maze of forces. Every creature from electron to man must extract its independence from dependence on others. Attainment of reality never results from avoidance of tension. Tension means simply that no one is alone. Integration of personality by no means brings to pass that peace of mind the disintegrated yearn for.

Acceptance of the real world, however, does abolish such strife as is unreal. Entrance into the universe means release from illusions about it. Most of the contentions are unreal whose ravages we are continually bewailing. These conflicts rage within the ego-body system which is closed to spiritual influence. It is the vexation of play that embitters us. The anguish the loser is punished with pierces so deeply because winning would have been no more real.

Nearly everything we read in the newspapers we have to read out of mind as futile and nugatory. Little is being decided though there is terrific fuss about decisions. Every four years we froth over a presidential election. Partisans foam in mad earnest. Progressives bluster that a thing can never happen twice; conservatives throb that nothing can happen for the first time. One listens to what the Republicans say about the Democrats, to what the Democrats say about the Republicans; then, believing both, votes for the nonobjective *tertium quid,* which doesn't require going to the polls. The day after the crisis there is handshaking all around, and the uproar subsides into the loser's sullen whimper that he could do the job better and will prove it a quadrennium hence. Whatever freedom we noncombatants enjoy depends on keeping as main issue who is going to be elected. The statesman who entertains a nobler idea than that of nabbing the job should be prevented from achieving even that. What the country always needs is a president who likes golf better. Politics must be kept as harmless and inexpensive as possible. And this curb is quickly jumped when a politician gets seized and suffused by the notion of a crusade, requiring us to be made over to conform to his conception of our good.

A political campaign certainly manifests the strife of opposites, a clash of teams and parties. As a political animal man must be resigned to duality, even a dictatorship engendering it beyond national boundaries if not within. Yet this conflict, despite its preemption of the front pages and the television receivers, lacks spiritual significance. Politics churn a spume of talk. Elections provide fun and profit for the winners, toil and boils for the losers. But nothing genuine settles from the gush.

A PARLOR GAME THAT IS PLAYED ELSEWHERE

The rule of the game is this: I toss you a concept, you bat me its opposite. Unless everybody nods assent to your come-back, you lose your turn, the player sitting next takes over, and you pay a forfeit—we will say spending the evening reading Aristotle's *Analytics*.

I say *good* . . . . . You reply *evil*.
I say *peace* . . . . . You reply *war*.
I say *health* . . . . You reply *disease*.
I say *play* . . . . . You reply *work*.
I say *freedom* . . . You reply *slavery*.
I say *God* . . . . . You reply (with some hesitation) *the devil*.
I say *heaven* . . . . You shout, oh, *hell*.

We have gone far enough. You demur on the devil and on hell. What I want to note anyway is this *either-or* swing itself, the up-and-down rhythm suggestive of children on their teeter-totter boards. If our game were confined to a parlor pastime, it would be innocuous, maybe amusing. But unfortunately we succumb to the witchery of language, deposing that verbal opposites are real opposites too. We fancy we can produce any desired condition by the elimination of its antithesis.

Such strife revolves about the pivot I have called magic. Magic consists of the attempt to control events through the manipulation of ideas.

Consider the antagonism we have nominated between health and disease. Here is a man who doesn't feel at par. He has tried all the vitamin pills ever broadcast, he has gone the round of the nostrums. He has touched the bases of the hospital clinics and crossed home plate with a clean bill of health. No describable ailment afflicts him, no medicine reaches him except at his pocketbook. He grumbles his way from specialist to quack, only to find nothing the matter. Yet he fails to find health.

On the other hand, doctors say it is possible for one to carry around a nest of easily diagnosed maladies still feeling fine and with no impairment of vigor. Health means a state of vitality that can contain disease, as a strong character can contain violent passions, augmenting its own strength by the obstreperous elements held in leash. The normal adult may be doing himself a service in harboring a cluster of focal infections somewhere in his anatomy just to keep the body on the *qui vive*. Certainly health is not to be defined as the absence of disease, nor is freedom from disease equivalent to health. Our *either-or* tug of war will not apply, much to the discomfiture of the annual check-up teeterers. An antiseptic residence under a bell jar soothes many minds because those minds are predisposed to superstition. Nothing but a love of magic may be disclosed during the rite of the periodic health examination.

The same sorcery befogs our politics of peace and war. It is generally believed that peace is brought about by hostile armies quitting their guns and the Senate's passing a resolution declaring hostilities over. We proclaim Armistice Day and get drunk on incantations. The Constitution naïvely states that only an Act of Congress can initiate war. This magical notion has long been overridden by the movement of events. Whatever be our fixed ideas on the matter, war and peace in international relations differ only insofar as the use of force differs from the threat to use it, a difference that has become so vague as to keep the world in a continual broil. The peace we have is playfully known as cold war. But our idea of peace is a shade more preposterous: the peace we pray for is the consummation of settling down and relaxing through the global extension of the cult of the quiet mind. This delightful idea is kept from realization, we think, by there being wicked people in the world. These enemies of mankind seem unwilling to let us sit on what we deem requisite for our quietude.

But real peace is no such gentle opposite of war. Real peace is no blessedness that is coming to pass by spiking the guns, though that spoofery be executed by the United Nations. Peace can provide no assurance that we will get without the trouble of fighting the boons we have been accustomed to fight for. This idea of peace is at once the opposite of war and identical with war, the idea that springs the trigger setting off actual war. Peace and war, as statesmen oracle the terms, have so much in common as to be practically interchangeable. Why not simply abolish peace by an expurgation of the dictionary: abolish peace, then war would go too, for there would be nothing to fight for.

Logomachy bedevils us again in fixing the relation between good and evil. Are good and evil opposites in the sense that by ridding ourselves of one we automatically clutch the other?

Moral education from the cradle on is enchanted by this formula, and deluded by it we hustle about the planet to set civilization aright. One day we chase Hitler off the premises, then turn on the Russians the next, with numerous sideshows for the extirpation of lesser hellions like gamblers, subversives, and racketeers. Virtue consists in running the vacuum cleaner. But indefatigable dirt-chasers often sweep the house so clean that the family has to sit on the back porch, the parlor being reserved for funerals and when the minister calls.

When the unclean spirit is gone out of a man, he walketh through dry places, seeking rest, and findeth none. Then he saith, I will return into my own house whence I came out; and when he is come, he findeth it empty, swept, and garnished. Then goeth he, and taketh with himself seven other spirits more wicked than himself, and they enter in and dwell there: and the last state of that man is worse than the first.

The conclusion Jesus drew from his story was, so shall it be also unto this wicked generation.

The frenzy to do good by doing away with its apparent opposite provides the fuel for the devil's mills. This perversion passes for idealism, of which there are two types, one relying on snobbery for the miracle, the other resorting to force. In the face of iniquity the idealist may either turn up his nose or clench his fists. Whatever his physical contortions, the same magical purpose breaks through: to realize good by blasting its ideal antithesis. The devil, however, is not to be scotched so sprucely. He cannot be driven from the world, for the driver himself is that same devil in a peculiarly malignant guise. Good ideas avail not to wipe out evil. Our righteousness must exceed the righteousness of the Pharisees. The Pharisee pulls out the weeds but his garden withers away as barren as a wind-ravaged sand dune. He swears devotion to his inner convictions though the world be destroyed. And the world tends to curl and shrivel wherever he touches it. The self-conscious do-gooder allies himself with the evildoer. Morally the relation between good and evil can be summarized in saying that the greatest evil is to work at doing good.

The tension of good and evil tells the central theme of man's moral life. But this tale precipitates no direct antagonism, and ends in a transformation of evil rather than its outright destruction. The victory of the good is never accomplished by frontal assault and the annihilation of the adversary. Triumph through tribulation, joy through suffering, good through the overcoming of evil, this is the story of man's moral adventure. And the first evil to be overcome is the idea that you know a formula how it is done.

That things are not always what our words say, you can see at a glance at the work-play couple. But here you cry, the distinction is clear and ineffaceable. Every schoolboy knows the difference. What else does recess ring out? The classroom signifies one world, the football field another. Why do we play but to escape the slavery of work? Why do we work except to earn the wherewithal to play, where we have freedom to expand into our glorious selves?

Work and play are admitted to be different. But the ends of a yardstick differ too. No points can be further apart on that particular scale of being. Yet no point so much resembles one end of the stick as the other, and if you do not consult the conventional scratches along its length, you cannot tell which end you hold in your hand. Work and play are opposites, true enough. They are opposite ends of what our ego-body dichotomy has stuck us with.

Both work and play are determined by rules governing the activities involved. In work and play alike the actor must abide by fixed mandates. Equally in both one is forbidden to feel his way. Ideas decide events in magical fashion, made possible by abstracting the field and seceding from reality. Work and play diverge solely in the rewards they bestow and in the motives that instigate them. Play is fun in itself, it is its own compensation, so it can be carried on with an appearance of spontaneity. Work, on the contrary, fails to thrill, yet it is economically productive and has something to show for itself after the effort is over. But does this difference in motive suffice to render work and play real opposites? Does it entitle play to exult in freedom, and condemn work to languish under the curse of bondage?

The dialectics of freedom usually involve shuttling between the bumping posts of a latent contradiction. A discourse on the subject resembles a seance with an astrologer. In order to have your fortune told, you must assume that the future is fixed. Your future is an object that can be scrutinized and known, otherwise there is nothing to foretell. Yet the reason you want to ascertain that future is to change it, and to divert a predestined course into channels of your own dredging. You are eager to know what the stars have to say so that you may do better by yourself than they are set to do. Thus the business of fortunetelling implies altering the unalterable. That this sounds illogical matters not a cent commercially.

Every game conceals the same surd. You feel free, and morally you are. You insist on knowing that freedom, which is impossible and which deprives you of it.

Peace of mind, the placating of fear, shaking off anxiety —these are the prancing steeds bolted on our merry-go-round. We long to gallop off to freedom, we buy our tickets with gusto. Some magic know-how lies in the manipulation of motives within and of natural laws without. But it is precisely these motives and laws that clap us in the clink. Can we lift ourselves by tugging at our fetters?

The founding fathers drew up the Constitution "to secure the blessings of liberty for ourselves and our posterity." The ink on that document was barely dry before the clamor arose for a Bill of Rights to guarantee freedom from the Constitution itself. We yearn to banish anxiety, to erect bastions against the onslaughts of worry: a country retreat, a bank vault bulging with bonds, the doctor's certificate after the semiannual duty. But having gloated over the treasures in the ark, we grow apprehensive about the ark itself. How strong is the fortress we rely on for our strength? We get caught in the trap we set to nab trespassers. We struggle against insomnia, and fretting to get to sleep wakes us the wider. The deadliest foe of freedom is the resolution to be free. The truly free man is as unaware of his freedom as he is of the servitude he is free from.

GOING BACK TO THE BEGINNING

Man is born free, but everywhere he is in chains. Since a new-born infant lacks any discernible faculty describable as freedom, we must surmise that Rousseau was referring in his celebrated dictum to the original parturition of the race. That takes us back to the Garden of Eden, howsoever you denominate that crib.

In the Biblical myth God gave his images a commandment long before anything was said about the famous tree. Adam and Eve were told to tend the garden, to increase and multiply, and to have dominion over the earth. In these orders was slipped the recipe for freedom insofar as such an elusive enterprise can be capsuled at all. There have always been multitudes of free people in the world doing just that. But these are not the people who sit for philosophers, nor the patients who pay psychiatrists their fees. Humanity is a vast deal better than its critics rate it, since these critics have scant sense of the freedom that lets the world go on.

The creator covenanted to share with man his own power of creativeness. Man became a participant with God in man's allotted sphere. In being God's image man is creative as a factor in existence; and out of such activity, the promise ran, man shall find his joy. The universe is God's, but it belongs to man as well. God and man meet. But this trysting place is never within man as an individual and isolated entity. God and man meet in the world, in that all-pervading spirit that encompasses it entire. God is free from the limitations of finite existence. He is free to be both what he is in himself and what he is not. God can be God, and at the same time the billions of entities that compose his creation. A creature, however, cannot be both himself and another. We have no power to create objects of our own by taking thought and aspiring to be what is other than ourselves. The so-called objective worlds we spew forth from our own insides can never achieve reality. Existence is more than idea; what more is just what we cannot contribute.

We attain freedom in being ourselves. But it is not so simple as it sounds. We fulfill God's intention, we know his love and appropriate his power, not by striving to be God but by occupying our proper station in the firmament. As the transcendental designer God cannot become an object of our knowledge. No idea of our minds congrues immediately with God's mind. When we project our idea of the One, or of the Whole, beyond ourselves, in a frenzy to grasp him, God becomes an object, called the Absolute or what-not. But this object necessarily excludes the subject that contemplates it. Reality, however, includes the thinker that objectifies. Hence the idea of God ranks as an illusion, for it alienates us from God. Man is forbidden to make any image of God; to project an idea of his own and worship it as God. Regardless of the fund of knowledge that inflates that idea, it can never be more than an idol, being counterfeit and supposititious. God has made images of himself. He alone can bestow existence upon an idea. These images are evident in ourselves, in each of us. The sole way to know God is to make good as his image, to be yourself. God exists in himself, but he exists too in every entity of his universe. He is the power that has made all things. Man can exert that power too, by allowing it to infuse and to possess him. What is prohibited the finite creature is the ambition to be more than he is, to identify his spirit with the spirit of God or with the spirit of any other creature. To do so is egotism, and egotism is man's besetting temptation. To identify one's self with God is the temptation of mysticism, with another creature that of romantic love.

God's spirit and the spirit of a creature are in communion, but only as long as they remain separate and distinguishable. Our freedom is to be sought staying at home and tending the garden. This smacks of the drab and cloddy stint of the peasant; we will have none of it. We can do better by ourselves than God has done.

This endeavor to go God one better, which is the nub of play, implies a psychic withdrawal from the actual universe. Though God can be both in and out, the finite entity is restricted to a here and now. Our aspiration to be more than we are wedges a separation between knower and known. The world is converted into an object, from which its damnation follows. From our pinnacle outside we can know the world in terms of science, we can admire it, judge it, scheme how to improve it. But we cannot genuinely love it, nor share it. We have saved our souls but lost our spiritual selves, and we find ourselves belabored with a burden. We have seined our treasure from the transiency of the flux; still, we are bored with our catch and frustrated by the flux. The world, of course, is to blame for our tragic fix. In a frantic grab to validate our self-won freedom we seize the sorry scheme of things entire in the desperate hope of remolding it nearer to the heart's desire. These histrionics entail both work and play, collectively known as culture. Dressing the garden makes a prosaic chore. So we condemn to slavery those of our fellows not so smart as we are, or we will invent a tractor. All this we can do on our own. God, being superfluous, is ignored. This is eminently proper, since the rejection of God was the initial drink that ended in the spree. We swell in pride at our agnosticism; in knowing nothing about God, we seem to know much about everything else. As for the devil, he obviously isn't; there is no such species nor spectacle. True, the devil can never constitute an object of knowledge. The reason is simple. The devil is identical with the subject that does the knowing. The devil resides nowhere but in man himself.

LUCIFER AND HIS GAME

According to legend the first person to escape to freedom was not Adam but an angel, Lucifer, an ancient alias of the devil. From his case it has long been clear that the will to be God merges smoothly into deviltry. On this head Lucifer has rolled up considerable experience. He has employed a wide assortment of tricks, with which the world has reckoned to its destruction.

But why, you ask, does the devil want to destroy the world? Your question shows you are full of the devil yourself; still I will answer as if I were not. The devil has only one possible motive for destroying the world. And this, incredible as it may seem, is identical with your motive in destroying it: the devil just wants to make the world better. Lucifer knows more about making a universe than God knows. His alone is the secret of freedom. Only he can compose the strife between soul and body, and create a harmony of opposites.

A possible way of tranquilizing the turmoil might lie in muffling the stirrings of the ego within the folds of the flesh. By constricting his total personality to its carnal section man might find respite amid the profusions of Nature, aspiring to nothing beyond his skin. He might surpass the animal through the idealization of his animal inheritance. Eating and drinking, not to the stomach's fill but to the mind's content, would then define freedom. The ideal man would be an ordinary specimen of the species grown fat beyond natural specifications.

This tack Lucifer has tried with results distasteful to himself. After all, the devil is as fastidious as the pure ego alone can be. He is a gentleman and a snob. Drunkards, prostitutes, and gluttons ignite no aesthetic glow in him. Besides he observed long ago, as you can by looking around, that such wretches do little beyond themselves to improving the world. Their avoirdupois disarms them. They are guiltless of world wars and mass massacres. Instead of inspiring others to deviltry, their corruption puts most people on guard. Thus the devil listens in mild approbation to sermons from Christian pulpits against gross materialism and sensualism. These inconsequential diatribes have the positive value of keeping preachers off subjects that might prove inimical to his interests. The devil wants the souls of men, not their stinking carcasses. No one can go to the devil through carnal indulgences; the devil won't have him. It was not that way that Lucifer got to be the devil.

It has served his purposes no better to siphon the will of man into its upstairs receptacle. Mysticism has its drawbacks, as the devil ascertained in his traffic with monks. Ascetics are too headstrong to harken to any appeal save reason. When they say to hell with the world, they mean literally that, and they refuse to raise a finger to help it. Besides, few mortals want to be saints. Such figures soar too haughtily to impinge on the mundane. Such chosen vessels carry scant cargo.

Aestheticism bodes immeasurably better prospects. Portions of existence can be pinched off and parted from the whole of it, and employed symbolically to panoply his purpose. The world can be remade by making segments of it autonomous. The world can be improved by destroying it piecemeal. That such a project entails travail deters the devil not a step, for the end conceived is noble and worth the candle. He will show God how it is done, though the exhibition be tented as a sideshow. The laceration involved is but incidental. Naturally Lucifer abhors the sight of blood; still the shedding of blood delights him if it aids his cause. Despite the havoc he spreads, every tyrant knows himself as the most magnanimous of men. The ideal goal he glorifies excels all others, the devotion to it he excites flowers in martyrdom. The persecutions he must resort to are designed merely to pry everybody's eyes open to the vision vouchsafed him. The devil never for a moment suggests that we actually kill the Russians. We are just to indoctrinate them in freedom and democracy, to do them over into nice people like ourselves. We have the right idea, and it is imperative to put that idea to work. Let justice be done, though the world be destroyed.

Anyone raises the devil who plays this wise at being God. He squirms at being a creature, he gets bored at the minor role. He requires as a motive for action the prosecution of an ideal end. He must know what he is doing and why. Detached from existence, he cannot take his part spontaneously. He never is, he is always to be blest. The Kingdom of Heaven does not encompass him, the devil feels uncomfortable within it. His kingdom must be strictly objective. Though its playground be billboarded with religious streamers, it proves sterile and stultifying, subversive of the spiritual life.

An impasse baffles us and disaster blocks us by reason of the impotence of our ideas to create the existential situation they envisage. Ideas do create objects; indeed, idea and object are identical. But no idea can confer existence upon itself. We plume ourselves on our ideas being timeless and eternal. But eternity merely feathers their ineptitude, the real universe being a temporal concern. Instead of being creative, the object which the ego fabricates succumbs forthwith to the determinism the ego rivets on all its products. The play world is never the plastic, viable work of God. Its strangle hold condemns every effort to attain freedom into a magic lantern show. The freedom it permits, far from being the opposite of slavery, designates the same condition tagged with a different ticket.

STILL, PLAY IS FUN

Both work and play belong to that objective sphere doomed by the ego that staked it out to be a land of serfdom. Any organized game, from a totalitarian state to sidewalk crap shooting, gasps in its tight encasement, its distinctive shell. These convulsions are not generally observed, for players want it that way. Released from the strait jacket, the game would expire. If rules were not laid down in advance, if decisions were made as we went along, that would be moral living. And that must be ruled out. Spirit ruins the sport.

Spiritual freedom is the real opposite of the freedom distilled from play. The latter condenses from players' renouncing minds of their own. They delegate decision to the referee, the dictator, the expert, the arbiter of good taste. Spectators looking on howl approval of the transfer. They demand that their stars be puppets, exhibiting some specific dexterity. Players must perform like animated mechanical contrivances, like trained monkeys darting through hoops. The good team and the efficient government function smoothly, automatically; they are lauded as a well-greased machine. And if genuinely all-American, the team gets likened to a rock-crusher, a steam roller, an atomic bomb. The acme of excellence is scaled by being more proficient than any robot ever conceived.

Where is the fun in this? Does it not smack more of work? The difference is not easily detected, the dividing line shifting under one's gaze. This line merely separates the winner from the loser in the contest that play inevitably is. The figures on the scoreboard tell the distinction between fun and fuss. When business is brisk, typing orders and hatching fresh skullduggery exhilarates the businessman. But business sinks into drudgery when red ink crimsons the balance sheet. Hitler's game of National Socialism aroused enthusiasm and abandon in the early stages of the Nazi movement, but the sport got tough toward the end. Just now our statesmen are enjoying the bluster against Communism, yet that play may turn into work before the final curtain.

Play and work call into operation different motives to sustain them. When the end sought is utilitarian, the means sigh into work. Play, on the contrary, acknowledges only the aesthetic motive of pleasure. The will finds the going easy. Play nullifies beforehand any purpose except the enjoyment of its process. The will must be put off; play is done in pretense, nothing being gained but the thrill of gaining nothing. This illusion clicks only as long as one is winning and having the good time. Even then an ancillary motive is liable to break through, the motive behind gambling. The winner may want something more tangible to show than phosphorescence of soul. Only the most doggedly egotistic succeed in maintaining the purely aesthetic attitude for long. And any ulterior goal makes work of play, tending to impair the peculiar tension on which the fun depends. To have an outside stake on the outcome binds the player to the stake of work.

Activity to be enjoyable must involve release of tension within a system of strain, this being true of moral living as well as of play. Spiritual tension obtains between a self and a situation possessing the same personal character. In play, however, this rhythm of strain and release is interiorized, occurring within the individual consciousness between subject and the object that the subject projects. For any play scheme to function, it is necessary that the objective field be fixed and amenable to law and foresight. The object must be determined for the subject to cavort within it. Whatever freedom play can claim is strictly dependent on this necessity. Where then is there room for tension and surprise?

The answer is that the fun of play hangs on the knowledge which grasps the event being incomplete. One plays scientifically but not too scientifically. While an indispensable requisite of play, knowledge is at the same time toxic to it. Too much spoils the game, both as a group enterprise and from the standpoint of the individual player. This accounts for the liability of games playing out as noted previously. All men desire to know; but knowledge crushes the desire for it and snuffs out even the interest that instigated it. If a little knowledge is dangerous, complete knowledge is deadly. Knowing it all kills all the joy of knowing.

Knowers tunnel into grouches. Pundits work themselves into drudges, being incapable of squeezing further fun from their trumperies. Housewives grumble over routine, over knowing every minute what the next will bring forth. When we have exhausted the ramifications of an ideal system and know every phenomenon it has to offer, no delight derives from further toying with it. Objects of play must be fixed and formal, yet in certain respects the player has to remain ignorant of the form, sufficiently so to permit tension between certainty and conjecture. Even the housekeeper finds a tiny thrill in finding a spot of dirt in a corner she was sure she had cleaned.

The causal series of a game operates mechanically beyond the player's ken and control. It is to be grasped only in that problematic grip of knowledge we call anticipation. The fun of the game depends on a continuous comparison of anticipation and actual development, the player running rapidly between an established sequence and a superimposed future of his own conjuring, shuttling between his expectations and their confirmation or denial. Certainty and uncertainty, his guesses and their validation or negation, vie for attention, and in this oscillation inheres the excitement of play. That anticipation is the gist of it is evident in there being more pleasure looking forward to a party or vacation trip than in the experience when it comes to pass.

As the knowledge of any object expands and hardens, anticipation contracts in scope and dwindles in intensity. Recalling the grim facts about last summer's resort, we view it with diminished zest and decide on a change this year. The play motive lashes violently, devouring its offspring as fast as it spawns them. The businessman wants business reduced to a science; he strives to stabilize markets, streamline methods, all of which eliminates waste and multiplies profits. We who are outside the cult take scant stock in such esoterics as Wall Street charts, Hooper ratings, and Roper surveys. Still, those in the know solemnly chant the creed; such sciences determine their miniature universes as objectively as physics determines physical nature. That this is magical the faithful never discover. What they do discover is that business deteriorates into a fearful bore. Paralysis creeps down the spine, and the spineless are soon attacked by depression. Top executives are as much afflicted by the plague as lowly toilers. The management, however, can secure relief through afternoon luncheon conferences, then quitting the office for a session of poker at the club. Wage slaves meanwhile organize for a strike and higher pay.

SCIENCE AND PLAY

There would be no fun playing cards if the spots on the pasteboards altered in crazy and unpredictable fashion, the ace of one deal turning up deuce in the next. There would be no fun either if players knew the exact holdings of every hand as would be the case if all hands were exposed prior to the bidding. The latter is a quaesitum only of professional gamblers who never play for fun anyway. The amateur, who does it for love not money, must anticipate the locations of the cards by leaping ahead in an imaginary time span before the order of their fall. The pattern of distribution is inexorably fixed, the rules governing their disclosure similarly so, to render play possible; but this objective configuration can be known only if knowledge be subject to ignorance and error. Perfect knowledge stultifies the game.

A detective story would pack no punch if the mystery were left unresolved and the reader were sent reeling to his typewriter to do the final chapter. But the build-up collapses too if clues are violated and the grand denouement is not rationally and ineluctably ground out, as the canny reader should have detected for himself. The upshot is there from the start, the last page being bound between the covers with the first. The sole freedom sold the reader is the freedom to tread a path already trodden down. The initial line of the tale dictates his sentence to serve time till the assignment is finished. But this aesthetic captivity is exactly what he wants for his money. He wants fun: the tension between anticipation and confirmation. The chicanery is deemed harmless, the transaction is pretense. The hoax, however, must be honest, in the sense that the reader finds adventure, though this takes place in the interior of his head.

Every player's beatitude is consummated in the post-mortem. The novel reader luxuriates in his ruminations to see how close he came to guessing the plot and where his conjectures went astray. Any play event must emit a sufficient flicker to light up a dissection of its corpse once its rocket has ceased to sputter. Science proceeds by autopsying the past, the living moment having expired when the scalpel of analysis touches it. From the historian's point of view the entire past has existed for the express purpose of fossilizing an object for his operating table. The exuviae of sports supply the data for the scientific exploits of the ordinary man, whose small talk smells cadaverously of political elections and fishing expeditions. If post-mortems of ball games were somehow interdicted and fans forbidden the fun of comparing what they thought was going to happen with what did happen, that particular pastime would pass into bankruptcy.

This interdiction does lurk in carrying science too far. You cannot perform a post-mortem when the object never was alive. Too much knowledge chokes the play. If I were a baseball proprietor, I would look with apprehension on such a streamer as constituted a full-page headline in *The New York Times*, the issue of October 6, 1951 (a long time ago but the last time I happened to glance at the sport page). The item may not bulk tremendous now, but that morning the account made no inconsiderable fraction of all the news found fit to print. Concerning the World Series classic the previous afternoon, the scientifically slanted *Times* deposed: "Curve Ball That Failed to Break Seen as Key Pitch by Jansen."

Now, if the thousands of spectators in the stands and on the radio had been privy to that momentous truth the instant the curve failed to break, the epic struggle might have collapsed then and there. Such diligent analysis convicts the game of being a mechanical sequence of cause and effect. This determinism may reign on the playing field. But it must not corrode the consciousness of purchasers of grandstand seats. There is no fun cheering if you know it to be a fatuous expenditure of wind.

No fun is extractable from playing with the law of gravitation. That unsupported bodies fall to earth is so generally accepted as reliable as to cancel the speculative factor that play requires. One cannot anticipate what gravitation will do; one knows and can predict it apodictically. Accurate forecasting annihilates the game, unless players can be inveigled into duplicating the feat of imagination I once heard of— a prankster who jumped from the fortieth-story window of a building and was heard muttering as he passed the twentieth floor, "Nothing's happened yet."

That such flatulence of imagination is no mere theoretical

contingency may be inferred from a glance at realistic art, which surpasses in some respects the dazzle of the jumper. Realism goes the pace with science, entitling itself to be called objective. The realist's world nowadays is borrowed from physics and psychology, although historically the artist preceded the scientist in laying down determinism. Why not, realism cries, accede to the truth gracefully? It is better to accept the universe. Why not hug the bogies of science to our breast as well as rattle them in our heads? Why not clasp the hand raised to smite us? Why not play with the very idea that seems to proscribe it, the idea of objectivity itself?

A notably voracious temperament is required of an artist to gobble down the dish of scientific materialism at one fell gulp. Yet it can be done, and if you stomach the load, you qualify as a realist, a term of prestige and of high snob value. Acknowledgment of bondage becomes a badge of freedom. Appreciation of fact for fact's sake blooms as the sublimest fantasy. The mill of work is embellished into an exotic studio of play. The absence of value starks into a supreme value for the delectation of the mind.

The ego is always capable of executing such a somersault. Realism can be observed in full swing when a child playing checkers turns a lost game into a winning game of giveaway. In our juvenile bridge days we improved the rule book by adding a rule we called *nullo:* the bidder contracted to take nary a trick—a difficult feat, by the way, which might put one on his guard against realism. If the ego cannot have everything, that same ego will make a bogus prize of possessing nothing. It will turn ascetic in a flash of magnificence. Awakening from his dream of beauty, the realist adorns the ugly nightmare that awoke him with beauty's fripperies, creating thereby a superior art. Why not?—fiction and fact are alike ideas, and the sole magic called for is the switching of labels.

Still, the switch is no cinch and considerable artistry is necessary to mystify the audience. Most people do not see it that way. Bending refractory materials to fit preconceived patterns makes work. For play purposes the materials must be pre-bent in somebody else's workshop and the will must find it easy sailing. Then only do the actual and the rational appear coincident as if through preestablished harmony, the track already laid and the train gliding smoothly over the rails. The diversion into the subject of what the realist calls will, and the will's volatilization in fun, is the prime rule of play. And your will needs a deal of discipline playing dead before you can enjoy a world as dead as the Stoics find it. Loving what is known to be unlovely may have been play for Epictetus and his ilk, but the sport is a bit strenuous for the unphilosophic. The realist's world is unquestionably objective. But it is thinly populated.

Science, in declaring its fixed order to be the single objective field, vies perpetually with art. Art promulgates objective worlds too, but these are as numerous as the artists themselves. The continuous strife of science and art, science and religion, is merely the sound track of the civil war the ego-body dichotomy is embroiled in. The facts of a reigning object—just now that of science—slaughter nascent fancies in the subject, and there ensues in internecine conflict between fact and value, the true and the good. *Fact* and *truth* are tokens of validity, titles signifying solid objectivity, that we crown the victor with. An army of concepts so crowned soon clears the field of all dissenters, leaving only the ceremony of burying the slain; of certifying, by snobbery of course, that all previous thinkers—in our day called prescientific thinkers—were demonstrably deluded and probably dubs.

How long any dynasty of thought will reign before reaching senility and decrepitude, when its reigning principles become inflexible and infallible, no one can foretell. An objective order fares better when being hotly disputed; complacency results from other contenders groveling before it (as for example Protestant theology now does before scientism), and causes it to lie down on its throne. How long will the scientific world-view view the world for us? Just as long as the rules of its game can be juggled with the free assent of those playing it; as long, that is, as knowers admit there is more to be known. Scientists get suffocated in their hot houses and emerge for a breath of fresh air, thereby renewing their youth. Such a wave of rejuvenating skepticism has rolled over physics during recent years. Nineteenth-century atomism got too oppressive even for those who had conquered under its banner, and the harness has been temporarily unbuckled by Heisenberg's Principle of Indeterminacy. The respite, however, will not last, and the now wayward electron will be complying with the nuclear physicist's idea of what an electron should be when it is behaving itself. A mechanical world, whose processes can be explained quantitatively, makes an unexceptionable demand upon man insofar as he is a knower. The exit of the playroom leads to a workshop.

Any activity when duly regulated by its specific science gets banished from the land of play: this holds whatever the scope of the activity. Political controls are sure to supervene as soon as economics gets clarified into a corpus of knowledge and economic laws deduced. These controls just as surely dampen the gaiety of business. Somebody's ideas, those of a brain trust that has swapped the snobbery of a cloister for the police power of the state, are objectified. The quondam free enterprisers are reduced to a routine of stacking tin cans on shelves and pasting on the correct price tags. What we actually abhor in Communism is not its political lore; what we resist can happen here under a different mythology.

In any regimented state a game beckons of outwitting the officials charged with law enforcement, and jockeying with the tax collector. This game is reputed to be wicked and unpatriotic. Political rulers prefer to rule by snobbery, making things snug for themselves. Since they, or at least their offices, are said to be sacred, flouting their edicts is equivalent to desecration and moral iniquity. Falling for this is to fall into man's most shackling superstition. Despite the physical force the opposition has at its disposal, all free citizens should feel a genuinely moral obligation to keep that contest going. Tax collectors should work for their pay. Resist, ye patriots, by all means fair or foul, resist out of sheer patriotism. It's the only way to keep our country young and healthy, it's the only way to keep the game agog.

Any form of play is constantly imperiled by actual play itself. Play tends to destroy the motive that sustains it, to dispel the illusion it weaves. It demands law and order, yet this law and order so petrify as to mummify the game. A culture wanes and ages. Eventually naught but a corpse remains for the succeeding culture to inter. The death throes plunge society into a series of spasms, an ever-recurrent cycle of stabilization and revolt against the rules that stabilize.

Play mirrors the Absolute that clusters all possible values. But the reflector must be tilted at a fresh angle now and then to give the impression of a novel view. Prisoners need to be regaled with a change of wallpaper in their cells. Perpetual agitation ensues against ennui, the agitation being mistaken for a creative urge. This it is not: play and work are not the opposites player and worker think.

GAMBLING: WORK OR PLAY?

The question, whether gambling be regarded work or play, is due to a hidden ambiguity. There are two types of gambling. One reduces play to work, the other is a frank species of magic.

The professional gambler does not take his game aesthetically. He does not play at it. His aim is not to have himself a time, but to garner cash. His attitude is sternly scientific. He works to squeeze every element of chance out of the event. If his chosen field be basketball, let us say, he strives to manipulate that game so that he can predict the outcome. His approach to the task ranks him with the technologist in any industrial laboratory.

Buying the players on the floor makes an obvious means to his end. No moral considerations impinge here. The discovery that gamblers do not gamble when they become expert in the craft shocks amateurs, but that shock scarcely justifies the imputation of wickedness. The proficient gambler simply exchanges opinion for objective certainty, good Platonist that he is. Knowledge pairs with virtue when it pays in dollars. The knowledgeable player invariably knows most about the machine that determines the final score. Knowledge is power. The game-fixer has merely contrived to push the frontier of knowledge a cut beyond the headlines of the sports editor. His methods bear the imprimatur of any possible science.

Branding him a fixer is supposed to expose him to disgrace. But the fixer is guiltless of personal wrongdoing. He has wrought no injury on others. Even the small fry who are spending only the time to watch are deprived of nothing. They can still have their fun. Chance continues to preside at the shrine as far as the immaculate worshiper knows. He does not know who has fixed the score or at what figure. His anticipation can run riot, and if he wants to bet, he can bet on what is in the bag of the fixers. From the point of view of the spectators, the fixer merely introduces a new element of contingency. More players are mixed in the scrimmage than can be counted on the floor, which really enhances the excitement. What went on in the hotel room before the initial tip-off—that can be known in the same manner as what will happen when the forwards face opposing guards, in the same dim feat of conjecture that lets loose the imagination. That someone has sewed up the game and carries it in his brief-case need rob no one of his fun in doping the result out for himself, no more than it does in solving a crossword puzzle which is fixed in advance too. Nothing immoral has cropped out anywhere along the line.

Admitted, the condition of being fixed spoils the fun of the athletes on the floor. Receiving money for their performances obligates players to conform to a bolted-down pattern, and the necessity to do so makes work of the game. But college basketball is hardly play anyhow from the viewpoint of the active participants. College athletics in the big-name schools operate for profits, not for amusement, save that of the audience; players are commercially employed and on somebody's payroll. Everybody knows it, including those who howl when the secret is whispered. For some occult reason slipping a novel quirk into the book of any game arouses the reaction that a grievous sin has been committed; even the clergy chime in with sermons against fixing. The uproar may be partially real: the remonstrance of the spirit and authentic moral revulsion. But what is morally protested against is the game as a whole rather than some petty infraction of its established prescriptions. Every game stems from the two sources of boredom and covetousness. It is not to the behavior of the child but to its parentage that the moral person objects.

When done for money, gambling must be classed as work. But as carried on by amateurs, gambling may accentuate the play motive that sustains the event. In this case gambling becomes a kind of magic. Spectators like to feel their side will win by virtue of its being theirs. The will never wholly yields to impotence and eggs the ego into assuming a spurious agency in deciding the contest.

Magic is by no means exclusively practiced by primitive races as we superciliously suppose. Watch a bowler bending his body when a ball rolls wide of its target, as if to push the erring sphere through action at a distance. Pretending that an idea influences the event is magic exactly. Betting is more frequently magical in intent than mercenary. When a partisan has exhausted all arguments in favor of his candidate, when he has tried snobbery by holding his nose at the mention of the opponent, there remains a supreme assertion of his ideal supremacy: he can challenge you to a bet. Put up your money: money talks. The player believes it can talk his way to victory.

The technical name for this stock magic is bluff. Bluff may actually function. To deny that magic may work is to work too hard at being wise. An idea often does determine the event—for instance, in a two-handed poker game. But magic peters out expensively when the game is in charge of those who know, whose objective grasp compasses more cogs of the machine. The odd-lot speculator does not bluff Wall Street. You are more likely to bluff your way to being elected a United States Senator than in building a garage. And magic fizzles dismally on the basketball floor when the score is fixed before the fracas starts. What's the use of taking sides, the disillusioned fans wail? This cry of anguish repeats verbatim what these same folks say about life all the way through: everything is futile, all is vanity, the show is fixed.

Resentment against the sport fixers issues from disgust at finding determined what we had fancied to be an oasis of freedom. The basketball cage looms as the same cage as the office. The mask is snatched off the face of play, and the grinning skull chatters the warning that the neck of play is wrung by the clutches of an alien power. We have been betrayed, though we are bemused as to the identity of the betrayer. Anyhow, we vow to fix the fixers. We will pass a law. Our side shows must be rendered safe by jamming them under the main tent of man's perennial circus: the government.

In the meantime exhorters will bombinate against gambling. It probably is true that gambling is a device of the devil. But to eschew the devil's way of doing, we must abjure not his shadow but the devil himself.

GAMBLING IN REALITY

Gambling, someone has written, is a biological necessity. We agree, without knowing clearly what is meant. And let us add on our own that gambling is a spiritual necessity too.

Real life can be envisaged as playing with God, in anticipation of what his will may disclose. The religious life can be likened to a game of hide-and-seek with a mysterious God whose nature is ever being revealed afresh. We do not know about God as if he were a stable and statable object we make stabs at pinpointing. God is no object we can tuck away just for the fun of ferreting out what was never really lost.

Nothing is to be known about God. God must be known in person as he makes his presence manifest in each and every moment. God must disclose himself, even as you and I must do when we are known by another. God is encountered in the burning bush, on the road to Jericho, the hill of Calvary. Hiding forever, he has no hiding place. In our quest of him we are to make no behest of tomorrow. This very night our souls may be required of us.

But this is loose living, it is laughing when there is nothing ostensible to laugh at. Not for us; we will keep a straight face with the devil. We conjure up a game of our own. We mistake arrogance for audacity. We shrill for freedom, but our mitts accept the manacles, provided we be allowed to cry for freedom. We go along with the rulers if they dole out liberty to squawk when we pay the tax. Real freedom is as much the opposite of this lusory freedom as it is of outright tyranny.

Behold, I will make all things new. If it comes true once in a million, it is truer than any sure thing. Who knows what

God can do? With God at the table, you may get a thrill from the sight of your wife at breakfast. Not every morning; that would be diabolizing God through definite expectations. An authentic glimpse of reality can never be expected. But no day glooms abysmally if a surprise shines through.

Man is a dual creature. There is no evasion of the polarity that vises him. But man must not darken the apprehension of this polarity itself. Man the worker and man the player cannot be paired. The worker is not to be re-created by play, nor is the player to be enriched through work. The play-work dummy needs be brought to life with the breath of God, and the insight and laughter God inspirits.

Player and worker are the same figment arrayed in different garb. To dress in such uniforms gratifies the deepest craving of the ego-body automaton. The free individual that philosophers prize and the mass-man they bemoan are identical beneath their denims. The craze to be unique culminates in melting indiscriminately in the herd. The free-born citizens of any ideological state rush hell-bent to conformity in thought, word, and deed. The sting of unreality must be poulticed by coercing everybody to converge in the same illusions.

The moral person makes no demand for uniformity among his fellows. Spiritual man is content for every man to be his own contented self. A gambler by commitment, he greets every event as a novelty of creation. He lays down no laws for the universe to follow. He judges no divagations to be monstrous. And when he listens he can hear the heart of God beating in any happening.

HEAVEN AND HELL

Here surely a perfect pair of opposites bobs up. And the strife between them flares so fiercely because each of the twain lights up as the antipodes of earth. Heaven is as high above as hell sinks beneath the terrestrial scene.

Heaven bursts with pure delight. Nothing can be thought of there save our final deliverance from the cares and worries that originally badgered us into thinking. Hell seethes with everlasting torment no thought avails to extricate us from. Heaven is enswathed in the soft music of a string orchestra, while in hell the screams of the damned are tuned to the cacophonies of a juke box. The contrast is complete.

There we might let our parlor game end. But someone in the parlor is sure to comment crisply and sagaciously that, after all, heaven and hell are just states of mind. That re-opens the whole subject and blotches the pictures we have drawn.

Hell is a state of mind. Hell is the state of anybody's mind when he sequesters himself from the universal mess and seeks his own composure in an elevation above that messiness. Man yearns for peace, for assurance, for security—all as-suredly good. He strives for certainty which existence seems to negate. But in demanding a kind of certainty existence does not provide for, this individual plows into a state of uncertainty existence itself does not inflict. Thus the stormer of the citadel of heaven plunges within the portals of hell. The emptiness of his soul makes it a wilderness where the devil can prowl. He soon harbors within its keep a progeny of fears, anxiety, and boredom. Hell results when one essays to create a private heaven, the vision of a heaven never to be indwelt. Hell is the idea of heaven. Hell is a state of mind. Hell cannot possibly exist.

But heaven is no state of mind. Heaven is as solid and authentic as the earth underfoot. Heaven comprises our own act when we enact the power of God. Heaven never symbolizes what our world might be, if it were not for other people's cussedness. Heaven resides in our midst. Heaven is our wholehearted, our whole-selfed, acceptance of reality, our heart's reception of the joys and sufferings of whatever exists. God saw everything that he had made and behold, it was very good. For us to make good as images of God, to be what we are, that is heaven, reality *in excelsis*.

VI

THE IDEA OF PURPOSE

WHY DO MEN ASK WHY?

SOME CENTURIES AGO much discussion raged concerning an ass introduced to scholastic society by one Jean Buridan. This fabled beast was hitched midway between two bales of hay, either of which his tether would let him reach when hunger prodded. Each bundle of feed, it was argued, would ply with equal motive this will-ridden creature: would he not, therefore, perish miserably in the midst of plenty, stalled between equipotential forces? Or was there within him a faculty of freedom, capable of breaking the deadlock by tossing its makeweight into one pan or the other? Nobody thought to try out his proof upon the object of it.

Nobody noted, either, the moral of the tale: the calumny it heaped upon the ass. What could be more asinine than to make a normal and respectable ass into a human being? Since the actual ass would scarcely bother asking why he should eat one stack or the other, he would help himself to both, treating himself to a feast rather than faltering into a famine. Animals are not bedeviled by wills upon which purposes act magically and motives mechanically. They do not corrupt

173

a good thing by substituting a fancy that is better. Man alone impales himself upon the barb of a question mark.

Raising the question of *why* calls a halt to whatever train of events traverses the crossroad of the present moment. *Why:* the signal demands a password from Nature. That *why* rummages Nature's pockets for a driver's license. Its traffic light beams red, aiming a shot at the heart of reality, at what is happening now. The actual must account for itself, either on the basis of the past or of the future. Ideas of cause and of purpose are correlative, cause explaining the existent by what has preceded it, purpose by what shall follow from it. By denying the right of the actual to stand on its own feet, both ideas compel it to limp and crawl obsequiously. Everything is determined by a push or a pull. Whether the actor acts from motive or from purpose, he has taken flight from his act. The cry of *why* frames an accusation against which there is no defense. It has already pronounced the judgment of the court, and that judgment is condemnation.

JUDGE NOT

To be agog with purposes that the world should be minded to attain exhibits the mind of the judge. The judge plays at being better than the object he judges. He knows better. That this makes a pleasant diversion accounts for its being so popular. Picking faults flatters the vanity of the picker.

In uttering his famous prohibition *judge not,* was Jesus not himself judging those who did judge? Does not the query *why do men ask why?* merely pose another why? Can the existentialist avoid the charge of being intricated in self-contradiction? Of entanglement in the toils of reason he explicitly renounces?

This argument we decline to continue. We will settle the

matter the only way possible of resolving a radical contradiction: we'll laugh at it, glad that it really does not matter. The intention behind my question is to put a stop to man's questioning propensity. The *judge not* of Jesus declares no rational judgment. It cries instead an existential fiat, a behest to smash the game of judging.

Presumably you will have to judge that fiat adversely. It spoils your fun and interferes with your work. If you are a lawyer, a psychologist, a preacher, or reformer, you make your living by judging. Business too consists in the manipulation of these motives through the engineering of salesmanship. This craft prejudges men by assifying them, the difference being that the sorcery works when men are the objects, as it never would on Buridan's critter. In its manifold ramifications the business of judging canopies civilization and keeps its show going.

Scientists are inclined to be complacent about their methods of judging. They identify their judgments with the mechanistic order they juggle. Scientists are realists: to know why events occur as they do delivers one from the folly of wishing them otherwise. Idealists, on the other hand, who find the roots of the present in the future, are disposed to exhortation and scolding. The ideal *ought* not only dictates excellence but reproves us for settling for less. Things might be as good as they foresee, and would be if we did not forsake their advice. The vertical dimension which directs aspiration upward can be twisted horizontally and used as a standard of judgment, its objective truth being transferred to the subject as a rule for evaluating experience. The fits and false starts we suffer from could be prevented by our appropriating these eternal purposes and governing ourselves accordingly.

Sometimes scientist and idealist converge in suspending

judgment, in the case for example of extending tolerance to a criminal. Every judge likes to temper justice with mercy, frowns and smiles whiffling on his brow without penetrating to his heart. The condemned criminal should be let off, the psychologist argues, on the ground that he could not have done otherwise. His complexes being what they are, blaming the victim of them only indicates a sort of complex in the judge. The sentimentalist wants to treat the convict leniently for the opposite reason: he could have done better and the next time he will, the motive being the spark of divinity within him. Realist and idealist concur in suspending judgment. But neither is pricked by the nib of Jesus' saying. Their idea of forgiveness is to remit the penalty judgment threshes out, to mitigate the sentence that the law has dealt; in short, to persist in judging but to make of it play and pretense. But this is not what mercy really means. Withholding judgment requires a moral attitude, which is equally unlike the aesthetic attitude and the scientific. Forgiveness is an act, not the idea of an act, good though this idea be. Jesus did not lecture the woman taken in adultery on the beauty of chastity. He did not tell her to reform, then give him proof of her reformation, after which he would love her. Jesus loved her, then and there, with all her faults.

The spiritual man accepts reality exactly as it is, embracing each moment without equivocation. The spiritual opposite of judgment cannot be reached through inventing excuses or diluting the harshness of judgment with insipidity. This spiritual opposite is love. Love is never caused, nor is love a purposeful transaction. You do not love a thing for what it may look like once you have recast it to fit your predilections. You love a person for what he is, at the very point where his life line intersects yours. You love the mangled body in the gutter on the road to Jericho, you love the gore. Love does not redirect the past in the service of the future. Love transforms the present for the sake of itself.

Judge not: this is no formula for human conduct; rather, it is an appeal to do away with all formulas whatsoever. The deliberate intention to do good and to lavish mercy soon palls. Its beneficiaries especially find it obnoxious. To understand all is to forgive all, the romanticist moons. But let anyone be filled with the purpose of applying the rule, he is forced to do his understanding at a distance. He seldom gets close if you see him coming. To love people out of the resolution to love them degrades the recipients of love into objects. That is to institutionalize the motive. And regardless of what its charter asserts, face to face with an institution man is demonized into the loveless and the unloved. You can never help another person if to help him is your sole concern. In deciding that he needs your aid and is worthy of your precious time, you have judged him adversely: you despise him first in order to acquire righteousness in serving him afterward. No handout can come from the heart. No ideal can be embodied so long as it enamors as an ideal, save in the abstracted sphere of play.

PURPOSE, PURPOSE EVERYWHERE

We are constantly belabored with books and spanked in speeches, lamenting the fact that our culture lacks purpose. We are chided with being frantically on the move but to no direction. Whirl is king. Modern man goes crazy chasing his tail. A closer inspection of these strictures reveals that what their authors mean is that we do not have the right purposes. These, oddly enough, turn out to be the purposes they incubate under their hats. We might fare better playing another game, who can tell? Yet this question hardly justifies a reformer for berating us for not playing at all.

That ours is a culture abounding in purposes is indicated by the low opinion we hold of the opportunist. No aspersion plumbs such depths of infamy as that of being a compromiser or an appeaser. To hug no principles dearly is to touch the nadir of wickedness. Yet should not an indefinable ability to get along together tower above the prosecution of particular goals on which we cannot agree? If society is forced to acknowledge any set purpose as its final end, that purpose, be it a moral one, must be the creation of free persons who are able to live by their own decisions—persons who are blandly indifferent to every conception society may entertain of itself. How splendid it would be, if our doings were actually as purposeless as our accusers charge.

Awaiting this blessed consummation, the best we can hope for is that nobody's purpose attains the monopoly everybody claims as his sovereign right. A government that is hampered by its own vacillations, not knowing today what it will do tomorrow, is to be preferred to a government that does know. A sensualist like Danton makes a better head of state than the grim logician Robespierre. Political liberty depends on the bosses being unable to settle among themselves who is to do the top bossing. It is better to swing at loose ends than to hang together as one. We should look with disfavor upon the now prevailing tendency toward church unity. If churchmen cease wielding their hatchets on one another, they are not going to bury them; they will melt them down into heavier artillery to blast the rest of us. Ecclesiastical organizations should be encouraged to keep on with their present game of sniping upon one another; it saves us from their ganging up on a common foe. Ideologists are dangerous whatever their brand of ideology.

No society becomes conscious of itself as totalitarian, this *ism* being the consciousness of a common purpose fervently espoused and sustained by clear objective loyalties. The populace of Germany was unaware of succumbing to Nazi overlordship. What the Germans were aware of was the grandeur of Nazi ideals and the ecstasy flowing through the channels those ideals grooved. No purpose intoxicates a people so wildly as one that has swept all cross purposes from the field. Then the divine event awaits only the decimation of the devil who lurks beyond national boundaries, in league of course with secret traitors at home. The longer the tremendous day delays, the more horrendous the spectral monster becomes, fictitious strength and barbarism alike being imputed to the enemy.

Quite sadly we are bound to note that we do subscribe to a collective purpose here in America. It may be a trivial purpose, every purpose being nugatory in the end. It may involve no more than demonstrating that the man Adam Smith made holds sounder ideas than his rival designed by Karl Marx. I call the issue frivolous, since neither *Homo academicus* bears much resemblance to the creature God breathed into his image. The Russians differ from us only in assigning another purpose to life and proving theirs, through snobbery or force, to be superior to ours.

The purpose of government is amenable to specific formulation. And this purpose has swerved little since politics originated under tribal chieftains. The purpose of any government is to protect its subjects against a government that is worse, and of whose yoke they stand in imminent peril. Government represents the projection of the ego's yen for security. To validate the security it confers, a government must first render its people insecure. The extent of the bounty of its protection is determined by the number of interests the component individuals want safeguarded, every government being alert to widen that field. That the political object institutionalizes more of man's will than any other device accounts for its persistence, its inevitability, and the vast power at its disposal.

As long as a society maintains a government, that society has a purpose, regardless of what preachers say. You can hear official spokesmen bespeaking that purpose whenever you dial the radio their way. In any form of work or play the good envisaged yields to precise stipulation. These goods consist of such counters as runs across the plate, marks amassed in examinations, dollars earned a share, concessions extorted at an arms conference. The ballplayer knows the score, the theater owner keeps tab on the box-office receipts, the salesman checks the day's take against last year's loot, and everybody knows his balance at the bank. Purposes assault us on every side. Philosophically minded scientists discern purpose in the universe. They descry progress in the evolutionary creep, in the climb up the stairs through matter, life, consciousness, self-consciousness, straight to the pedestal of the philosopher doing the discerning. Nihilistic novelists write with a purpose, to unveil the absence of purpose except in themselves, in their purpose to construe reality as an aesthetic spectacle. What do our contemners mean, that we have no purpose?

Heavens, I may have some purpose in writing this. There is no escape.

PURPOSE IS DOOMED TO FRUSTRATION

Frustration epitomizes the predicament and the tragedy of humankind. No way opens to avoid purpose, and no way either whereby any purpose can avoid futility.

Every quest is doomed to end short of its goal. The thrill of achievement wears off. The game stales and stinks. That frivolity inheres in a checker match breaks nobody's heart, but devotion to Aristotle's metaphysics is disheartened by the same vanity. Any idol hammered out of gold responds no better to man's real needs than an idol whittled out of a rotting log. Neither answers his prophets with fire, and snobbery alone can finesse a difference between them. By nature, man is a spiritual self. He finds nothing enduring except in relations that are personal, those with his kindred and his friends. And this love is without purpose and without design.

The objective world, constituted by one or more egos, must furnish the seat of every purpose. There alone can ends be pursued by the manipulation of means, whether the end be a game of checkers or the Lord God Himself. God, conceived as an object, may delight the thinker and elicit a glitter of rhetoric. But in a crisis of existence, in the hour of death, that god, like the Baals of old, is found sleeping and cannot be roused. Peace of mind does not supervene though a thousand pages give a thousand reasons why it should. Man asks for bread and is put off with a stone; is it not a put-up job?

Ascribing the vacuity of our lives to materialism is easy;

idealists talk themselves into reputations doing so. Their
judgments notwithstanding, there is nothing wrong with the
materials consumed in our vital activities. Through intercourse with the physical world alone can human beings communicate with one another. Solely in the production and
use of the fruits of the earth do personalities meet and
merge; solely in the love of God's world can we reveal our
love for our fellows and of God Himself. Since we are in
Nature to our necks, why should our heads wag so magis-
terially above her? Idealism is precisely what ails us. Our
ills do not derive from the materials requisite to our needs
but to the symbolic properties we impute to these, distorting
them to conform to our artifices and resorting to magic to
get them to do the trick. It is not Nature that foils us but the
follies we have foisted upon her.

Nobody outside the books he writes corresponds to the
philosopher's idea of a materialist. Preachers are never more
idly engaged than when they vituperate the congregation
for caring only for money. No grubber of it wants money
as such. People are beguiled by the notion that money is
equivalent to power, to prestige, to security, to the very
desiderata the idealist craves. Money symbolizes static, ulterior values. And in our magical world money actually fulfills
its magical purposes.

But it does so speciously. Consequently any purpose to
make money is bound to be as self-thwarting as it is self-
gratifying. Money doesn't grow on trees, we tell children,
when teaching them how to get it. Still the admonition is
more profound than we think. Money is no natural substance,
money represents purposes which become false as soon as

they are objectified. Material goods are good only in consumption. Saving for use tomorrow what is ours today results in its corruption. Money will buy anything except what the man who has it actually wants. The rich man depresses himself into a slough of poverty the pauper may never sink into. The materialist is condemned by his very idealism. He compounds his sin when he blames the material world for the anxiety that infests his soul.

To behold in accumulated wealth the attainment of an end invites betrayal by the idol of one's own manufacture. Rich men gather into barns, then endeavor to mute the dull presentiment that eventually their souls will be required by screwing locks on the barn doors and staffing the warehouse with a cordon of police. They are seduced by their purpose into planning the impossible. Existence makes no comparable provisions for transcending its own transiency and contingency. The real world shows no concern to confirm the theory which the symbol of wealth is based on. The rich man plays at being God, he prefers his conception of what a world should be to what it is. His antics are magical.

To corroborate his figment and render the symbol plausible, certain conditions must be brought about, those that determine any playground. The community where the symbol functions must accept it docilely. An effective majority has to assent to the game. If the Russians balk at the idea, that rules them behind the curtain. When someone on our side of the drapery sulks or raises too many questions, the idea must be buttressed first with reason, then thumped in with brute force. Revolution is liable to attend the suspicion that no real sanction inheres in the object, as indeed it never does.

The primary purpose of any purpose is to applaud itself. Those within an institution must harden their hearts to resist change and exploration. The inner and invisible grace which inflates the symbol cannot risk being punctured by the prick of existence. A millionaire depends on miracle to vindicate the supernatural power he attaches to his riches, the miracle of entering heaven through the eye of a needle. The service of mammon, which implies reliance on the devil, puts one's trust in the potency of his own ideas. One hoards security in an object which has been created for the specific purpose of hoarding.

Money in itself does not debase nor defile. As a simple medium of exchange money does no evil. It is not vile so long as its use is restricted to facilitating commerce. Men can be no more innocently engaged than in making money, provided that money be not polluted by the hereditary taint. Even the love of money is not the root of evil, despite the excellent authority for the adage. The idea of money is the germ of the disease infecting it. The purposes we inject into money incubate its virulence. Rich men strut as notorious idealists.

Every purpose exits in frustration. What shall it profit a man to gain the whole world, though he manages to convince its two billion inhabitants that his ownership is just and lawful? His possessions are lacking in his own major lack, and Nature fails to pay him proper respect. His treasures shine only as a reflection of his motive in acquiring them, and his soul remains unrescued from a specter that beckons: the certainty of death. The universally agreed-to premise of the textbook syllogism, that all men are mortal, negates every conceivable purpose to elude the temporal lot. The bitterness with which one contemplates his final dissolution is aggravated by the success the ego has made in embodying its ends in objects of its own invention. Earthly accumulations avail but to render more imposing the mound of ashes that shall inhume one in the end.

Cannot the subject that played with one world so nimbly work the same stunt on another? Through the back door of immortality egotistic man makes a supreme effort to take flight from himself. A theory of survival projects both the obstacle and the ambition to overleap it by a mighty jump. No one comes back with tidings of how the program pans out. We can observe on our side of the dust curtain that the arguments though rationally cogent do not allay the pangs of death nor diminish the peril. Professors who write the books are still beset by the demon they profess to have banished. How can anyone be sure of a hereafter who has never been sure of the here?

To the spiritual person death brandishes no terror, nor does death pose a problem. One world at a time: the sting is extracted. All things come to an end, and he has never imagined special treatment for himself. The spiritual man has no time to worry whether there be an afterlife. That word *after* unsheaths no dagger to assassinate the present. Wheresoever it bears him, the aftermath of existence cannot take him far from his self.

The purpose "to get away from yourself" knocks that self to pieces and knells the forfeiture of heaven, the heaven of this life and of the next. In carrying out that purpose, say by going to the movies, you relinquish the actual experience that might make you a real self. Sometime when you are scanning the screen for tape to paste your parts together, reflect what genuine adventure might be yours on the street outside. And if on the way home a beggar asks you for a nickel, do something for that self of yours. Instead of knocking it out with an uppercut, muttering perhaps that the welfare agency answers that purpose, do something for that poverty-stricken self: give your coat, then give your cloak also. What did Jesus mean? I have no idea. You will have to find out, then and there. You're on the spot. But it is there alone that you can find yourself. The way to escape frustration is to make your lowliest act identical with your loftiest purpose. Every square foot of earth marks the spot of that city that lieth foursquare.

PURPOSE AND MAGIC

It is an oddity of our culture that everybody strives for power, and that everybody agrees that power is evil. Power corrupts, absolute power corrupts absolutely: parrots patter the platitude. Yet by power we simply indicate that things change. Power is what keeps existence going. The universe is a system of powers, and as long as time lasts, the universe will continue dynamic.

Power politics are execrated by idealists. But how can there be any other politics, even in the Kingdom of God? An event culminates a struggle of forces. Whatever exists owes what it is to an equilibrium of opposing tendencies. To declaim against power expresses a yearning for a static realm of essence where nothing can happen. A world bereft of power would lack everything else.

That an assertion of purpose does not result in that end coming to pass is responsible for the ambiguity attaching to power and for the anomaly of its being sought and simultaneously decried. Ideas are weapons, the pen is mightier than the sword, provided we take it out in wishing. Ideas cannot create existence. And whatever prevents events from complying with the positings of reason must be bad.

How shall the process of Nature be reduced to rational order? Plenty of good advice jets from every tap, but Nature's flux streams from another source. The congregation is pleasantly pattered by the sermon, then goes about the ways that have been roundly condemned. Preachers when they condescend to practice make out no better. To cite a memorable case, Plato wrote an immense treatise on politics, informing mankind how to manage its affairs. Still, on the only job he undertook himself, the affair at Syracuse, Plato emerged a dismal flop. Plato clearly perceived that wisdom would function solely on condition that those with the right ideas get in the right positions. But how to wrench this to pass, has snapped all the tools political science has forged. Hence *The Republic* must be adjudged a compendium of magic, and in politics the upshot of magic is despotism. The purpose sought turned out to be the Spartan tyranny, which Plato admired so tenderly.

Magic should by no means be scorned as an addiction of savages. Elaborately civilized societies fall prone before it. The Pharisees of New Testament times can scarcely be snubbed as barbarians, yet they soberly affirmed that if the Sabbath were perfectly kept for a single week end, God would dispatch his Messiah to earth and peace would reign forever. Outworn purposes appear stupid to the enlightened who have issued improved editions. Wherein does our belief differ, that if we stockpile sufficient bombs, peace will supervene? Magic inheres in any notion that a rationally conceived purpose carried out according to plan is effective in bringing that conception to embodiment. When an army general says that we had "far better risk a war of possible annihilation than grasp a peace which would be the certain destruction of free ideas," he is trumpeting magic. Peace through war, whatever the charm of its phrasing, tinkles as an incantation. Though we speak with the tongue of an angel and have not reality, we become as sounding brass.

These cymbals reverberate the confusion between play and work on the one hand and moral behavior on the other. In the former sphere ideas are determinative, but the objects they are identical with are illusory. Real peace is not the creation of the military arm but of the whole man. To realize this peace requires the act of the people who are to live in peace. This peace could dispense with the ponderous agenda of a peace conference. These give ample notice that summit diplomacy flourishes in the supernatural realm of magic. Authentic peace does not hang on good ideas but on men's being good at heart. Peace is consent to existence, without endeavoring to prove that somebody is right and everybody else is wrong. Peace means assenting to what we by nature are.

Rational goodness and spiritual goodness seldom jibe outside the textbooks. The pious Sunday believer in the God of love wriggles himself into an exceedingly crafty fellow for Monday morning business. The Golden Rule he has ingested exudes in the rule of grab and greed. Expatiating on brotherhood renders nobody fraternal to the touch. Pondering essays on virtue rarely makes for virtue, and no book has ever papered the delivery room for the second birth. Purchasers of peace-of-mind manuals do get something for their dollar, but it is nothing that makes a difference their friends can detect the morning after. Nor does shouting them more raucously serve to drive ideals in. One never becomes a real man by exercising the play man more vigorously. The fanatic whose purpose explodes in the sky doesn't differ essentially from the plodder who totes it along in a wheelbarrow. The slowpoke, indeed, may be more desirable for a next-door neighbor. Hypocrisy, which we denounce so vehemently, is actually the most agreeable trait of the Pharisee. When the hypocrite resolves to wax sincere and to animate his mask, forcing his good ideas upon others, you had better move to a quieter part of town. The idea he is going to realize is trouble. It is easier to take his snobbery than the beating.

Idealists undoubtedly do wield power. The objects they have constituted respond to their wills. The ego can determine the paths of moving bodies by interposing other moving bodies and employing the laws of kinetics. An expert technician may contrive to blow up a city by pressing a button. He releases energy outside himself, mastery of which he has acquired through knowledge. Knowledge is power. The advertising wizard succeeds in moving his trash. Get people obsessed by the same idea as the pusher, they can be deflected by mechanical pressure and pushed around according to his design. The heaviest artillery wins the battle. Ideas receive material embodiment and produce effects. This is the power idealists berate, despite such power being ideal and the only power the ego is capable of exerting. The obvious reason for mankind's adherence to magic is that magic does work, within the limit of the game. The pills the medicine man doles out cure his patients, enough of them to keep his reputation healthy. The ruling ideas of every generation are the ideas of its ruling class.

Now, there is another kind of power. This power is available too. This kind we ignore, partly because the exercise of it cannot be explicated in any science, partly because explicators themselves seldom possess it. The technician who holds the fate of a city under his finger may be unable to compel obedience in his six-year-old son unless he gets after him with a whip.

An integrative force within Nature, analogous to spiritual power, is revealed in the speculations of science, whether scientists see it or not. If this were lacking, there would be no Nature to speculate about. How, amid a host of moving bodies as lowly as electrons, one entity can, by ceasing to move and strive, acquire a tremendous attractive force and become proton and nucleus of the tiny colony, organizing the motions of its fellow electrons around itself and establishing a community where previously only individual repulsions had obtained—how this can be, no thinker will ever know. Inkling of the mystery is not invoked by taking thought. The mystery is revealed in the actual experience of affection and good will. This is power too, creative power, though it eludes rational explanation and is never to be grasped as an object of purpose.

The momentum possessed by physical objects represents a kind of power. This is the only power any technique can master. But righteousness is power also. Spirit wields power. This is the power that has swung the stars in space and keeps them steadfast in their orbits. God belongs to the universe, God is creator of it. Yet he produces his effects neither magically nor mechanically. God is no empirical object which scientific research can bark into a corner and bargain with: this science has discovered. God is no body displacing other bodies. In any configuration of objects God does not figure. Still, all Nature is his handiwork and he indwells the whole firmament. Any vehicle of God's will abounds in power, in the power that the winds and the sea obey.

A purpose that aims to secure a moral act through any power save God's is perforce magical. To possess God's power the purpose to possess it must be abandoned. Righteousness is power, provided we do not pretend to know of what either righteousness or power consists. Right makes might, when we smelt both to a fluid state, without institutionalizing or objectifying our meanings. Man must perpetually engage in recasting his ideas, melting them afresh in the crucible of God's judgment. No trim and eternally valid separation of good and evil is permissible. Any living process exhibits aspects of construction, aspects of destruction. An abrasive member may be plucked out, voided, cast into the fire, irrespective of what the best people think. The influence of good ideas being well-nigh negligible, it behooves man to conceive of good not in terms of human values but of God's favor. Humanism redounds only to human pride. It merely stiffens man's neck and renders his decapitation slicker. Man's security is not to be bought in any insurance policy, but has to be sought in the trust the sheep repose in the shepherd. Planning life out plans one out of living.

Yet, to repeat: knowledge is power, ideas control events, magic does operate. We may contrive to drop the bomb on the enemy before he gets the drop on us.

Our purpose is to win, and win we may. But winning implies something to win and someone to win over. We can work so hard at a game that it ceases to be a game. War has been the stage for the drama of civilization to be played on; who wins if we blow up the stage? To win: aye, there's the rubout. That the purpose to win is doomed to frustration is as plain as the air-raid shelter in your building. Whet your mind too sharp, you may cut your own throat just flashing the blade intended for the enemy.

For knowledge to be equivalent to power, Nature must be degraded to a mechanism. Only then does Nature run in the grooves of her manipulator's self-interest. We perform on Nature the same operation that has split our own selves. We stuff the universe into a retort and distill off the volatile component of the psychic. This the scientist lets the philosopher have to play with; in the workshop psychic entities snag the works. The residue left from this fractionation is inert and destitute of mental quality. We call it matter, and it is immaterial that matter is artificially produced in man's mind. Esters of the soul can be sprayed back upon the characterless mass, perfuming selected segments as media of work and of play, making the objects of our purposes.

What we craft through such technology are the secular provinces of business and industry on the one hand and amusement resorts on the other. Over the surface of this material world reason may romp and brood. Every thinker is free to conceptualize it according to his convictions. Still reason is impotent to command its objects to come to life. Man cannot duplicate the feat of the Living God. No idea can confer existence. The role of cognition is adynamic. Magic stalks when we fancy anything really happens in obedience to the laws we lay down. The power to create eludes scientific apprehension, and artistic romancing too. This power is to be seized by a spiritual being alone.

Idealism and materialism bifurcate as the twin lobes of the devil's brain. To suppose they are opposite in any real sense makes a favorite ruse of his. Spending half our time fashioning an environment and the other half trying desperately to get away from it, summarizes the predicament of us modern men. Each half is found to negate the purpose of the other.

THE OTHER KIND OF KNOWLEDGE

To the two types of power two kinds of knowledge correspond. Objective knowledge and the power consequent upon it we have surveyed. Personal knowledge, its real opposite, yields to no simple resumé. This knowledge must be gained first-hand and immediately experienced to be known. That the inexperienced can scarce be persuaded of its genuineness is attested by the fact that we scarcely have a name for it. As already mentioned, spiritual knowledge is hinted at in the archaic Biblical expression, that a man knew his wife and she conceived. This phrase conveys two insights: first, the body is involved in the act of knowing as well as the mind; and second, that knowing is generative. Procreating a child is different from excogitating a theory. Spiritual knowledge I have called nonobjective: the subject is not detached from its object, one person participating in another, and the environment of each partaking of the same character as himself.

Traditionally our bodies are excluded from the hallowed precincts of epistemology. Still our bodies know much that we do not know. We would be inestimably less egotistic and unlovely if we muted our minds occasionally and attended to the intercourse the rest of us has with Nature. When our deeds bespeak the impulses of the flesh rather than the purposes of the ego, we derive ineffable glory from self-surrender and from joining in the flow of the cosmos. The Lord gave, the Lord takes away, blessed be the name of the Lord. The stuff that comprises the body of any man has served others before him and will offer the same service after he is gone. A fraternity enfolds Nature, of which our ideal of brotherhood casts but a pallid and flickering reflection. One species nourishes another, the lower sustains the higher. The grass rejoices in being assimilated into the lamb, and the lamb may exult, too, to be enfleshed in man. Death is not mourned as a grievous occurrence, as a dour note in Nature's symphony. Nature smiles at her funerals. And she may be laughing outright at the wise and prudent of the upstart species which is resolved to segregate its own affairs from her sovereignty.

How can evil be overcome by good? No one objectively knows. The mind can depose no recipe. Yet our bodies know. The transformation takes place after every meal. The food we swallow is an alien substance. Injected directly into the blood stream, a protein is highly toxic. The stomach, however, sets about restoring the harmony the inundation has disrupted. Equilibrium is rapidly recovered, tensions are relieved. This is accomplished with such ease as to produce a pervading sense of well-being. The body harbors a seethe of conflicts, and health depends on the transmutation of evil into good. The cause and cure of cancer has deployed into an all-out campaign on the objective level. Yet the body knows

the secret. Incipient cancer is probably an everyday occurrence in the normal organism. In the huge majority of
these uprisings, however, the rebellious cells are subdued
and their divagations are suppressed—all without the knower
knowing anything about it. Within the body ideas are dynamic.
The somatic will is a real will, being embodied and embedded
in physical existence. Knowledge there possesses the power
to create. This sort of knowledge we are prone to neglect.
The more grimly we grind out one type of knowledge, the
less we glean of the other.

The deeds we do without knowing how or why loom significant above all others. Such a deed is the act of falling in love.
Love and marriage come about without purpose or effort.
The fall is inevitable, but its inevitability is a genuine expression of freedom. Self-interest may oppose the mating;
this is known objectively. Parents and counselors advise
against the union. They are listened to politely, but the motives appealed to are objective as well. As such, arguments
are discredited and discountenanced. The person loved makes
no suitable object for the knowledge of outsiders to tamper
with or to prey upon. The beloved is a person independent
of one's self yet constituting one's self. Inside knowledge
supplants and supersedes outside knowledge, the real self
dominating his subject-object liability. Criteria of goodness,
of beauty and truth cannot take the measure of the infinite,
the beloved makes no specimen to be weighed and tested.
Judge not, is the lover's retort to any judgment.

What does he see in her? The lover overhears the question
being asked; how silly the gossip sounds. Why do men persist in asking why? The only answer surpasses understanding
and the faculty of communication. What is thy beloved more

than another beloved? Tell me what you see in her. I will parade a hundred women with the very specifications. What is thy beloved more than another? Be objective about it.

The lover knows a thing or two, though his knowledge be nonobjective. That knowledge defies analysis, flouts catalogue values, dispenses with the category of purpose. The beloved resists verbal capture and captivity in any tabulation of merits. If the lover endeavors to objectify his feelings, his account does not dwell on details of psychological dissection. Instead his diction becomes poetic. He beholds in the beloved the whole creation, alpha and omega, stars and rivers, lilies and precious stones. His vision encompasses the universe, his gaze the eye of God. The lover may seem overly expansive unless he stirs you to the same amorous mood. Still he is stabbing at an unutterable truth. All love is the love of God, every love is a loving with God. The beloved person manifests the sum of creation and love sheds insight into the structure of reality. The lover beholds what the Lord has made. And, lo, he finds it very good.

GOODNESS WITHOUT PURPOSE

Any act done in prosecution of a purpose cannot really be good, if goodness bears a moral rather than a utilitarian or aesthetic signification. This thesis is challenged by credal and sacramental religion. Religion holds that certain acts, specified by formula, are intrinsically good and are bound to be causally efficacious and to produce promised effects. Rites like churchgoing, performed according to rule, never fail of their high purposes.

When religion talks this way it must be silenced to give God a chance. Though esteemed sacred, these performances may excite only aesthetic reactions, possibly boredom, which are disconcertingly difficult to distinguish from the phenomena of secular play. Whatever be their impact, it is exhausted within the mind of the individual subject. The worshiper may be inflated to feel good. A wave of ecstasy may attend the act. But if this be regarded as amusement and self-indulgence, the behavior of the worshiper, once the thrill has evaporated, does little to refute it. If you meet a man Sunday afternoon, it is hard to tell, unless he tells you, whether he went to church that morning or washed the car.

Real good is not to be elicited by circling through a round of motions, whatever the purpose assigned to the routine. Real good comes from allowing the forces that encircle the world to include you. Ordinary happenings are the very stuff of spiritual goods. There are no distinctively religious acts. God is not to be sought in certain sites, in certified spots. To find him you have only to keep your eyes open wherever you are.

Suppose, for instance, you board a bus; the driver slams the door, squeezing one of your extremities and volleying harsh language at the other. What do you say to my saying to you that you were as much to blame as the driver? Had you actually been the person you thought you were, he would not have behaved as he did. Testy and irritable though he may have been, your presence should have calmed him and dispelled the miasma of his grouch. Could he not feel you coming, in the antique sense of know, in spiritual contact? Goodness is power when it is real. Its power is amply conveyed by its presence.

Since you were not really what you purposed to be, you retaliated in kind. You know bus drivers, you consoled yourself, licking your ego. You know they are a discourteous lot, menials by station. You exhibited your superior breeding by pretending to pay no attention; *noblesse oblige,* you played the game of snobbery, you were too proud to fight. So you extricated your coattails and stumbled over other passengers' feet, in a mood to thresh out revenge on the man you were rushing to keep an appointment with. The driver too was left no better off for having rocked your soul. He was a bit more surly at the next corner.

So we blunder through the day, jostling with bus conductors, tripping over clerks, customers, pedestrians, all plain ignoramuses. We seldom pause to suspect the part we play in the mess. We classify everybody to death; we never meet persons, human beings who are sensitive to one another's approach, each one an adventure, each capable of reflecting the joy of God if we present God's face to him. We know what the good is but our ideas get sidetracked in our knowledge of them.

Why do good, why be good? Only one sufficient reason can be given and that is no reason at all: doing good is the way to enjoy yourself. Doing good augments your power, it releases your self. Authentic good is spontaneous and inevitable, it bubbles from the depths of being, gushing forth without motive or purpose. This good is dynamic and the source of existence.

Flagrant vice is not so repulsive as a false kind of virtue. A lusty sinner is more pardonable than a lackluster saint. All righteousness is not the same righteousness. Three grades can be distinguished, spiritual righteousness alone being genuine. The other types pertain to the terminals of the ego-body complex man makes of himself.

Nearly everybody behaves righteously as far as the police can see. Righteous we have to be to a degree, to stay out of jail. We pay our bills, we give up half of the road. We do not jibe with the picture the uplifters daub of us, since we are neither gross sensualists nor materialists. Our world blears so desolate not because we do no good, but because that good is torpid and sterile. We barren our lives not by caring unduly for sensations and materials, but by caring really for nothing at all. We reach right over the present moment, wherein any event must take place, in a delirious grab for the future. Even our pleasure we take out in purposes, extracting from them an insipid satisfaction: are we not as good as the next man, and better than the man next to him?

Conspicuously we rate good enough when we inspect our intentions. We love mankind, we belong to church, we think the United Nations is probably a good idea. Still we must keep reviewing our intentions to get a view of our virtue. Immediate joy and the surge of power we sadly lack. Our brand of righteousness can be taught but little inspiration accompanies the lesson. Robert Ingersoll once said that if he had made the world, he would have made health as contagious as disease. God had that idea before it occurred to Ingersoll. Health is contagious, righteousness transmits power. That our goodness does not spread without the auxiliaries of snobbery and force signifies only that it is sham and sinister.

There are three kinds of goodness. To discriminate among them, let us observe people executing an act generally admitted to be righteous. It is difficult to select an act not disallowed in some quarter; the only act whose virtue I have never heard impugned is eating spinach. All spinach eaters are righteous people; you would dissent as a minority of one. Yet considerable diversity prevails among spinach eaters and the type of virtue they attain in performance. Objective research will confirm my own conclusion that righteousness may pertain to the hands and feet, to the head, or to the heart.

Children eat spinach because they have to. The law-enforcement officer stands hard by. It is dangerous to leave the green glob untouched at the edge of the plate, and no means is available to conceal the crime of its rejection. Eating spinach makes work but the idea is backed by force. The penalty is incarceration in the dog house. Thus hands are coerced into compliance, the strongest motive determines the will, and the distasteful task is gobbled down.

Growing to maturity consists in transferring the weapons that extort proper conduct to the province of the mind. Concepts of duty and purpose take over the job of the police department. The adult splits into a higher and lower self. The ego harnesses the hands and feet to the reins of reason. Virtue is reposed in the head. Spinach matures into an article of diet good for one's health. The stuff tastes vile. Still, virtue is naturally repellent and cuts across the grain. Stoics like Kant propound this as the supreme principle of ethics: what you like and what you ought proceed from your opposite ends. Goodness lies in taming and muting the passions. You know; science alone is qualified to define the good. Think of the vitamins and minerals in that there spinach. This objective knowledge may be a hoax, hatched by spinach growers and their advertising agents with medical hirelings suborned to make the game more profitable, but such a suspicion smacks of subversion. The experts know. You are inclined to agitate for a law making it compulsory to eat spinach, at least to punish defamers of the vegetable. Defamation indeed is a more heinous offense than disobedience: while it is an evil to violate an obligation, it's a greater evil to deny that the obligation is valid. Anyhow, you are convinced, and your purpose towers firm and ardent. You get the bitter portion down. But your righteousness is stuck in your head.

Now, there is a third class of spinach eaters—not a thickly populated class, to be sure. Still, if you dine around, now and then you meet folks who honestly relish the dish. They devour their spinach without pretense and without pretensions to virtue. Their act is neither a legal mandate nor a philosophic chore. It is a free expression of the peculiar selves they are. Blessed are they who hunger and thirst after righteousness, for they shall be filled. Blessed are they whose goodness resides in the heart. Doing God's will consists simply in enjoying your own.

The rare times I have hankered for spinach and felt disposed to sample a bite have been those occasions I sat at table with a lover of it who could not get his fill. Righteousness proves to be contagious if it can leap from plate to plate.

That practically everything in our world languishes in need of improvement we all agree. That only man's righteousness can accomplish the transformation we assent to, again unanimously. From there on the going gets nonobjectively rough. Real righteousness envisages a milieu without assignable purpose. Its sphere is fluid and pliant, freely malleable if man be free himself. Without joy in his heart, no deed can be truly good. Man's joy is but his sense of God's power.

THE END OF THE WORLD

Concerning any purpose the only sure thing that can be said is that it, along with the purposer, shall surely die.

It was scarcely necessary to await the advent of Freud to detect the death instinct in man. That man tires of his playthings and wills surreptitiously to destroy them, is fully evinced in the history of civilization. Death is foreshadowed too in that hopeless despair we sense as boredom.

No game sustains our allegiance permanently. The warning whisper of death cannot be muffled by bandages. Culture, being man's burst to defy his own mortality, succumbs finally to the bust of that defiance itself. Our technologies turn out to be superficial and deceptive, and disillusionment balks our resolution to construct. The subject-object creature, roaming the void alone, begets the purpose to annihilate its progeny, to burn the score sheets and the bridges, and to exit into the nothingness it had evolved from. The sole alternative play man cannot comprehend: to regard death as a real act of a real person. From no other viewpoint can death be met without violence and with acclaim.

An obscure strain pervades the Bible which rebuffs our understanding. We nail the glimmer down by calling it eschatology. Eschatology is the doctrine of the last things, of the end of the world. A queer being hovers uneasily, whose name is Messiah, the Anointed of the Lord. At the cataclysmic moment, he will dart to a footing, to terminate this sorry scheme and reshape it nearer God's. The Messiah is at once creator and destroyer, a spoilsport who will show men how to play with God. In the Biblical picture these aspects are scarcely separable, his spirit being identical with the spirit of God himself.

Exhuming and codifying ideas concerning Messiah have consumed the talents of sundry scholars. The Messiah has been revamped into a symbol of supernatural power, of the Absolute shafted to a point. All speculations get the idea but miss its impact. The Messiah can be nothing in all the universe except a man, an ordinary man, perhaps a carpenter, doing God's will and suffused by God's power. He cannot be a symbol of anything beyond himself. God's power cannot possibly be symbolized. It inheres in no object whatsoever, being possessed by a person.

And the eschatological climax cannot be projected into the future. No plan can be laid to bring it to pass. The world is forever coming to an end. That end is occurring every instant. Death is as continuous and inevitable as the passing of time. This very moment celebrates the grand finale. The Kingdom of God is in our midst.

VII

THE SPOILSPORT

COMPLICATIONS IN LIVING

MAN SPLIT HIMSELF long before he split the atom. The rift within himself is responsible for the havoc the riven atom portends. Cities are ravaged by the civil war raging within our skins. Pulling ourselves together would not relieve us of tension and conflict. Yet when we rally to meet a situation morally we can face it with faith, hope, and charity.

The self and the ego-body structure are the poles we oscillate between. To ease our conditions by the obliteration of one of these aspects of ourselves tempts as a solution. Why not decide to be either a person or a player, one or the other? Can we not achieve integration through the amputation of the opposite member? This is no new proposal; and since it is a bright idea, you can guess which pole is doomed to excision. The idealist votes for the ego's monopoly.

The monk makes his egotism exclusive. Nothing concerns him except his subject and the objects it protrudes. Other people, not being his own creations, strike him as a nuisance; he may even adopt a rule forbidding such casual recognition of them as conversation. We call the monk an introvert. He seems wrapped in his ideas, and his objects completely enwrap him. Still only the flimsiest line distinguishes him from the similar-souled extrovert.

The high-octane, top-plight business executive conforms to the same pattern as the monk. The objects of the extrovert's consciousness are more generally recognized as objects, that is all. A marvel of ingenuity, this executive expresses himself in pushing buttons, throwing levers, opening and closing valves. He is a master of details as long as these remain mechanical, that is, ideational; as long as they are destitute of personal quality. Other people he regards as objects to be summoned when he needs them, then whisked away after serving his purpose. He responds to the faintest market signal, he is sensitive to delicate fluctuations in the economic ebb and flow. His eyes rove keenly within the field of his own objectifications. Yet this so-called extrovert would not notice if his secretary appeared of a morning with her arm in a sling, provided the fractured limb did not disrupt the office machinery. The modern industrial age came about through turning loose, their insides stuffed with different dressing, a flock of birds which in the Middle Ages would have been cooped in monasteries. Jung's famous classification of introverts and extroverts amounts to little more than play with prefixes.

Egotists, whether they inhabit a hermit's cell, a university, the Pentagon, or Rockefeller Center, are ruthless in action, since their actions are logical and logic is inexorable. Upright they usually are—heads up. Scrupulosity rates tops in their table of values. They illustrate principles for cataloguers to admire. Though dazzled by their doings, we still sense an emptiness. Despite the heat they generate, we call them cold. They like being addressed by their first names, such spurious intimacy concealing their knotty and impersonal cores. Can you imagine yourself getting chummy with John Calvin, Immanuel Kant, with Stalin, with anybody you read about in the morning paper? Warriors, tycoons, philosophers, or saints, these men are players and their acts are theatrical. They have capped their spiritual poles with ice. That their worlds are undeniably objective does not mean that they are not unreal as well.

Might it be possible, on the other hand, to reject this egotistic pole and to dwell wholly on the moral plane? So to cast away the counterfeit dualism man is heir to? Probably more people make heart-way in this direction than make head-way in the other. But their ways are of slight cultural note. No Cassirer can write books about them. They do not count in the census of the great. Their deeds are unspectacular, unsuitable for inking newsprint. Still, we do possess a torso of biography of one man who did just that. That man was Jesus. He will be considered here, among the spoilsports, though being consummately one he even spoiled the sport of writing biography.

Most of us zigzag our way through. Real persons at times, it feels good to be true. But utilitarian interests intervene. Our consciences get hurt in the squeeze. We regret doing what we cannot help doing. We seek relief, not by moralizing more of life, which is always possible, but by endeavoring to reorganize the objective sphere on a moral basis which is equally impossible. We scheme to escape the mystery of existence through the exit of the known. But the only place to spiritualize the world is where you are, the sole way by leaving existence intact. Theoretical reformation accomplishes naught but bewilderment and frustration. The reformer, however, does spoil some game or other, and the spoils of his skepticism is a theme of this chapter.

Transition from a personal to the objective plane is subtle and may be sudden. You are, let us suppose, the father of a just-born son. You love the little tyke. Yet when your pride and pink takes to squalling in the nub of the night, he is transformed into an object, in a class with the radio in the apartment upstairs. Now you have a purpose in dealing with the brat, you consult the book for means to keep him quiet. So you shift back and forth between the poles, the infant sensing which predominates better than you do. In a few years the bairn will be packed off to college. You may continue to love him dearly, but at that juncture he falls into that disagreeable class of objects you owe money to. Love bulges with complications.

These complications stem from the contradiction of regarding people both personally and objectively. The most poignant tragedies lie in the failure to make proper adjustments on this score. Such propriety is not brought about by requiring those we love to meet objective standards of perfection. Quarrels within the family, precipitated by this demand, exceed in rancor any arising elsewhere, since one spasmodically loved resists total objectification. Hate is a personal attitude too. It comes about through affirming what you personally dislike to be an objective evil. You can hate only a person whom you genuinely love. Thus the rupture of marriage arouses an aversion more intense and insidious than either estranged partner could feel toward a business competitor.

The home must be heavily ballasted with the personal element if it is to remain afloat, since utilitarian and aesthetic motives are gusty and can drive any houseboat on the rocks.

Outside the home, however, we belong to hosts of groups which are ostensibly objective and institutional: play spheres, such as the church, the state, lodges and clubs, corporations wherein we are shareholders and employees. These are far removed from the spiritual pole, and importing moral quality into them but leads to befuddlement. Such organizations of togetherness rest on utility and are designed for egotistic satisfaction.

No player, however, succeeds in being exclusively playful. A soldier, for example, cannot commit murder in that role, as long as he kills only the enemy. Indeed, if he is notably ferocious and sanguinary in the right place, we hail him a national hero and pin a medal on his lapel. Yet we vacillate even in this clean-cut case: when we see a khaki uniform approaching bespangled with a purple heart, we do not dash for a dugout; that soldier shoots only under conditions specified by the game, other times he is capable of decent behavior. Outside the playground all men show a moral side, which side the game requires putting aside for the duration. But the requirement is never wholly met. Anyone can doff the uniform society makes him don.

Play is autonomous while it lasts, at least in theory. Nothing either moral or immoral can take place. The soldier commits no murder. When the President of the United States tells a news conference what he knows to be a whopper, is he lying? Now, lying consists in bearing false witness against one's neighbor; lying is a personal matter. But a politician has no neighbors, his political role is impersonal. The President is surrounded and abetted by his team mates, he is challenged and unhorsed by his opponents. How can one lie under such circumstances? A player does not lie when he false-cards in bridge. Are psychic bids not permissible? Is not any game psychic? A politician's utterances are no more than gambits. Stealing votes is no more heinous than stealing tricks at the card table. The vice imputed to the strategy means no more than the snobbery of the losing side. Platforms are intended to be shredded into sawdust for stuffing shirts. No form of play is amenable to moral methods. When anyone dictates such pseudo morality, he degenerates into an ill-tempered faultfinder, thwarted by his very purpose to achieve righteousness. The spirit forfeits its power in being converted into an end. All that truth can mean in politics is somebody's idea attaining objectivity, inasmuch as none more compelling comes upon the scene.

Sundry questions snap and crackle whenever the poles of man's being tug at the diameter. What about cheating? Within the confines of the game, clearly, one cannot cheat. His opponents are there to match him and to watch that he doesn't. Contending egos straddle the board; whoever wins plays fairly. Eternal vigilance is half the price of victory. If cheating be charged when minor rules are violated, the culprit can plead that any organized play not only tolerates and condones but actually invites this loose conduct. The do-good censors are merely angry because they have lost. The laxity they are peeved at serves to keep the game going, making it flexible and enhancing its make-believe. What does more drastically imperil the integrity and the vitality of the game is insisting the law be observed to the letter. Any organization with both feet out of the grave placates an insurgent, laughs at the cribber, instead of ejecting him in a huff.

Cheating becomes a moral matter only when a person is cheated. Come with me to the Automat for lunch. The woman at the change booth flips you eleven nickels for your half-dollar—it happened to me once. Now, that woman's nickels are counted; she must account for every one. If you pocket her mistake, she is out of pocket. And there she sits, a human being, prone to error like yourself. Having done the right thing, I trust, you stand before the tier of vaults that glass in the pumpkin pie. A door swings ajar. The mechanism has slipped a cog, and an unguarded slice beckons you for free. This also happened once, and soon I was guttling the tastiest tongue of pie I ever ate amid that clatter. Did I do wrong? Horn and Hardart are not persons at all, being a fictitious entity whose stock is traded on the exchange. I have engaged in numerous tilts with that corporation, and for the first time ever I was enjoying an advantage of weapons. That outfit is well able to take care of itself; quiz the boy that carts away the dishes. You cannot cheat a restaurant chain. It is jolly on the job to see that you don't. I suspicion the company plants an open door now and then just to graft a new sucker. I admit having sneaked back regularly for a month, enticed by my crumb of luck.

When the maxim, honesty is the best policy, is applied to business, honesty is divested of moral implications. Honesty means merely overt assent to the rules of the game. If the player's heart is in the right place—we say *heart* though we mean *ego*—a measure of trickery around the edges adds to the hilarity. Only in this borderland of unwritten law can activity wax zestful: seeing how far you can stray from the straight and narrow without diminishing returns. Do entrepreneurs really believe the astounding claims they scream for their products? How ridiculous to ask. Persuading you to brush your teeth with rhetoric works no moral evil, and it keeps the wheels of prosperity spinning. Moving customers by mass propaganda is no more wicked than any other bull-dozery. No objective appliance is either pro or con the moral self.

A morally honest businessman would aim to produce the best possible article at the lowest possible cost, being convinced beforehand that the commodity was one that human beings needed. His purpose, if he theorized one, he might state as the fulfillment of human wants. Industry, of course, would then operate within a spiritual matrix. But then, too, *profit motive* would become an unintelligible term belonging to the language of an extinct race. Of such a spoilsport contemporary business always stands in terror. To moralize economics would extinguish the game we have made of it. Anyone who essayed to do business honestly in that sense, could deal with friends and neighbors alone. Such neighborliness would incur the wrath of all present players, and congressional action would quickly sharpen the teeth of fair trade legislation to snap off the menace. But even speedier strangulation would check the enterprise in the good neighbor's getting caught in his own trap. A moral concern is abandoned in institutionalizing it. A personal relation cannot be idealized, it must be lived existentially. The game the reformer decimates reassembles under his mace.

TYPES OF SPOILSPORTS

Three sorts of game-busters can be distinguished. Two of these are composed of skeptics. The third one collects the great believers.

The third class first: the player who kills the game beyond all hope of revival is, ironically enough, the one loudest in proclaiming its virtues. He demanded unswerving loyalty to the rules, maybe on the ground that these rules have been divinely revealed. Nothing short of sheer rigid conformity, meticulous adherence to the code, will do. He stickles for tradition, or for whatever the proprieties be. Innovation he denounces as a sin, and he has a perfect right to cast the first stone against the sinner. Often the doughty defender of the past poses as a prophet and upon his followers he may throw a mystic spell. By way of example, he can be identified as the one hundred percent American. Eventually any perfect percenter will topple his own house of cards or palace of principles. The inquisition he inaugurates, if he manages to seize power, strangles the very creed his aim is to ensoul. The tin horn of the despot finally sounds taps at his own interment. The great believer is a spoilsport despite himself.

The second class makes more trouble to round up, and to round off in a characterization. Reformers belong here: spoilsports of this stripe want to preserve the game but by improving it. Their scheme is to alter its prescriptions, perhaps beyond recognition if you listen to the wails of players who are prospering under the established book. Conservatives yell that the universe is being overturned by the innovations, being tumbled from some sacred gold standard. This spoilsport looms as a downright cheat according to the word of the opposition.

Iconoclasts are to be put here. They get things done. They produce historic effects, though lesser ones than historians tell of. Iconoclasts smash a lot of ornaments, but they wangle a similar stock to pile back upon the altars they have denuded, leaving worshipers to recite the same prayers before a different array of idols. The net result, for instance, of the iconoclastic movement in the Eastern Church was to impose a ban on statues—which merely rehabilitated the use of pictures as religious symbols and decorations for the church. This settlement proved significant for artists, compelling them to employ the brush rather than the chisel. But the result was hardly commensurate with the uproar. Iconoclasm involves an assault on incidentals. The play survives intact despite shiftings of stage scenery.

Stock-item reformers differ from iconoclasts in being impelled by genuinely moral sentiments instead of aesthetic prejudices. By original capacity reformers are real persons. Still they hang on the fringes of reality; they do not protest against the game as such but against such pestilential consequences of it as they have discerned. The reformer feels a strong sense of kinship with his fellows, especially those who are faring badly in the fray. The pains in their backs he suffers in his head. Their poverty and sordor he blames on the worn, well-thumbed deck. He calls for a New Deal. A wobbling society, he believes, can be propped into a welfare state that looks like a morally going concern.

In this he is mistaken, and grief overtakes every reform movement in the end. But for the nonce the ship of state is kept paddling. The illusions of the game are fortified, its most glaring chicaneries are curbed, its pretensions decently draped. In politics a reform movement has the primary purpose of moving in a reforming dynasty. In no democracy do the free citizens vote responsibly or even intelligently. They regard freedom as the chance to pursue self-interests; indeed, they have never been told otherwise. Their very cupidity renders the masses gullible. Thus the electorate is easily victimized by bloated promises and blatant bombast.

When the voters reach for the two-birds-in-the-bush and do not get them, the reformer raises the lure to three birds and makes their plumage brighter. The rules allow a candidate to buy votes by promises to increase the voters' pay once he is in, but the rules forbid the candidate to buy for cash the votes to get in. Does this not make it too cheap for the candidate? Why not make him pay through the nose instead of through the mouth? Reform, however, never runs in a costly direction as far as the reformer is concerned.

The reformer opines that the pretensions of the game are praiseworthy, the damage being wrought through technical maladjustments in play. New rules will repair the damage. No one can deny that such tinkering redounds to the good, objectively speaking. Though the repair job has no relevance to the moral life, the services the reformer confers are not to be lightly disprized. Civilization would grind to a horrible halt if it were not for somebody's tireless work in abolishing evils and putting off the evil day. The rebel stabilizes society by making the seats on top uncomfortable. Sometimes reformers actually alter the course of history for generations; other equally good times they get pitched out of the game for their pains. What factors determine their reception makes a fascinating enigma; why, for example, John Hus flopped, while a century later Martin Luther roused a howl of success.

The third genus of spoilsport contains whosoever refuses to play. The skepticism of these plumbs ultimate depths. They decline to play at improving the play. Play is futile, a waste of time, it gets nothing done. Its treasures are objective, of this world, of sounding brass. Such spoilsports do not propose to moralize the game, their insight penetrating deeper than this superficial purpose. They live spiritually themselves, often impressing as extreme individualists. True, they are different from other individuals; but there is, literally speaking, a world of difference between the real spoilsport and the conventional individualist.

Jesus belongs here. But before turning to him, we will consider as a foil a classical reformer Jesus is often, rather obtusely, associated with. Christians like to compare Jesus with Socrates. It makes Jesus seem respectable.

SOCRATES

The fifth century B.C. in ancient Athens was a period similar to the period humanity is always barging through. The tail of an age of enlightenment and liberalism, it was witnessing the collapse of what are referred to as the pillars.

The best society was overrun with Sophists, all resolved on self-expression. That one man is as good as another, each being the measure of all things, is the idea that everybody provides his own autonomous and self-evident end. This end is to be approached through knowing what it is. The game consists in so cunningly adapting the means to the advancement of self-interest that the greatest happiness accrues to the greatest number. Each Sophist constitutes a cult of self-improvement, each slyly improving his own position in peddling information how his customers can improve theirs. The refrain of Greek sophism was a tune familiar to our ears: how to win friends and influence people. Success in the wizardry is dependent on acquiring the know-how. And to know how to know how is the golden nugget most anybody will pay handsomely to nuzzle. No trade flourishes so fabulously in an age of sophistry as helping folks to help themselves. The idea flatters the vanity of the simpleton, and he reckons the cost of the course on the side of gain.

Upon this Athenian scene hove Socrates. A spoilsport he was undoubtedly. He encountered little difficulty in exhibiting as shysters the big shots in the racket. They were advertising self-knowledge as a recipe for wisdom, yet self-knowledge was precisely the commodity whereof they were short. From every verbal bout Socrates emerged the winner, infuriating his victims by insisting on his own amateur standing, the gist of his pose of humility and ignorance. Even more irritating was his refusal to take pay for his services, money which he could obviously have used to advantage. A university professor welcomes controversy from his peers, the refutation of his views being recognition of his worthiness. But to be shown up as a dunce by an illiterate vagrant, that is a disgrace which no snobbery can shake off. And Socrates was a hick from the sticks among city swells, an uncouth stone-cutter, a roughneck cutting a swath in the high-rent district. Naturally he met with resentment at the hands of those who had institutionalized self-knowledge into a lucrative profession. His repulsive appearance and rude manners made him an easy target. Socrates lacked good taste, always a top item in the Sophist's roll of virtues, good taste being what tastes good to the particular Sophist. Thus the bomb of self-knowledge exploded in Socrates' face. He blew up a martyr to his own ideas. He talked himself to death. At any time up to the downing of the hemlock Socrates could have got off by consenting to keep his mouth shut.

Socrates was the life-of-the-party type and doubtless he had enlivened many. He was at his best on the party level, which he preferred to the personal, having his wife and child ejected from his death chamber, coolly ordering them out, so he might spend his final hour in quiet discussion in the company of his equals. His own death Socrates regarded as a good idea, for, said he, "If I shall live a longer period, perhaps I shall be destined to sustain the evils of old age, to feel my intellect impaired and to grow inferior to others in all those qualities in which I was once superior to them." *

The wisdom of Socrates winds to the conclusion that self-knowledge should be imparted not by dubs like Protagoras but by experts like himself. As a spoilsport Socrates was far less radical than historians credit him with being. Divers philosophers rushed into the agora to gather the rocks he had hurled and out of them to build mansions for themselves. One of the marvels of human ingenuity was the deft maneuvering of Plato to hack the erratic individualism of his master into rubble for concreting a totalitarian state, a feat so cleverly executed as to have ensorceled Platonists ever since.

Socrates accepted the salient rule of the Sophists' game: knowledge is the supreme quest of man, his highest good. Since no man can know the good and resist its goadings, virtue is identical with knowledge. To become adept and adequate in any pursuit, one must amass ample information pertinent thereto. Virtuous living requires merely the sharpening and trimming of those concepts which determine the ethical realm. The actual world can be moralized by revising the dictionary. That most people have continued to think so does not prove Socrates right save as a thinker.

The gimmick lies in confusing existence with the artifact of work and play. In work and play essences may determine

* Xenophon, *Memorabilia of Socrates*, Everyman's Library, p. 150.

the course of events, and knowledge may be virtue and power. At a formal dinner party, for certain, etiquette governs whatever happens, which certainly is not much. To know the proper move is to move in the proper circle. Artisans also, like the shoemaker and navigator, rely on knowledge for the prosecution of their crafts, and ignorance is tantamount to vice, possibly to calamity. Socrates could make out the same case in respect to politics. Since the basic purposes of the state are to collect taxes at home and to make war abroad, a competent statesman is one skilled in these sciences. Knowledge makes for virtue as long as life proceeds on no other level than that ranged by a plumber or a United States Senator. But real life differs from and is incommensurable with any work-play roundabout ever devised.

That the spiritual personality pertains to quite another dimension, Greek philosophy saw no more than a faint glimmering. Plato and Aristotle, it is true, did glimpse the Achilles' heel of Socrates' doctrine. But their remedy was to hold the rest of Achilles longer beneath the surface of the Styx. If the moral life be envisaged in the simple terms of loving your neighbor, in discerning beneath the armor of your enemy a human being like yourself whose will can be transformed by sharing it, if this be the moral way, no gentile before the advent of Christianity had more than the dimmest inkling of morality. Plato never got beyond the objective field of politics in his search for the good life— thereby clamping upon Western man the superstition that rules him still, the idea that these domains are congruent. Plato's ethical consummation was identical with a stable and ordered society, made sacrosanct by having its seams cemented by thinkers with trowels. Known man and real man were one and inseparable. Hence classical learning makes but a manual of magic and a poor one at that. It did not function then, and it will not function tomorrow. No incantations of psychology will empower Americans to coexist with Russians, or show any man how to get along with his wife.

One Socratic gambit players in any game should be wary of: the pretense of being dumb. To know nothing is the familiar pose of the open mind, of the tender soul free of prejudice and seeking the truth at whatever cost. Descartes worked the same stunt some centuries later with such magnificent effect that philosophy has never quite rallied from the scare. The play consists in hiding all the apparatus of one's system, announcing in startled voice that everything is lost, then organizing a hunting party which proceeds to discover, as if by miracle, every item exactly where it had been secreted before the tour got under way. Any player who bleats he has nothing in his head has plenty up his sleeve. The man that professes to know none of the rudiments of the game is apt to pick them up with very rude speed and at your expense. Be skeptical of skepticism when it speaks with the assurance of omniscience. The genuinely religious man has more doubts than most solid atheists.

Socrates belongs to the type of spoilsport I have called the reformer. Philosophy he did reform and reinvigorate, giving it sundry shoves in diverse directions. But he never aspired to be anything the Sophists were not. The rules of play he essayed to alter, but the game itself he left unchallenged. He looped his knot in that cordon wherewith philosophy was tying man's hands behind his back, leaving him the otiose diversion of staring helplessly into the infinite realm of ideas. How man could be both what he was and what he was not, remained a riddle. Ancient thought wound up, rent between Stoic fury and Neoplatonic weariness, snorting defiance at one world and exuding a mystic yen for another, torn between work and play.

WAS JESUS A REFORMER?

Their both having suffered violent deaths threads the connection in popular imagination between Socrates and Jesus. There the strand of resemblance must be severed. Both were spoilsports, but of these there are various kinds. Socrates was a reformer. He quirked current modes of thought and queered that game.

Clergymen today say Jesus did the same. He gave legs to an idea, he upheaved society by novelties he scattered about. This is a fashionably objective interpretation of him. Still, fashion apart, no originality attached to Jesus' ideas. He showed no inclination whatever to revamp the games then dominant nor to tamper with their rules. What Jesus did instead was to repudiate these pastimes, just as he might repudiate our pastimes, including the one of patching out theories about him. The preeminent man of our tradition who refused to play, he envisaged life as a continual playing with God.

That Jesus proposed to improve the customs he was brought up in, is an idea commentators elicit from their own heads and not from the Gospels. You will scan these records in vain for evidence that he advocated any program of reform. The mores of Judaism which we consider so onerous he adhered to steadfastly and gracefully. On one point alone did Jesus hint at rebellion, and that hint was so subtle we overlook it: it hardly seems proper to laugh at Jesus even when we are laughing with him. The point concerned the payment of taxes to the Roman overlords.

The reason for the incident's being ignored can be traced to an oddity in our mental make-up. We revel in the puffery of doctrinaire freedoms: the freedom to worship a god of our whims, freedom to think and to call it thinking. We are jubilant that the government shall not decide what church we are going to stay away from. These freedoms blarney our egos. But they ditch the rest of us. The same benevolent government, without infringing our precious liberty, conscripts us for war, swipes our pocketbooks, and chucks us in jail if we do more than grumble at the outrage. To bestow freedoms that do not matter, then dictate matters where there is no freedom, makes a neat trick the Romans stumbled on long ago. Jesus was sufficiently clear-sighted to penetrate the sham. He countered with an even slicker device to cheat the tax collector. His ruse is both vivid and obscure. Those who are fishing for schemes to match wits with Internal Revenue might ponder St. Matthew 17: 24–27. Jesus apparently had a new move in that perennial game; it is regrettable the narrator so garbled the details.

Barring that single episode the Gospels have no suggestion that Jesus propounded any change in the social order. He went through the same motions as everybody else, kept the commandments without complaint and without producing better ones to take their place. At his trial no illegal acts were charged against him, no infractions of law or precedent. He was not alleged to have corrupted youth nor to have fomented subversive organizations. He had attacked no sacrosanct rackets. The accusations of his tormentors were vague and addled, so badly balled up that scholars who spend years straightening out the report of that trial can make scant sense of it.

There is no sense to be made. No one in Jerusalem deliberately willed Jesus' execution. It came about by its designers having forfeited the capacity to will anything at all. Choose this day whom you will serve: this was the imperative Jesus had iterated. But players cannot choose. Their personalities have been blotted out, their selves blurred and blotched by the mechanical process they have set in motion and been enslaved by. Killing a man is not actually killing when it is done for the good of the state. Jesus had broken up their game by withdrawing from it. He had left nothing in its place, thus leaving his assailants helpless, bereft of their purposes, a mob propelled by brute force. Evildoers do not choose to do evil, they are unable to choose at all. A reformer does offer an alternative, within the limits of the familiar game. Jesus allowed none.

Socrates was executed legally. His judges even tempered the sentence with mercy, opening avenues of escape. But the condemnation of Jesus lay quite beyond the province of the law. No law was reigning; the objective world had come to an end. The death of Socrates was not inevitable in the tragic sense of the Crucifixion. For a player to run into a fog of hard luck marks a mere contretemps, howsoever grievous it may appear. An outright clash between a spiritual person and a sphere of play is something else. This is tragedy in existence. The cosmos groans, causing the earth to tremble and, rumbling, open the graves of the dead.

JESUS AND THE PHARISEES

The Pharisees were good men. They spent much time on their knees and more time brushing off the dust. Their teachings were verbally identical with the teachings of Jesus, as irenically minded Jews today are agog to point out. The maxims of the Sermon on the Mount were copybook material, golden texts in schoolrooms then as today. No doubt Jesus did utter them. But the congregation had heard them else-where and they were duly recorded because the evangelists knew them by heart.

Had Jesus done no more than to edit these precepts, had he been the winsome idealist of contemporary Protestantism, he would have died, as his ministers will in due season die, safely in bed. The Pharisees would have listened then as they listen now with approval and delight, nodding their heads as if to seal a valve at their necks to prevent further penetration. What Jesus did in addition, did not consist in giving the Pharisees something new to talk about. What caused the trouble was Jesus' telling them they talked too much already. Their babbling stank of the gentiles. God knows men by their fruits; the Pharisees were amusing themselves with fruitless flowers. Their good ideas rattled audibly in their heads. But they were a generation of vipers, differing from rattlesnakes only in that the snakes rattled at the other end.

For their dismal ineptitudes Jesus never held the ceremonial law accountable, as preachers say; a good idea, by the way, of theirs. The Torah he accepted, naïvely it seems, as the divine will of God and governed himself accordingly. What he did rebuke and execrate was the law's getting shunted into the head of an expert on it, the law's deflection into a toy for the tinkering of idealists. No reason could be excogitated for the law's being what it was. No reason could ever be assigned for the universe's being what it was, or for there being a universe at all. Existence is nobody's idea. The law was made for man, to fix his habits and enrich his life; man was not made for the Sabbath. His freedom lay in enjoying the Sabbath, not in pestering himself by idealizing it. Jesus might remind his liberal coterie today that idealizing the abolition of the Sabbath seems to be going the Pharisees one better. The Pharisee thanked God he was better than other men. We thank God we are better than the Pharisee, eventually thanking ourselves for having no god to thank.

Originally Judaism had meant the bond of moral relations within the holy community which made manifest the covenant entered into with God. Traditionally there had been no Jewish state. The science of politics was unknown in Palestine, the Jews being a people rather than a nation. But the Pharisees were institutionalizing that people, thereby volatilizing the covenant into what we now extol as spiritual religion. Its real spiritual quality was being dissipated into the exquisite experience of saving one's soul, into an inner glow and fluorescence. Each worshiper got tied into his own tight knot. It manacled him no less because the law of Moses supplied the strands that laced it. Every Pharisee was as proud of his own dexterity fashioning bows as he was captious of the ribbons bedecking others. The Pharisees were idealists— stunted and deformed perhaps, for the soil of Judea dwarfed a species that reached full bloom in Greece. Still, they were speedily talking themselves into a swarm of New Thought cults. A group known as Essenes, semiascetics and world-forsakers, were frantically chasing the salvation of their souls around the deserts. Far from being a revolutionary such as these, Jesus was an archconservative. He took his stand on the ancient oracles of his race, appealing to the worthies of antiquity against the newfangled ideas of his day. His followers linked him intuitively with Moses and Elijah: Jesus' God like theirs answered with fire. No one sighed for peace of mind when Jehovah was around. The presence of Jesus had the same scorching effect.

Yet Jesus questioned no customs as such. He never fancied, idiotically, that real freedom is to be miraculously achieved by pottering with the rules men invent for their own enthrallment. Communal habits are no evil. No community can survive without them, instinct itself providing man with no pattern of behavior. But these cannot be institutionalized and declared articles of faith. The body must have its ways of doing which can be at the same time the deeds of a real self. The law has to be existential rather than objective. It is to be taken in one's stride instead of becoming an idea straddling one's mind. In making an objective of the law the Pharisee used it to subsidize his ego. When so objectified into a permanent system of values, righteousness was deflected in a single swing into mechanism and purpose. And, so debased, righteousness lacked power. It produced pinched faces, headaches, and boredom. The more optimistically the Pharisees vaunted their own virtues, the more pessimistic they waned about the world where, alone, virtue could be expressed. The closer they stole to God, the sharper the devil nipped them from behind. However, Jesus never blamed the law for the legalism of its proponents. The Pharisees possessed a petrifying touch and damned even God to stone. Far from being its antithesis, legalism is identical with the ideal-

istic quest. While the ego romps in play, the person perishes
and legalism is what we call his corpse.

Anyone who aspires to be good for the sake of goodness is
condemned by that very purpose into a tedious drudge and
the dourest of hacks. He fails in the one thing needful: power
to accomplish the cherished end. A keen observer like Jesus
quickly detected the hypocrisy inseparable from this plight.
To play with the idea of the Kingdom of God and to work
for its realization are equally frustrating: the Kingdom of
God is already in our midst. God himself wearies as a fearful bore when godly people sweat to make him known. The
Pharisee was burning his way to heaven; he should keep
cool, he must consider the lilies of the field that neither toil
nor spin. Jesus hardly meant that men had to stand in corners,
faces to the wall, engrossed in pious contemplation. What
exactly did Jesus mean? He never says, no man can say.
There arc no recipes for freedom. But freedom is a recipe
for bringing the Pharisee's game to an end.

Jesus never advised breaking the law. It is, therefore, at
my own risk and on my own account that I tell the Pharisee
it is better to break the Commandments than to be broken by
them.

A DIGRESSION WITH THE DEVIL

The devil is an unpleasant name for the urge to get away
from yourself and to escape from spiritual reality. That
Jesus met the devil at least once is attested by the story of
the temptation. Here the record is plain. There was a second
temptation too, but when the Gospel writers got to it, they
were full of the devil themselves and he mangled their accounts. We will survey these episodes in turn.

Jesus, probably influenced by the Essenes, went to the wilderness to be alone with God, and to wangle certainties from objects angled from his own mind. That had often been tried before Jesus' famous escapade. It has persisted as a favorite device for the alleviation of frustration. In the instance of Jesus, however, the record rings authentic, for its outcome departs from the normal. Jesus did not find God at all, which is normal; he did not think he did, which is highly unusual. Jesus instead made a momentous discovery: the digression brought him face to face with the devil.

What of it, you say? Nobody goes to the wilderness any more. Maybe not geographically, still people do crawl off to bed with books on peace of soul. Such books are tremendously popular, and recourse to them indicates rebuff. The games we are embroiled in cease to thrill, so what remains but to withdraw further? Nothing we can do will avail to save the world. It is jogging a dizzy course to war and bankruptcy. Perhaps we can rescue our own souls from the fated crash, elevate ourselves above the din and rubble; perhaps we can arrange a private peace by defining peace correctly. God will give his angels charge over us, lest at any time we dash our foot against reality. True, our righteousness runs thin and washy. Yet this need not suggest that our righteousness is humbuggery. It suggests that others are delinquent. That the world scoffs at the ideals we garnish it with, confirms us in the conviction of our own superiority.

The devil whispers just that, vanishing from sight in telling us what we already know. He beckons us to join him in eternity. In his *Human Life of Jesus* John Erskine writes, "It was the Devil's hope, in the symbolic account of the Temptation, that Jesus would demonstrate his divine origin by strictly temporal choices. . . . When Jesus put the temptation from him, his decision was made to live at once as he wished to live always, to live in eternity now." All that may be said to this is that the writer knew the devil better than he knew Jesus. What the devil proposed precisely was for Jesus to live in the eternal indefinitely, to make the wilderness his permanent address. Inasmuch as nothing is going to happen anyway, one might as well aim for the best, and in the wilderness the contemplation of an idea is tantamount to its fulfillment. Why not gently ease himself from the gross concerns of men? Those were good ideas, those ideas of the devil's. Jesus loved his fellow men—everybody does in the wilderness where you don't have to look at them. Why not exhaust that love by making bread for them out of stones? there would be so much of it and it costs so little? What would please God more, the loving father of mankind? How is one to tell the difference between God and the devil when both say the same things? Wherein lies the deviltry of the devil?

The perspicacity of Jesus evinced a remarkable endowment. This is theologically accounted for by the theory, devilish perhaps, that he was the Son of God. But need we go so far afield? Jesus was a Jew—sturdy, old-fashioned type. Traditionally the Jew had no taste for solitude; to this day he has scarcely been cultivated into it. The Jew's religion had always been his people. Jewish society had avoided, as far as humanly possible, the mortar box of play. No phase of life had ever been granted autonomy, not even religion itself. Indeed, the Jews had no word for religion. None of the flowers of the inner (or objective) life had blossomed in Palestine: there was no art, no science, as cognized and recognized disciplines. References to sports and games are as notably rare in the Bible as they are abundant in Plato's dialogues. Politics, economics, etiquette: all were indissolubly mixed in Judaism, and religion—a term the Jew never invented—was simply the sign of the organic union which meant true spiritual fusion. No real Jew ever got off by himself either physically or psychically. No Jew pined to be ideal by renouncing his personal character wherein individual and community were inseparable.

Thus Judaism preserved a firm attachment to the existential world, deprived as it was of indulgence in the luxuries of a higher one. The Jew had his feet on the ground and his prophets told him his head should hang in the same humble direction. We call the Jews materialists still, altogether superficially, for materialism is a brat of gentile begetting which was never spawned in Jewry. Ever battling in the thick of the cosmic struggle, the Jew did not claim for his ego the privileges of a conscientious objector. Jesus knew that bread is not to be baked from stones by the yeast of taking thought. The devil's proposition sounded phony.

The ideas of any sojourner in the wilderness lean toward the good. The evil wrought by the devil cannot be ascribed to the malignancy of his proposals. From what source, however, is the power to realize those ends? The moral person acknowledges but a single creative power, that power being God himself. The devil detaches the spirit of God from God's person. The devil of it is naught but the righteousness of God bereft of God's power.

The devil possesses no power except the power his cronies

contribute to him. He has been much flattered in being depicted as a puissant figure, equipped with vast armaments of destruction. Such a picture pleases the devil, since it makes it possible to locate him where he is not. The devil seems always to be crouching within an object that is foiling our wills. He stalks in the dictator overseas, in whatever prevents us from having our way. And where shall we get the power to banish the devil from the planet and to make our ideas regnant? From ourselves, from nowhere else. The devil's power issues from man's aspiring to be what he is not. The devil can function only in a field where man is playing at being God.

The devil's subterfuge is to preach that power is evil: coincidentally that is what preachers say too. Power corrupts: if external forces were not blocking our motives, thought would be actualized in merely thinking it good. This fatal bifurcation of supernatural and natural, ideal and material, was avoided by the Jews. Hebrew monotheism, a unique phenomenon in the annals of the human race, declared righteousness and power to be identical, properties of the same person. Any idea sundering them caused a cleavage within the cosmos wherein God ruled morally. Hence images of God were forbidden. To conceive of God under any symbol was as unreasonable as the ambition to do so was intolerable. God can be represented in art or sacrament only if God is an idea. But the God of storm and battle, the God who speaks by fire, is no idea. This God is power. He makes things happen, and anything that really happens is God himself. Such a God no man can play at being, if he has ordinary common sense.

Power is evidenced in existence, and existence cannot be

symbolized. It is, or it is not. Power is or it is not. The sole
way to represent power is to possess power. Power pertains
to the present, to neither past nor future. Power belongs to
the actual, never to the possible. A column of wooden soldiers
does not symbolize the army; those manikins win no battles.
Their parade may fill a certain type of officer with immense
delight, but such an officer fades under a real cannonade.
Similarly any scheme to symbolize God converts God into
a toy, and relations with him into artifice. Art, not power,
is guilty of corruption. God is what God does, and a deity
painted on canvas or stained in glass is shackled to a stand-
still. He may have the punch to make his votaries feel pious.
But the enjoyment of aesthetic objects entails a digression
from the real.

Idolatry cannot accomplish what the idol promises. A
known God is not the real God. The righteousness of God is
not to be sublimated into human values. Conjuring bread out
of stones is a splendid idea, but the devil cannot pull the
trick. In the temptation lurks a patent fake, a hoary hoax.
Whatever be the excellence of the project, it excels only as
magic. Jesus would have no such bunk. The devil is bunk.
The devil is an alias for man's ego, and that ego's power is
restricted to magic.

The devil still rampages despite that decisive repulse. An
impatient motorist honking his horn in a traffic jam is full
of the devil. A church convention passing resolutions to out-
law war is full of the devil. The devil flourishes in legislative halls, where through the sorcery of making laws politicians seek to accomplish what Nature interdicts. Every bu-
reaucrat hugs a new idea for diving from the pinnacle of the
temple without hazard to his neck. Bunk is a play of thought,

irrelevant alike to man's moral life and to the existential universe.

Jesus went to the wilderness to be alone, and alone he met the devil. The devil, unsought and unseen, companions every self-made man. In affirming the independence of our egos, we pay obeisance to him. Solitude is incompatible with personality. Whatever authentic dignity accrues to man, whatever equality obtains among men, depends not on each man's possession of a magical divine reason, but on each belonging to his people. Believing in God means accepting joyfully and valiantly one's status in the human race.

Jesus left the wilderness unspoiled by his engagement with nothingness. But he left a spoilsport. Henceforth he must exceed the Pharisees' conception of righteousness as playing with ideas. Righteousness was equivalent to the power whereby good ideas could be made existent.

THE SECOND TEMPTATION

The Gospels are hardly biography in the usual sense. On long stretches of Jesus' life they give no information whatever. Reading them is like leafing through an album of snapshots. On one point, however, these shots converge: they show us Jesus in possession of extraordinary power. The wonders he performed astounded all witnesses including himself. The lame walked, the blind had their sight restored, the deaf heard again, and the poor found life worth the hardships it incurred. His deeds showed up the Pharisees as ciphers, their power being limited to producing scowls, wrinkles, and twaddle.

The Pharisees could not stand so much going on. Power corrupts: their piety preferred static perfection. Jesus ruffled their placidity of mind. The Pharisee is always jolted by mere mention of the word *miracle*. Though never insisting on Nature's being good, he does demand that Nature be law-abiding in her adversity.

Against the popular roar for signs and wonders Jesus protested. No act of man could signify God's favor. Every event was God's immediate doing, even the fall of a sparrow. To appeal for an unnatural show of God's power voiced doubt that his was the natural power the whole world showed. Faith, being but ordinary vision, could not be engendered by an extraordinary operation of prying men's eyes open wider. No one need build a theater where God might stage an act, for the lily of the field bespoke him fully. The idea of miracle is chimerical since it severs the creator from his creation. The lack of faith that raises the question whether miracles happen debilitates the spiritual person who alone can answer. The Pharisees can work no miracles; the same pride that alienates Nature keeps them from acting naturally. Jesus spurned the role of miracle man; he was a real man, playing with the Living God, revealing the world that God had made. To enter reality repentance pointed the way. Men must get off their high horses and walk humbly. The mechanically determined object represented no handiwork of God's; it was the masterwork of pharisaical thought, wherein man condemned himself to a petty game of his own.

Soon Jesus had gathered a tumultuous following attracted by his mighty acts. In the excitement the effete Pharisees were elbowed aside, and another party, the Zealots, stormed into their places. Jesus was inflaming an ancient purpose. The nationalists spied in him what they had long been planning. Political ambitions were being fed and were fattening rapa-

cious. Here was the deliverer, Messiah, sent by God for the
express purpose of driving the Romans out. No longer would
the Chosen People squirm beneath a foreign heel. A revolution was forthwith brewing. Plans were well advanced, for
James and John, two of Jesus' closest friends, appear to have
carved out jobs for themselves in the new regime. The devil
was assaulting Jesus again, this time frontally, and coming,
I opine, nearer to success than at the siege in the wilderness.
Jesus' physical power was being augmented by the brawn of
the mob. Besides, was not the rescue of a captive people
from the tyrant's yoke clearly a laudable idea, the very reign
of God, foretold by prophets of old?

The records do not enlighten us as to what went on, for
an understandable reason. When the Gospels were being
written, Jesus had already been cast into a cult. Worship
was being accorded him as the eternal Christ. He was being
deftly withdrawn from politics, so that the Romans might
find no offense in the new religious movement, though Jesus'
crucial decision had been political. Silence concerning politics seemed the safest course. Emperors have no objection
to what goes on in church provided it goes no further, and
Rome granted toleration to any religion so long as it was
content to be a religion and did not interfere in imperial
business. Silence was a plausible course too, not because
Jesus had showed no interest in politics but because his attitude toward politics was so baffling: instead of reforming
that game he chose to smash it entirely.

Presumably the triumphal entry into Jerusalem, engi-
neered high-handedly by the nationalists, was the occasion
that forced Jesus to say yes or no. What he said left the im-

mediate situation unaffected, yet it overturned the checker-
board. His decision favored neither the Jewish patriots nor
the Roman conquerors. It was leveled against both. Jesus
refused to play their game. He proposed no new laws to
mitigate the injustice of government, he lent no hand to shake
off its weight. Still, he did not withdraw in the aloof sniveling
manner of a monk or pundit. What he did was to repudiate
politics utterly as an arena of play. Jesus chose anarchism.
His kingdom was not of the world he saw in Pilate's court-
room.

The Hebrew prophet had never been a mystic. He was not
wont to receive special intuitions of the divine within the
cryptic recess of his inner consciousness. The prophet was
accustomed to read the will of God on the scroll of events,
rather than to deduce his politics from the logic of ideas as
the Greeks did. Jesus was seared by the burning conflict between Rome and Judea, and in the flames he discerned the
righteousness of God. Righteousness was power. But the
troops his countrymen had at their call were puny compared
with the legions of the empire. If his people mechanized,
or idealized, the political order and resorted to arms, they
would surely lose that test. The armies of Rome were stronger.
Since God was both just and omnipotent, man's ideas on
both subjects required revision. God did not intend rebellion.
The Jews could fulfill their historic mission only by abandoning all thought of a military mission. God would send
no succor, and their own resources were insufficient. Only
by rendering unto Caesar what Caesar extorted could they
render unto God the service he required. Solely in submission
to Rome lay freedom. Government is irrelevant to moral

living. And the irrelevant is entitled perhaps to the tribute
of compliance as long as it is paid with the irreverence of
a laugh.

Thou shalt love thy neighbor as thyself: but who is my
neighbor? Jesus had once answered: the first man you met.
But suppose this man chanced to be a Roman? Why call
him a Roman? That is to condemn him already before you
have met. Nationalism is diabolic. The devil is an American,
a Russian, Jew or gentile. The devil is equally pleased at
being any or all. Such tags are daubed by the devil's brush.
One choice confronts man supremely at every decision: the
choice between spirit and the sportive substitutes for it.
Politics cannot be allowed to fence off a separate and autonomous domain. To acknowledge a political motive merely
propels political bodies, and these are inhuman. The way to
get along with a Roman is to get him away from Rome. They
that play with swords shall die playing. That the meek shall
inherit the earth bespeaks God in creation. If politics denies
this, let politics be damned.

Jesus' decision ranks as the most incisive made in man's
evolution. It was a creative act, bound to effect creation, and
we resist it to our own ruination. Patently the political game
was not permanently shattered that day in Jerusalem. The
apparatus was speedily rehabilitated. The play has persisted
2000 years as the devil's favorite diversion. But, had Jesus
fallen to the second temptation, we should certainly never
have heard of the first. His name might have died a lingering
death in the footnotes of historians, but the power he dis-
played could never have oozed through their tomes.

A generation later the Jews did rise in fury against the
Romans, with consequences Jesus foretold. Jesus too fore-

told his own fate. Caught in the squeeze between disgruntled Pharisees who pounced from one side and rebuffed nationalists leaping from the other, both of whom he had deprived of their toys, Jesus was delivered unto Pilate. And Pilate did not long waver for a move.

God could not have prevented the Crucifixion. God can control Nature. But God meets man only when man is free. God meets man only within the spiritual environment which both Romans and Jews had nilled and annulled. The will of God cannot be transformed into a human motive. But when it is said that God did actually reverse what we regard as a natural process, and that he raised from the dead the victim of that Crucifixion, I am not one lightly to refute the report. I know that the devil could not have done it. But what God can do takes a better man than I am to tell.

Who crucified Jesus? The query propounds a riddle. Christians have stolidly accused the Jews. The Jews have exculpated themselves by framing the Romans. Pilate on their behalf washed all blame from his hands at the time. Judas surely would plead innocent; he was just plying a stunt to put Jesus on the spot and prod him into self-assertion. Who, then, did crucify Jesus? Nobody, of course. The same people crucified Jesus who started World War I, World War II, the same people who will start World War III. And who are they? The other fellow, don't you know? It is the devil of it to behold the devil in someone else, never in yourself. The evil we do, we do not intend. No man, indeed, can will the commission of evil. We do evil because we decline to act freely. We have the devil on our hands when we have played God out of our hearts.

JESUS THE SPOILSPORT

Jesus has confounded all manners of rationalizers. Interpretations of him have ranged from making him the Second Person of the Holy Trinity to making him out a paranoiac fit only for an insane asylum. Every rationalization excites disdain except from its author. A mystery can always be objectified into an infinity of problems.

What is so mystifying about him stems from his having been at once the most worldly of men and the most unworldly. Such a combination of opposites fits none of our patterns of thought. Jesus was so entangled in Nature that even the winds obeyed him, yet his own declaration sounds authentic that his kingdom was of no world he knew. His was an active career, multitudes pressed upon him, and he swayed throngs to do his bidding. Still, he impresses one as having been a quietist at heart.

Jesus founded no institution; he did not seek to reform those he found. He advocated no veering either to the right or to the left. The customs of his people he adhered to docilely. Despite the ardency of his Judaism, he chose in the end not to challenge the gentile lordship. He never agitated for abolition of the legalism that had enfeebled the Pharisees; he was no conventional liberal who instead of idolizing the law idolizes his superiority to it. An elusive and impalpable trait in his teachings made them unsuitable to copying. The freedom which formed his life can be affirmed in any environment where one exists. Freedom consists in dealing originally with what is many times secondhand. No gain can be expected to accrue either from sculpturing the façades of human institutions or from hacking away at their foundations.

Man's cultural trappings are creative in their place: which is beneath his feet, else they spin a gossamer of witchery to befog his head.

All elaborations of the ethics of Jesus are not only vapid but basically diabolic. The ethics of philosophy lay beyond his comprehension. His Gospel heralded a power that made for righteousness and a righteousness that generated power. But apart from God, man was incompetent to define either of these terms. Man could not know his end, and his knowledge grasped no definable purpose. He who did the will of God would know the doctrine soon enough, not he who thought to determine it from his own ideas. Those who brandished the sword of their conceit would be pierced thereby and perish. Good must be done without motive. Knowledge of faith must supplant knowledge of science. We dilate dolefully on the purity of Jesus' principles. We bewail the fact that because of their absolute character we cannot apply them in such relative and rapacious realms as business and politics. True, it is all very sad and sodden, this predicament we dig for ourselves. Our distress will increase until we realize that the Gospel contains no formulation of principles, absolute or otherwise. Jesus calls for a *retreat to reality,* principles be damned. But this spoils a lot of sports, professional and otherwise. It requires that men be free, and merely playing with freedom is so much fun.

Players maintain their aplomb—regardless of who is getting the plums—as long as the game is rolling along according to Hoyle. Let a rule be broken, however, and shattered complacency gives vent to rage. No group organized for play likes being disorganized. Men must view their institutions as everlasting. The losers hope for a turn in the tide,

they prefer to suffer the slings the game inflicts than to
question its sanctity. We long for an infallible church, a
written constitution, a fetish of flint, a god of immovables.
However, the more tender the trust we repose in an idol,
the more rickety that idol becomes. Rationalizing the bond
of unity renders that tie treacherous. The big idea behind
any institution eventually becomes the idea of perpetuating
itself and immortalizing the incomes of its officers. Hence
heroic measures are finally summoned: the self-interests of
the individual constituents must be subdued by snobbery
or crushed by force. Yet no jugglery of egotism can jell a
moral situation. The reformer can never accomplish what
he designs, though by greasing the gears of an institution
he may prolong its duration and defer its demise. Struck
by his lightning, the game may right itself and sprint along
again. And the obloquy spat upon the innovator dries to
bronze whereon is etched the legend of his deeds.

Occasionally vituperation activates muscles more potent
than the tongue, and the reformer comes to a violent end. This
happened to Socrates in Athens. But this is no more than an
accident. We revere Socrates as a martyr. He perished in the
cause of free speech, and we like to speak freely. That he
did die for freedom of a sort is less obscure than the case
of American soldiers who die on battlefields abroad.

Still, in the trial of Socrates, only an idea was at stake.
Morally his death was no different from what it would have
been, had he expired snugly in bed or been done in by
Xanthippe. He preferred to pass out rather than pass up expressing his opinions. Socrates may have been defending
a noble idea or a pestiferous idea; have your pick, realizing

that you may pick the other the day after tomorrow. The alternative does not pertain to the spiritual universe at all. Socrates' suffering commits us only to a sigh that he was a good man and that his tormentors were wicked men not to know it. Surely there must be a higher realm where the ideal somehow prevails. Despite the mauling it receives on earth, eternal truth is vindicated in heaven. Nature swaggers along her aimless track, but we can fortify ourselves against her bumps by inhaling deep draughts of rationality. We are duly and dully sorry for Socrates. We would be glad to expunge the incident from the annals of mankind; we swell in self-righteousness inasmuch as we would never do such a thing ourselves. But, that is the world we are living in, though today—fortunately—such terrible people inhabit the other side of the curtain.

Was Jesus the same sort of spoilsport? Did the Cross parallel the cup of hemlock? Did Jesus merely assert his own views against those whose ideas were inferior to his own? Had he made the discovery every philosopher makes, that life is nugatory if bereft of values which are indispensable to happiness? Did Jesus just happen to know more than the Pharisees knew? Was he resolved on revising the rules of that game?

Behold, said Jesus, we go up to Jerusalem. What motive impelled him on that rash journey? Must the mind plot the body's curves under the guise of motives? Scholars elucidate the purposes of Jesus, his Messianic consciousness perhaps. Our segmented personalities, our tenuous ego-body structures, incapacitate us for recognizing a free act when we see one. But there are times when prying for reasons and rummaging for motives manifests only the vulgarity of the searcher. Triflers know what they are up to and why; they play for the sake of patriotism, to snatch a dollar, to snare a trick. Jesus had no purpose nor motive. He was a person in tension with the Living God, a man in love with the lover of all that exists. The inevitability of his act lay nowhere in the future, nowhere in the past. In the stark and unrenounceable plenitude of the present Jesus found freedom. God had spoken. God gives no reasons. He has none to give.

The Crucifixion can be torn from its spiritual matrix and objectified as a spectacle. Upon the contemplator of it, Calvary casts an aesthetic spell. The gruesome sight softens when descried through the haze of centuries. The blood has been clotted by the winds of time. The scene can be arranged for the stage, to be witnessed as a drama, with drenches of Aristotelian purgation dripping from the rafters. The death of Jesus thrums a sublime Miserere, a lyric threnody in an opera. How could such a dreadful thing ever have happened? murmur the mourners at the Three Hours on Good Friday. Then they hop off their knees and scurry about last minute shopping for Easter. Playing with the figure of Jesus generates no more moral power than cutting out paper dolls.

Reason can operate in its distinctive fashion upon the objective world, for that world reason has created. We can know what is amenable to being known. But the creator of the real world slips off the operating table. God can never become an object of human cognition. Having pushed to the outposts of the objective realm he conceives, man, if he chooses to know more, must lay down his tools. Man must cease laying down the law, and yield his soul to receiving the Word of God. Man can determine his choice only by allowing that choice to determine him. In such wise do righteousness and power teeter on the pivot that is God. Man must be perpetually resigned to being overruled in his surmises, wringing fresh faith from the fragments of the old, waiting for the coming of the Lord.

VIII

ADVANCE THROUGH RETREAT

BE NOT ANXIOUS . . .

IF A MAN were actually the Socratic soul with the capacity to know himself and the duty to utilize that knowledge, short-coming in either respect might cause him chagrin and embarrassment. Ethically he might be expected to suffer a penalty. Life would then be the problem it is known to be, the task of a schoolboy tussling with his number work. Poor marks would goad one to sterner effort, or divert one's effort to more promising endeavors. Inadequacy, however, would scarcely infect one with anxiety. Anxiety disqualifies you either for plugging ahead or dodging aside.

Besides, anxiety seems to be intensified by success in solving the problem life is supposed to be. It creates the very situation you are helpless to flee. The more you know about yourself, the more unsatisfactory both knowledge and you yourself become, and the more desperately you cry for release. According to a recent analysis by J. W. Krutch,* man shrinks in terror of himself as that self is revealed in such explorations as Darwinism, Freudianism, and other "isms."

* *The Measure of Man* by Joseph Wood Krutch. Bobbs-Merrill Company, Inc., Indianapolis, 1954.

One fears knowledge tells a true story and the whole truth. Our jitters are to be attributed, not to ignorance as Socrates would have it, but to knowledge it is as difficult to accept as to reject. We have ferreted out the correct answers, only to smother in the hole we have bored. The revulsion that anxiety symptomizes is really aimed at the Socratic soul itself and to its diabolic skill in performing the job assigned it.

Knowledge is said to be power, and power is for action. But anxiety tends to put a stop to every start, even to false ones. Anxiety clamps a brake on action; unless, through a reverse lever, anxiety girds one into fanaticism.

Anxiety arises when the purpose or project the ego objectifies is too vague, too remote temporally or spatially— too nihilistic, let us say—to engage the will in its prosecution. Whatever you are anxious about you cannot help, yet you cannot help being anxious. Fanaticism means whipping the will to greater effort which appears to bring the object closer to its grasp. Worrying over having cancer is a typical case. Whether you have it or not is problematic, and if you do have it, not much can you do about that either. So you watch, fanatically, for "danger signals," you pester the doctor for frequent check-ups, and you check in liberally to the cancer fund. Fanaticism allays anxiety by getting you tremendously active doing nothing, deluded however that this nothing is actually your object.

But anxiety vanishes completely when one moves out of the sphere where it constitutes the atmosphere, out of the world that anxiety itself has created. Any man is always free to mind his own business. You can live existentially, and existentially no man ever died of a cancer he did not have. Just living where you are will cure cancer of the mind, and may stand us in better stead than we suspect in curing cancer of the body.

To this spiritual dimension of being entirely in the present humanists like Mr. Krutch are blind. The humanist knows too much about humanity. The humanist knows you to death. Patently, the more you know about yourself, the more that *you* is jeopardized. That *you* is ultimately shrouded in mystery, and in dispelling the mystery the knower destroys the real person. The known self is not the real self, the latter being neither the subject nor the object of knowledge.

The real self hovers above all explanations, affirming or denying any explanation at his pleasure, accepting or rejecting the faculty of explanation, considering it all a good joke. His polarity with the subject-object artifact defies description beyond calling it a state of tension. To objectify this tension, or the real self, is impossible. But acknowledgment of this impossibility marks an advance beyond objectivity. In this tension between the poles of man's being lies the sole constant in a universe of change. In laughing over his insecurity he feels secure.

This conclusion of the matter makes no claim to truth in the scientific sense. But since it flaunts no such pretensions, it is invulnerable to scientific disproof. It can be called valid knowledge, but knowledge in a nonobjective respect, knowledge insofar as knowledge and life are one. The sole ethical formula to be drawn from such knowledge flouts all rational ethics: let yourself go, let yourself alone. I am not offering this, however, as a slice of advice. Proffered as a precept, you will not take it, for the sufficient reason that you cannot take it. Man is impotent to act morally according to knowledge. To be free spiritually all one needs know is that the universe is as plastic as he is himself. But no one can be knocked by argument or kneaded by exhortation into such awareness.

Do the twenty-five centuries of philosophy serve to answer the simple query, what does man really want? Pursuit of objects we think we want stokes the engines of culture and industry. Our sundry objective configurations—the state, amassed wealth, amusement gadgets—these know what we want and undertake to tell us. But they delude us, betray us, bedevil us: they know what we want, but they do not know us. Culture raises ladders to the sky to rescue us from the roof of a burning house, the conflagration having been kindled by our playing with matches. What do we really want—to see a fire? Our real want, which the pondering of knowledge keeps us from probing, is: just what we happen to have. The place whereon we stand is holy ground. It is here we are destined to meet God, it is here and now that existence shines with eternity. Be not anxious for what you do not have. *Carpe diem,* be not anxious for the morrow.

Such immediacy, however, can never come about through any objective medium; immediacy is no occult dimension of an objective domain. Humanists, like Mr. Krutch, seek to allay anxiety by diving beneath the depth determinists so far have penetrated. Science, they say, has turned up facts which to date science has been unable to explain; the known is forever bounded by a vast haystack of the unknown wherein man is free to search for the needle of freedom. Humanists, for example, argue that no infinite tribe of monkeys pounding on as many typewriters through infinite eons could tap out *Hamlet.* But man's shudders are not to be quelled by the argument that he should not be shuddering. And any determinist can cage such vagrants at his convenience, breaking their necks with a simple twist of his gnosis. The rejoinder of a mechanist to the *Hamlet* argument is so obvious as to be startling: a monkey once did the trick and the monkey's name was Shakespeare.

The sad case is that whatever is objective can be explained objectively; that is the essence of objectivity. It advantages little to lug God in the humanist's back door, even though God be put up splendidly in the guest chamber or a higher story be added for his private abode, as old-fashioned supernaturalism had it. God, too, can be snuffed out by explaining how he functions, and his corpse buried in the cellar of deism. Man's unrest is due to his own confinement in the objective world, and his squirmings are not to be quieted by tampering with the ground rules. Whatever be its furnishings, the objective realm is designed to domicile the knower. The real man wants no such quarters, regardless of any gingerbread front or bric-a-brac interior.

On the humanistic plane the single way out is by way of self-imposed exile. To save himself from life imprisonment, the dogged knower must seek egress in mysticism. By blowing the subject up to infinity, the mystic can soar superior to the facts, both the nice ones and the ugly ones, taking refuge in the empyrean where nothing can happen. Thus mysticism issues as the counterpart of materialism, the other end of the same stick. Determinism suffocates the mind but lets the body gallop out its fated ride, while mysticism extinguishes the body within an infinitely expanded consciousness. Being extremes of a false antithesis, mysticism and materialism tend to merge into a single system, properly labeled by either tag. Among classical thinkers Spinoza discerned most clearly this correspondence, deserving to rank therefore as the supreme philosopher. Call him a determinist or a God-intoxicated mystic, either seems appropriate. The purest idealist was wed to the crassest mechanist in one and the same book.*

Still no peak of philosophy can elevate us above the objective level. The well-intentioned humanist must somehow get the intention of abandoning his own humanism. There is no rule how one can come by this intention. The humanist has to escape from the captivity of his knowing self. In the arena where he has accepted combat the determinist will thrust him every tilt. The humanist needs see that Shakespeare's writing *Hamlet* is one thing, the fact that he did write it is another. The fact of *Hamlet*'s having been written is naught but an idea. The status of the idea is the same whether its contemplator is or is not familiar with the play, and has precisely the status of the fact of what Shakespeare had for breakfast the morning he started. The knowledge that *Hamlet* has been written fails to communicate the joy that accompanied the act nor does it confer power to do likewise. The knowledge that some men appear to have attained freedom renders nobody free. Knowledge transmits facts, but no fact can resist the onslaught of determinism, every fact being just this onslaught and testifying that determinism is itself a fact. Freedom pertains only to existence. No fact can prove it, the act alone is free. But how can we act when we lie flat on the back, supine on the floor of objectivity? Still, are we not free to get up? To mount to your feet is tanta-

---

* On the remarkable vogue of Spinoza in contemporary Russia, see *Spinoza in Soviet Philosophy* by George L. Kline. Routledge and Kegan Paul, London, 1952.

mount to freedom. Be not anxious. . . . get up. . . . let
yourself go. Go where, do you say? That is unknowable. If
you insist on being told the fact where, all I can say is that
you can go to hell.

The humanist must confess that the factual stakes objectivity rests on are driven by the sledge of his own egotism
into the bottomless bog of nothingness. Strictly speaking, we
should refer to the objective world only in the singular, for
we are referring to the specific one that is our own. Snobbery
sniffs that ours is the one and only. That ultimately and universally objective world, the truth that was and is and ever-
more shall be, unmasks into an empty abstraction, being but
the forms of our reason. Taken concretely, objectivity displays bewildering variation and is subject to the fluctuations
of the subjects projecting it. Every objective order wears
thin and wears out: it wearies of interpreting experience.
Every age is an age of revolution. Which is true: Catholic
theology, whose key concepts were sin, grace, salvation;
the eighteenth-century certainties of natural law, the rights
of man, the Supreme Being; the nineteenth-century program
of matter and energy, evolution, progress; or our contemporary ideology of relativity, electrons, complexes—or what
do you say? Which is true? The as yet unthought-of will be
just as true for the as yet unthinking tomorrow.

A chastely respectable objective world may be begotten
by a single subject—how else can one get launched?—whose
objectivity is to be enhanced by the selling job that puts it
across and constrains other subjects to buy the spectacles.
When Galileo contends against the church, he is within his
rights in charging the balkiness of the establishment to ob-

stinacy and malice. But his own obstinacy should not be-
cloud the facts on the church's side. Every strife of egos
is ringed by the ropes of fact.

Facts can be counted the solid citizens of objective society;
an apter metaphor might be its warriors or storm troopers.
Facts are fighting words. A fact packs a polemic, to be hurled
into the teeth of the defenders of an objective army em-
battled against your own. The bombs of fact are ignited by
goblins of the past, they are fused to torpedo somebody else's
present and to explode his complacency. Facts are pinch
hitters in your line-up. They break up an objective outlook
at variance with your own. Within your camp, facts are allowed to doze, to be aroused by a sentinel's alarm that a
hostile subject is on the march. Does anybody believe that
Occidental science for the 2000 years prior to Galileo's attack never suspected that the acceleration of a freely falling
body is independent of its weight? Lucretius, if I mistake
not, actually noted it. The fact was known; but nobody of
importance could see how it was important, hence it was no
fact at all. Facts await the baptism of utility to be regenerated
as children of eternal truth. Your best defense against the
let's-look-at-the-record argument is to say it first.

No objective world gives up the ghost when it gets trounced
by another one. Instead it slinks as a ghost, occupying the
skulking status of a superstition in the new reign, crouching
behind the throne, poised for a pounce. Once an object, always an object. The thesis that thirteen is an unlucky number
is just as objective as anybody's law of gravitation, though
its validity be more esoteric and is only to be attested in
centers of sophistication like New York City where buildings

lack the thirteenth floor. Yet, who knows, someday our no-
menclature may be revised to excise the horrendous numeral
from the ordinal.

Be not anxious that thirteen is an unlucky number. But
be not proud because you know it isn't.

REVIEW OF PLAY

No objective sphere can be deemed real; each one obtains
solely for the purpose of play. Such a system is constituted
by mutual agreement, by all players accepting a configuration of ideas which determine the rules. Indisputably any
organization can assert its right to write the code whereby
it is to be governed. This embodies a collective will which
must be maintained else that corporation vanish. We have
surveyed the various means available to confirm such objectivity; rational appeal, snobbery, and physical force.

The motivation to support such an order can be rationalized
into the law of rewards and punishments. The profit motive
furnishes the incentive to compliance, fear of reprisals the
deterrent to rebellion. This is to speak a platitude; business-
men and politicians say so whenever they get the chance.
They are so horribly right; where they go wrong lies in
fancying that there is a moral way of doing what actually
repudiates the moral way of living.

Every device of the kind fulfills a purpose: the self-
interests of the individuals engaged. A theory of pre-estab-
lished harmony is tacitly assumed, the theory that the egotism
of each redounds to the egotism of all, this hypothesis weaving
a decent garb for naked selfishness. But such finery may
quickly be torn to tatters in the rough-and-tumble of the
game. Only philosophers who stay safe in their studies see it

that way. And players who get their eyes put out have a
perfect right to agitate for a change of rules when any
regimen becomes oppressive. They can legally petition for
reform, if that seems a feasible tack. Or they can operate by
stealth. Both overt method and subterfuge are permissible,
for the end sought is the preservation of the end the game
must serve to endure. The pattern has to remain elastic if
it is to persist, and any means to stretch it is justifiable; not
morally for the moral person is not involved, but objectively.

Winners prefer the setup as it is—aren't they winning?
The trump card they play exhibits the slickest joker the
intellect of man has ever crafted. They identify the *status quo*
with such out-of-the-world values as probity and honor. They
ascribe the plight of the sufferer to sin, which losers com-
pound by their reluctance to accept defeat as the judgment of
God. The winners smuggle in such pseudo-moral concepts as
fair play, good sportsmanship, the sense of honor, loyalty to
one's self—all sheer snobbery. This parade of virtue on the
part of the victors avails not to transform play into a moral
enterprise. This sacred sense of honor merely glues a mask
the ego is to don. The angelic paint should scare nobody. In
play, all is fair which the player can get away with, it being
understood that opposing players have a right to keep him
from getting too far. Eternal vigilance on one side is the
counterweight to temporary virtue on the other. The essence
of play is the contest wherein separate wills check and
contain one another. Play is neither good nor evil. It paves
a diversion from reality, however, and from a spiritual point
of view lacks all significance whatsoever.

TO PLAY OR—WHAT?

To play or not to play poses a problem each man **must** settle for himself. Decision has to be existential, it cannot be hypothetical. I cannot tell you how to decide nor when the time shall come to decide. But I do protest against sneaking moral considerations into play itself, this being an insidious brand of snobbery. Doing so is directly responsible for man's major debacle, that of putting the Pharisee into the pulpit as a spokesman of God.

Acting morally is never equivalent to having good ideas. Moral behavior is in actual deed, and the deed is specific. It concerns persons and pertains to the present. Such terms as love, hope, and faith degenerate into rhetoric when used nonmorally, abstractly. One cannot love humanity, one cannot put his hope in princes or bureaucracies, one cannot repose faith in an evolutionary process. That is pharisaism: to plump for a state of mind.

Still, if you find the illusions repugnant that play imposes, you are up against more than your weight. Your fellow citizens will regard you an eccentric, if not a downright menace. If you refuse under all conditions to deceive your neighbor, the deceit being no wise palliated by the explanation it's done in pretense, you cannot play cards. If you hold it morally abhorrent to defraud any man, even one unknown to you by name, you cannot trade on the Stock Exchange, where the rule brazenly promulgated is to buy low and sell high. If you decline to kill your fellow man, though the blood you shed spurts from the veins of your country's enemy, you cannot take the oath of the armed forces. If you do not consent to lie and steal, it is impossible to play politics. But what in the world is left?

I do not mean to assert categorically that soldiers are murderers, card players crooks, stockbrokers cannibals, and politicians bandits, though I'm tickled it sounds that way. The epithets apply only to the games they ply. The individuals caught therein are just pretending, submitting to the rules and renouncing incidentally their moral selves for the duration. Emerging from their nasty dives, they may vent their disgust, showing another side to their families and their friends and wishing life were not the gruesome grind it is.

Yet it advantages naught to play at moralizing what is inevitably nonmoral. Such spurious virtue glides into man's chief vice. It amounts to no more than trilling everybody a Merry Christmas—every such wish is tainted with the meretricious. The day after Christmas Santa Claus is back at the North Pole, having cut no ice. The greeting cards are stuffed in ash cans, and the artists have returned to their trumperies. No motive fizzles so futilely as good will, a fiasco that ensues whenever that good will commits itself to a cause. No situation need constitute the cause of a reformation. If men would merely choose to be moral, their games would go and the reformers with them.

In the meantime, reform movements flourish as gambits in every game. Just before the fall elections a passion for virtue overspreads politics and suffuses its landscape. Corruption in office is disclosed by the party outside that plans to ride in on the back of the disclosures. Despite the consternation, the pledge to abolish corruption amounts to no more than a move in chess. When the Democrats wax too daring and glaring, whom shall we blame but the Republicans? Who is to protect us from the depredations of one side unless it be the other? Our liberties consist in keeping the teams evenly matched and both in fighting trim. Corruption represents no alien motive extraneous to politics, it is politics itself. Our way of life is not being threatened, it is just being illustrated. Governments thrive on emergencies, and to keep them coming makes a sure move toward the public purse. Any attack on government, either by subversives within or by enemies without, renders the need of government impressive, a need to be met only by more government if only to keep functioning the government that already is. *O tempora, O mores.*

Maybe you choose not to play. Come now, you must relax, you must relent. You cannot crawl into the cave of the inner life, that is a game too. After all, we are living in civilized society, and concessions from time to time are no more than civil. Every man has to take a part in politics. Turn the rascals out to make room for other rascals; keep the turnover high. Having created a sphere of rascality, let us make shift within it.

I am venturing to state the relation the real self must constantly bear to every artificial self. This is a rational attitude the spirit extends toward all possible forms of play; it is, I repeat, rational rather than emotionally cantankerous. In a previous chapter I have called the point of view I am advocating radical skepticism; it consists in denying as absolute any play order, in questioning the postulates of every game. Whatever is objective can be accepted, but only provisionally, as expedient. One may play provided he strips off the pretensions play takes seriously, provided he plays morally naked. Though one has to pretend for the purpose of the game, one is pretending without pretense. If this sounds complicated, the rule can be simplified in saying that spiritual man finds culture to be comic. Spirit finds the sense of play identical with the sense of humor. When you are overawed by the pomp of any objective monster, laugh in its face. Instead of taking it for what it is cracked up to be, crack it into what it really is. Keep smiling; the difference between God and the devil is God's smile.

In the actual fray the playful spirit usually slants its support to the underdog. Since the sole difference between sides is that one is winning and the other losing, join the side that needs your help, just to avoid the devil of it. That may be God's side too: remember the gay and giddy words of the Magnificat:

He hath scattered the proud in the imagination of their hearts. He hath put down the mighty from their seats, and exalted them of low degree. He hath filled the hungry with good things; and the rich he hath sent empty away.

Should you be a pagan and brook no back talk from the Scriptures, I append from Vergil the same exhortation: *Parcere subjectis et debellare superbos.*

How can you hesitate? No man shall be allowed the luxury of fancying his own game spiritual just because it benefits him materially. Turning the tables is the game moral man exults in. I chuckle over the blockhead who diddles an A on examination day; the old duffer at the teacher's desk is slumped under the table. What difference how the boy contrived it? I snicker in glee at the fabled New Englander who stamped out to every town meeting just to vote *no* on each warrant: nothing, he averred, was going to be unanimous as long as he was around. The majority gets to thinking too highly of itself, making off with the prizes for correct thinking. Let us stand firm against tyranny, foreseeing the power the tyrant will wield. If opposition to determinism entails a wile or so, let us not quibble on that count. If the self-righteous deem trickery dishonorable, that is but slyer trickery on their side. Snobbery inspirits the trickiest move ever devised. No mortal is so good that dropping him a peg wouldn't make him better.

This, of course, has nothing to do with moralizing the world. The only way you can act morally for society is to live spiritually right where you are. Humanity cannot be improved by good ideas, but solely through the influence of good people. The little fellow, therefore, from a cosmic point of view has the same opportunity as the loftily stationed top shot. Indeed, were it not for the integrity afforded society by the multitude of nobodies at its bottom, the somebodies at the peak would soon have nothing to play with.

The profoundest sociological document ever written lies tucked away in the 18th chapter of Genesis. Sodom and Gomorrah were marked for destruction, and Abraham appealed to God on their behalf. The judge of the whole earth could do no wrong: would the Lord slaughter the righteous with the wicked? No, assented the Lord, if fifty righteous men could be found there, he would spare the cities for their sake. Abraham haggled and bargained. He beat God down in his price, till God finally settled for a scant ten. Only when these ten were lacking did fire and brimstone rain upon the cities of the plain.

Presumably Moscow and Washington are dens less foul than Sodom and Gomorrah of old. It would be rash to estimate how many righteous men would be required for our salvation now. But I conjecture they are just as scarce and that the Lord would have the same trouble rounding them up.

Now, I do not know exactly what a righteous man is. All I feel sure of is that we would recognize a righteous man if we saw one. Dogs probably would acquaint us of his presence, and the birds would perch on his shoulder. Certainly he is not the respectable fellow who goes to church and pays his bills. These things he may do, but there is an indefinable surplus. The disciples, we are told, beheld Jesus as he walked and exclaimed, the Son of God! Maybe righteousness is but a special way of walking. Whatever it be, righteousness manifests the presence of God. But to exhibit the presence of God, one must live in the presence of God and one's world must be empowered by God's being there.

Ten righteous men does not seem an excessive number, considering our one hundred and seventy-five millions—not till you look around for them. The Biblical minimum abroad in our land might not justify dismantling the federal leviathan at one swoop. Still the decemvirate might be worth a sizable chunk of the Department of Justice, including the FBI. The humblest citizen can be, if he chooses to be, one of the ten. Such a choice would, of course, imply a retreat from what trots on under the name of civilization.

WHAT THE RETREAT IS NOT

I have descanted upon the bankruptcy that ensues on selling out to the future. But I have said relatively little on the sell-out to the past. A *retreat* may suggest a backward march, a reversion to some good old day whose glory is heightened, like a towering mountain peak, in being viewed from a distance.

No one could live on that snow-capped summit. And patches of outworn orthodoxies can be sewed only into the tawdriest garments. A conservative reaction sounds so obviously fraudulent that eloquent exhorters always abound to commend it, pleading that we recover the defenses our fathers found secure, but burking the question of why then they ever left them. An antique patina magnifies the value not only of furniture but of piety as well.

The endeavor to live in and on memory, whether individual or collective, forfeits vital existence. Old age titillates in reminiscence, senility revels in the repristination of misspent youth. But there is really no such experience as the consciousness of the past. In memory you are presently conscious of what is gone by and done for. Objects of recollection can be surveyed aesthetically, but the series is no more alive than a wall of pictures in an art gallery. And what is more depressing than a trip through a museum unless one has been antecedently depressed into the permanent fatigue of an antiquarian. Nostalgia is the name of this peculiar affliction. It involves a play of the mind, tension between what was and what is, the past emerging the winner and the object dwarfing and deforming the person. Whatever is known in conscious recall is sterilized in being so known. Let the dead bury its dead. Bid be-gone to bygones or be a goner yourself.

Every cultural group is besieged by collective nostalgia when its culture is playing out. The church makes a religion of it, universities make a flourishing trade. But who is vitalized learning languages nobody reads except pedagogues earning their living teaching them? Why extol as classics books that snobbery alone sustains as pillars of an academic palace? A splendid plan, it might be, to burn all extant copies of our numerous Bibles once a decade, then start compiling them afresh. The sections not being reproduced in contemporary living were better lost and forgotten. People know by heart the good of any sacred text and recite it in deed. What gets shelved in books overhangs as a peril and a scourge. Amid the dust the devil slinks, in the ambush of any object that is venerated out of existence. Every dogmatism affords him a hide-out. The sense of security we derive therefrom baits the trap that trips us. Uncertainty happens to be the lot of any man who chooses to dwell in reality. Remaining insecure is his sole security. Inevitably we will grave idols as long as we are men. But as an antidote against the venomous sting of idolatry we might strip our altars clean each morning, smashing yesterday's accumulation, thus plying our craft more innocently and probably more intelligently in today's reloading. Let us join heartily in the creeds, provided they headline only this day's edition. Sufficient unto the day is the ritual thereof.

Our *retreat* is not immediately concerned with institutions. The works of men are irrelevant to the spirit, which exults in a strange and holy indifference to them, one and all. They make a convenient road to travel over, they are fit for stopping places, but never for settled residence. Man's inventions are not wicked in themselves. Their power for evil comes from his expecting from them a positive good. Our own confidence discomfits us. Umbrellas can be sanctioned for occasional use, on condition we realize they leak, usually turn up borrowed on a rainy day, and that they never can wing you to heaven.

It is silly to decry civilization as an obbligato to the return to the natural life. You cannot return to what is real in nature, for you never left it. The opposite of civilized man is not "natural man" but spiritual man, and spiritual man assimilates unto himself anything that is truly natural. To eat with knife and fork is no less natural than to eat with your fingers. Motoring at 60 miles an hour, or flying at 300, is just as natural as hoofing it. Pascal was quite right that "custom is a second nature that destroys the former; nature may be only our first custom as custom is our second nature."

Thus the *retreat to reality* makes no cause out of returning to the simple manners of the forefathers, especially the four-legged ones. The retreat goes all out for technology, for bigger and better gadgets, provided we be braced for bigger and bitterer disappointments too. The noble savage of revolutionary lore represents merely an inverted utopianism, the idealist standing on his head. No riding the dimension of time into either past or future will deposit us at the present moment, and riding paraphernalia never help nor hinder us in its realization. We would be made no wiser by destroying the means wherewith we are accustomed to implement our folly. Primitive man seems to have been no way morally superior to his successors. Science cannot be blamed for our fribbles and our foibles. Whoever chooses to live spiritually can start right where he is, atop whatever junk pile he has collected.

Institutions redound to man's immense advantage in his spiritual self-expression. Life is expedited and enriched by customs and established ways of doing. An ingrained habit stands you in better stead than a servant at your elbow, and an electric appliance may be worth a dozen. Tying your shoelaces is no moral feat, your fingers can execute the task more deftly than you can, and if a gadget is invented to do the job, be not the last to lay aside your digits. Why should we not have our meals at regular hours and pick from a uniform menu, sparing ourselves petty bickering and the resulting indigestion when we dine together? Custom takes its cue from Nature; bizarre individuality Nature does not prize. Embodied ideas are expedient and wholesome. Patterns of regularity and order can be descried on Nature's face. No objective world should be told off as wicked as long as we keep it from falsifying reality itself. Without benefit of objective knowledge the spiritual life could not proceed. Knowledge forges an indispensable instrument of adaptation. No man can be really real without thinking and thinking soundly. The intellect is not to be denied a function in the person. The retreat envisioned here does not prescribe the amputation of the brain. It merely aims to restore the circulation that links the brain with the body, into a total self.

The spiritual man, therefore, gets no delight from razing institutions just for the fun of hearing the crash. Jesus did not play at demolishing the Judaism of his day, and he would probably deal with the church of our own in a similarly off-hand fashion. Presumably he would attend its rites with whatever diligence people deemed proper. He might drop hints that the church would be less boring if it talked of something besides itself. He might point out that nothing is sacred save in the sense that everything is sacred.

So, let us keep our institutions, cuddling them with the very skepticism they view with consternation. Let us cherish each and all, till each blows like an autumn leaf from the tree, withering in its tiny blaze of glory. When the frost descends, let us enjoy that too, gladdening in its colors, confident that the coming summer will grow new foliage just as luxuriant. When under any organization's roof, one can take off one's hat, sit down for a polite chat over a cup of tea, or a merrier one over a cocktail. But one does not undress and go to bed in any such place. The *retreat to reality* bypasses the conventional fields of play. To play together with no institution laying down the rules is the real thing: that is playing with God. In spiritual society everybody plays, nobody knows what. All can be at ease in Zion, for Zion itself is no disease.

Our retreat means sinking deeper in whatever you have, instead of seeking depth in the distance you interpose between yourself and reality. Were you ever caught in a blizzard, say a northeaster on Cape Cod? You curse the weather, level your ammunition of bad names at Nature. Soon in unloading the arsenal you have made an implacable enemy of existence. You struggle to keep your umbrella from capsizing. You button your coat around your neck, tightly and defiantly tuck its collar beneath your chin, flick a puddle from your hat, stamp the clogging sand off your shoes, snort the moisture laden with imprecations from your nose. You survey your disheveled corpus, your accumulated disgust declaring war on the universe. Minutes more, you are wet through, thoroughly drenched. Your bulwarks have been washed away, every defense you trusted in has vanished. Suddenly, for no reason you can know, you give up the fight. You heave the umbrella to the winds, cast your hat into their rapacious maw. You fling your coat open, rip it off and hurl it into the gutter's torrent. You spread your face upward to the downpour, raise your palms in welcome to the heavens. Lift up your heart, you shout, it's wonderful. Thou art wonderful, *thou art*. Miraculously, but just as naturally, your self has confronted another self in the advance to reality.

"No method," wrote Thoreau, "no discipline can supersede

the necessity of being forever on the alert. What is a course of history or philosophy, or poetry, no matter how well selected, or the best society, or the most admirable routine, compared with the discipline of looking always at what is to be seen. See what is before you and walk on into futurity." * That is all the retreat implies: the story of a nut breaking out of his shell.

MAN AND TIME

A few pages back casual note was made that consciousness pertains only to the present. To suppose we can be immediately conscious of the past or of the future is an illusion, though a prevailing and a convincing one.

What we actually mean in speaking of memory or anticipation is that we are conscious of an ideal image of the past or future as an object of present contemplation. This objectivity fosters the notion that the subject is a time-defying substance, a Cartesian soul. All distinctively human problems can be traced to man's apparent time-superseding capacity. This faculty permits him to organize formal orders to regiment his own conduct.

In the flux of Nature what we call time gives no evidence of existing; if man's life could become a continuously creative act, there would be no time for him either. Nature pays out no thread whereon the beads of passing moments are strung. Nature is hobbled by neither past nor future. Remorse over what might have been, anxiety about what may be, these do not impede her doings. Nature does not act for the sake of appearances, being no different from what existentially appears. Nature is never shackled by oughts aspired to or

* *Walden* by Henry David Thoreau. Everyman's Library, p. 99.

violated. Man, on the contrary, is perpetually beset by a craving for what is not; he is enthralled by nothingness, enraptured by ideals. His ideas create values, which are real in the sense that he does value them. But they are disvalues inasmuch as they tend to impair what they purport to preserve, that is, life itself. To reverence any means to living, or even life itself, shatters the immediacy of actual experience, and causes life to founder on the rocks of fate.

The ego we accost in solitude and reflection appears timeless and spaceless. The subject within us transcends the vicissitudes of youth, maturity, and old age. You might have belonged to the days of the Caesars and been the same knower; you might dwell on the surface of the moon without effect on that thinking center. The ego ranges above change. Change it perceives without being changed, change it may master without altering its changeless character. Existence is doomed to transiency and death, but the soul is immortal, beyond the reach of the violent hands of any clock.

If the knower were resigned to letting the world go by, blissfully wrapped in the contemplation of his own essence and the realm of possibility it has encompassed, his contemplation would be of no effect. Indeed, no other knower would so much as know about it. The cleft between known worlds would be complete. But this gap each individual knower yearns to bridge. Each ego transfers to the flux a pendant of itself, projecting thereupon ideas of objective fact, of fatalism, of a past that remains intact and indelible. The moving finger writes, then moves on; but that is not the end of it. Your piety and wit cannot erase a single word that was written, for you know for a certainty what those words were. That which has taken place does not vanish by relinquishing its place. The past survives to plague the contemplator of it. Transiency hardens into the illusion that the flux is fixed, the fluxion being mere appearance. The body, that part of one's self in direct contact with Nature, is dumped into a dungeon of facts, within a prison of laws that connect those facts among themselves. The past cannot be washed away in the sewer of time, however copious one's tears. Time does not flow; the past crams each now, quite beyond your power to alter but potent to alter and to determine you. The objective order is made up of such an array of inexpugnable facts, each stiff and static, each glowering a bit unworldly, the array as solemn as monks marching to chapel.

Thus the idea of objective fact arises as the projection of the time-dominating ego. Ideas of necessity, theories of predestination, of scientific determinism, apply alike to the past and to the future, being the spawn and heirs of the concept of fact. From worship at this shrine emanates idolatry, albeit the idol of fact rates high in the modern pantheon of science. A fact is a fact is a fact: we chant the liturgy in unison.

This self-subsistent ego, however, detachable in life as it will be in death, has troubles aplenty making good its sojourn on earth. Far from being the master of time, the ego is exceedingly vulnerable and fragile, fleeing at the slightest tap of existence. Right at the moment you are engrossed in ideas, but that spell would be quickly broken by a child's sticking a pin in your leg. That prick would pitch you into direct relation to an actual world, robbing your mind of its ideas and all concern with objectivity. The pin-in-the-leg situation you might an hour later consider a fact, but no fact feels quite like the pin. Precisely because the ego is so evanescent, it imposes upon us its demand for facts that do not feel, facts that are morally irrelevant. Collectors of facts gather no emotions to stuff in their bags. Pining for peace beyond the vale of pains and pins, the ego gives man none, its vacuity issuing in anxiety.

In reality there are no facts whatsoever. The happy hunting ground of facts is the paradise of the ego. In the spiritual universe the present moment alone exists. Every instant pinpoints decision. You jump into action. The entire cosmos is wholly reconstituted. What shall perish of its predecessor and what shall survive, each moment decides for itself. That which is not borne along within the drive of existence does not remain to dangle in a malicious time order. An event done with is the event done for. The real world evolves into a morally going concern. The nonexistent object can never be a present obsession. Scientific history lacks existential significance. Dealing only with formal time, it incurs a waste of actual time; it's a mere diversion.

The formal time of thought, this vessel that receives all objects of reflection, is empty till filled with the mind's own products. Every item lodged therein is immutable. The ego gazes upon the assortment with satisfaction, with longing, with anxiety and regret. But this ego must exhaust itself in private and adynamic reactions. The ego and its objects lack efficiency in the real world. Stoics make quite a play of their obeisance before facts. But what else can they do unless they cease being Stoics? What can one do with a fact, save to talk about it, perhaps intimidating someone by the talk? Facts wield no power. No special virtue attaches to submitting to facts. One is just being polite to one's self.

In existence nothing is fixed, everything is fluid and flexible.

Each day preserves all that yesterday has left—not in the mausoleum of memory, but in the thews of living flesh. The power of any creator is dependent on his ability to forget. God forgives men their trespasses, though men think it is asking the unreasonable to forgive one another. Mourners are comforted. Evil is overcome by good. The dead nourish the living. The existentialist, seizing this clue, lets things happen. He lets himself go. He disarms violence by refusing to bear arms against it. He softens what is hard by outpourings of his spirit. He suffers no defeats through a hang-over of failures. Time heals the wounds it inflicts in its scuffles. Every moment bulges as sum and substance of all that has ever happened. The trash of has-beens does not trammel one with a halter and a drag.

Man's domination of time drives the wedge that splits him. Spiritual man surpasses time, but not in the way intellectual man thinks. Objectively conceived, the past and the future do man out of his present. Since the present alone is real, if men cannot come personally to its point, they cannot meet at all. Time-defiers defy one another with the same frenzy that embitters their defiance of time's flow. Everybody has his own ideas and writhes in exasperation when others have words to say too. Despite the objectivity of values—how could values be otherwise, the object being by design the depository of values—values are subjective also, each individual willing his own. Eternity is every man's private estate, its bliss but the echo of the monk's quietude in his separate cell. Ascetics by the duality of our nature, we readily revert to monkery; ask any casual group to tell what happened in their midst ten minutes ago, each reported is certain his own account is correct, that account being determined by the predilections of his subject. The magic word *fact* comes tightly wadded with the explosive of egotism.

The panorama we call objective looks tenable and habitable when we completely identify our inner and our outer views. Nature reenacts her appointed roles, she goes through the paces, she appears to be mechanical and dons sciences of herself. Nature trips gracefully across the stage we have built, dutifully modeling the gowns we have garbed her in. But existence shakes off the vestures of our knowledge. The living person can never become an object. To any possible psychology, whatever the popularity of its facts and their indisputability, your only comment should be: it doesn't mean me. Facts are indisputable just so long as nobody disputes them.

In such a science as history, for example, when scholars direct their guns upon a selected spot, each savant shoots the bird of possibility he had already in his bag. It turns out there are as many facts at any point as there are historians rustling the leaves. The more objective hunters profess to be, the more strident and rancorous the wrangles that animate them. Could Russian pundits and our own concur on what has happened during the last four decades? On whose side are the facts? No science can say. But science might caution us that whosoever searches for the living among the dead shall steal back from the cemetery attended only by the data gathered by his own ego. This quest for objectivity I have previously called the predicament of egocentric incarceration. In striving to know, one does not cease to be a finite creature; in striving for universality, all one does is to alienate the dynamic component of himself into the will, whose finiteness

and rapacity is always more evident in the other fellow than
in one's self. In seeking the truth beyond himself that shall
make him free, every man falls victim to the enslavement of
his passions that set him in opposition to others. The pole of
objectivity is a stake the possession of which means war.

STARTING WITH A CLEAN PATE

Certainty has both an objective and a subjective reference,
the latter sometimes called certitude; these are ultimately one
and the same. When you are certain the fact is so-and-so,
you are duty-bound to make its acceptance a matter of conscience, of your conscience and of everybody else's: it is
universally true, to use two words where one would do. The
denial of the truth is tantamount to evil. He who doubts it
or disavows it, does so at his peril, and to protect the erring
from the consequences of error rests as an obligation upon
you. Knowing is indistinguishable from judging. The knower
is as prompt as he is deft at sorting men into such classes
as clean and unclean, Christian and heathen, orthodox and
heretic, saved and damned, elite and vulgar, champion and
chump, snubber and snubbed. In place of the natural unity
that obtains within the species, of the reality that binds men
together, we substitute a supernatural basis, creating artificial
unities according to standards of belief and intelligence.
The knower finds himself pleasantly discriminated from the
ignorant, elevated above the untaught herd. He is entitled to
the peculiar privileges pertaining to a particular aristocracy.
To be so stationed, superior people must defend their title
against such as are depraved and patently dangerous.

Thus faith in any propositional order, in any God who is
known, whose predicates are determined, whose ways are

catalogued, the faith that this God exists pits believer against unbeliever. Every creed is arrogant and adamant. Its dogmas are supernaturalistic, designed to destroy one world in the certain hope of another world's appearing where the mess we are in will be happily missing. A creed accordingly which affirms that God is love is the diametrical opposite of the existential discovery that love is God. The philosophical doctrine that God is life is the very antithesis of the experiential insight that life is God. That we use the same word, faith, for both a metaphysical idea and for religious perception, shows how quaggy our quandary is.

The philosopher's God may be called less ambiguously the Absolute. This Absolute is an object. The Absolute is to be known through the operations of discursive reason, through logical inference, or by identifying one's self with Being and mystically realizing the Absolute within one's subjective consciousness. There is no harm in philosophy provided the thinker admits the diversionary character of the pursuit and regards it as an amusement, played on the same board as chess.

The harm comes to pass when he essays to live in his cozy cell. Mistaking this for reality, the philosopher drains the ocean of mystery on which his raft of knowledge is afloat. The duality between Absolute and relative he lays out cold, but a further duality stares from the book that has resolved duality, rendered more enigmatic and acute by the solution itself. This polarity obtains between man as a person and the composite entity dealt with in thought. After his task has been disposed of and he has retired emeritus, the thinker exists in tension with the moral person the world summons into action. The ethics he has deduced do not equip him to meet the real test. When the thinker condescends to contact with the real thing, he finds his wisdom dashed into the spray and spume of play. His principles convert existence into a game, a theatrical performance. Nobody actually wants to be virtuous according to knowledge. Aristotle's magnanimous man cuts a sorry figure everywhere except in print. His rule of moderation results at best in a moderate creaking of his joints. A china gentleman, he is ill at ease in the bull shop.

The Absolute stands above reproach as an object of contemplation. And contemplation rewards its votaries with its distinctive goods: with peace of mind, with logical clarity, with divers certainties. I have no wish to despoil such treasures or to disparage the exploit of scaling the ramparts of heaven. The worst I have essayed is to point out the danger of toppling from the heights and landing on the business end of a sharply pointed stick.

Any creature is so imperiled when, convinced of the identity of his spirit with a spirit that is infinite, he descends to action on the mundane level. The Infinite is self-contained and self-sufficient, which means without relations beyond itself, which means further without power to affect existence. The Absolute is obsolete by the time you get it into motion. Virtuous beyond all possible embodiments of virtue, the perfect good is evident enough to thought, but the thought of it does not make it existent. Being wholly ideal, such a God cannot mix nor mingle in the flux and furore; aloof from the contingent, this God affords no real help to those who fumble within it. The thinker, reverting to the relative sphere, has the right ideas, but no power invigorates him from his visitation with the divine. Seeking to incarnate the vision he has glimpsed, he trips over his finite feet. In the existential

circle every man is decidedly circumscribed. His sole potency
resides in that torso of himself which the ego has antecedently
rejected. All a man can do is what his body can do, and that
body has been foredoomed to mechanical enmeshment. He
has moved out of his emotions.

Spiritual man's commitment, however, is simply to be himself. And such a self possesses capacities far greater than the
energy that stokes his body. Man's real powers are tremendous compared with what he thinks. Such moral force the
egotist scorns and spurns in denigrating one aspect of himself to ennoble another. Thus he becomes so good at one end
he is useless at the other. One who aspires to be God has his
wish fulfilled solely in fantasy. In attaining the Absolute, he
invites frustration because of his futility in coping with the
relative. All he can do is to play. In this wise there comes
to pass a strange meeting of opposites: in seeking God, man
finds the devil. When he attempts to spend the gold he has
filched from the wilderness, he discovers the haul to be counterfeit. The devil pops out as God's righteousness without
God's power, as God's essence without God's existence. The
self-righteous man can boast a surplus of righteousness but
he must take it out in talk. And that talk proves dull and boring to listen to and impresses as bunk.

Anyone who conceives of himself as pure spirit, that is,
spirit in the supernatural sense (which is not my own), the
man for example who insists that religion be spiritual, must
rely on the mechanical equipment of a fallen world to implement his good purposes. The same people who want religion
to be kept pure, uncontaminated by business or politics, cry
the loudest for the police to clean up these secular dens. They
do not look so pure when grabbing means to advance their

holy ends: note the tender affection and mutual esteem the clergy and gendarmerie show for one another. Idealists scurry about for somebody's artillery to reinforce their own puny air rifles. Their certainties are amply certified in their mania for persecution. As a consequence idealism fails to get done what it aspires to do. Despondency soon overtakes, and the idealist echoes his original wail that all is vanity and the case is hopeless. Peace is not rammed into nations by the sword. The liberty we dream of extending planet-wide hardens into totalitarianism under the pressure of a war to make men free. In this world, verily, the devil is prince. This world vouchsafes no rendezvous for saints. Philosophy exits, moaning for redemption, folding its hands and flipping an S O S into the stratosphere.

Such purity of spirit sterilizes the cosmos. It consigns the living matrix to the perdition of scientific naturalism, to fate, to deterministic enamels, to a gladiatorial arena. Who can say, the wedge that splits man his full length may drive deeper than we opine or opt, it may rend the universe from top to bottom. Is God the opposite of the devil, or of the Absolute, or of both? The devil may be but the ego of God. Perhaps God is implicated in the same existential situation we are in. God may become an object of contemplation, of intellectual knowledge, of mystic rapture. But in ceasing to be personal, God ceases to be God. To see God so detached and abstracted from his deeds would be, as the Bible admonishes, to die.

To project the whole of things, the all-inclusive One, into an object of thought or aesthetic appreciation, necessarily excludes the projector's self from that whole, even though the subject swells to be coterminous with it. Reality, therefore, can never be adequately known, for the knower is omitted from the construction he objectifies. Religion follows a different path from science and philosophy. Its knowledge is nonobjective. The tension designated by the term *religion* obtains not between a subject and an object; its tension links one self with another self. Religion is a personal matter. Religion cannot be played at, it must be actual and existential else it be false. Any shrine its God indwells is mounted on wheels; in the movement of the ark and not within the moving ark abides the spirit of the Almighty.

Duality describes the human lot and any effort to eschew it is vain and void. Life cannot be fixed. But we can fix the poles that bound our oscillation. This, however, is not to be accomplished by polishing one pole to our logical or aesthetic satisfaction, through refining our knowledge to make it more plausible and widely acceptable, thus inveigling outsiders to join us inside; nor through playing with such an idea as tolerance, which means muffling or minimizing the annoyance we feel in the presence of stupidity and exercising restraint over the impulse to exterminate its source.

Productive polarity calls for quite a different tack and talent. We must find strength in suppleness, in the agility to glide from pole to pole in the twinkling of an eye and with a twinkle in the eye. What is the sense of humor but a magic carpet route between the perfection of a superreality and the imperfect reality, between the universal that embraces nothing and the existent that can never be universalized? Such an act of adaptation provides no final solution to man's persistent problems, and it does propose a miracle which **no** solution can take into account.

It is becoming easy to envisage our planet's population eventually divided into two warring camps, each equally certain of its certainties and each depending upon the antagonism of the other for whatever unity it possesses. One host shouts for God and freedom, the other for God and equality, though just to be different one army may cry its God to be no God at all. I can imagine further two hostile dictators facing each other in the final showdown before the final blowup, each fulminating the convictions of his side. Freedom versus equality, theism against atheism: imprecations bound back and forth, fusing the bombs of the sacred shells.

Can we now conceive, at such a moment, a miracle? One spokesman—it matters not which—turns to his adversary, his countenance enlivened in a smile.

"Freedom and equality," he drawls, "are both good ideas. We know they are good. Sometime or other we have known them as realities, as really holding between a father and a son, let us say. Father and son are equal though unequal in every assignable magnitude. And both are free because they are bound together in ties of love. Equality and freedom are nowise incompatible if each is real. But abstracted from existence and cast into political bombast, what do these ideas become? Equality becomes the equal right to sink into the grave, and freedom becomes everybody's privilege to do so. Just how idiotic can human beings get? Let us start with a clean pate. Let's be friends."

A miracle? Perhaps only a miracle will save us. But the miracle will truly come to pass only if all concerned are stunned into not asking what friendship implies, what we are to *do* about it, only if no one proposes an international organization to see that it is done right. Friendship must be accepted in the lowly sense of dogs rubbing noses and wagging their tails.

Between the devil and God there lies simply a laugh.

A CONCLUSION IN WHICH NOTHING IS CONCLUDED

A book which does little more than point out that the real self and the known self are antagonistic may seem little more than superfluous. When you make an object of yourself, that self is distorted and destroyed: everybody is aware of that to start with and nobody has left his starting post.

A pretty girl who knows she is pretty just isn't.

A scholar excessively cognizant of his learning impresses others with his studied stupidity. A jackass bearing a load of books is no wiser than another beast laden with bricks.

The virtuous man who is conscious of his virtue is the self-righteous hypocrite properly regarded as the Evil One's masterpiece. Who is less likely to bring peace than the proposition-plated Pharisee who knows precisely the conditions of peace?

Surely there is nothing esoteric about objectivity being the antipodes of reality, about egotism being the antithesis of Nature. What have I done except to call the obvious to notice? But perhaps I have dealt with the problem man has made of himself in a manner different from the usual. I have not denied that we are as good, as beautiful, and as true as verily we opine. I have promulgated no dogma of Original Sin to disparage man and slap him back in his place. What avails it to get people thinking meanly, instead of highly, of themselves? One is as egotistic as the other, and there are as many prigs who got that way by calling themselves sinners as by calling themselves saints. I have phrased the question to read: how can we be at once both what we really are and what we know we are? How can we actually be as good as we think we are? And my answer consistently has been—well, why repeat it when you probably have taken it for a joke?

How often and how fluently we say of one another: Who does he think he is? Who do you think you are?

This *who* everybody—save the accuser—identifies himself with is a much detested being. *Who* seems to be at once the object of everybody's pride and the object of everybody else's odium. *Who* has every great and noble quality, yet *who* lacks power and influence to make those qualities real. *Who* makes righteousness repulsive; *who* makes learning look silly. *Who* speaks with the tongues of men and of angels but is a sounding brass and tinkling cymbal. *Who* has the gift of prophecy, *who* bestows his goods to feed the poor, *who* gives his body to be burned, but it profits *who* nothing. *Who* is that ideal being, that paragon of perfection we identify ourselves with in taking thought. *Who* is what we love in ourselves and hate in our fellows.

I heard a voice from heaven saying unto me: Write, *who* is dead.

Could it be possible that you have not yet heard of it: *who* is dead. *Who* has been stung to death by the *bee that be-n't*.

Behold, I show you a mystery: *who* is dead and the living God reigns in his stead. We shall all be changed, in a moment, in the twinkling of an eye. The dead shall be raised incorruptible. Then shall be brought to pass the saying, Death is swallowed up in victory. O grave, where is thy victory?

Our victory is not to possess God but to be possessed by him. Man's vocation is not to penetrate mystery and to resolve it by thrust of his knowledge. Being penetrated by the mystery of God is knowledge also.

The true self lies embedded in mystery. This mystery the individual ego disputes and attempts to dissipate. But this ego is a leaf clinging tenuously to the tip of a tree whose roots are sunk in the firmament that is God. At those depths we do not suck pride from our uniqueness, we do not play at showing off. We do not make objects of our fellow men by calling them names. Being aware of God's presence as the ground we grow in, we meet one another face to face.

In being persons we are conscious both of being together and being apart. We are closely linked yet we remain free, each of us distinct. Is the self not wholly present in both hands when hands clasp in united effort? So God is existent in every union he creates. Still he is outside too; his presence and absence both is the mystery of it.

In judging not we allow God to do the judging by transforming us through the power of his love. When we are ruled by him, we are no longer obliged to lay down rules. His service is our freedom. If we do God's overarching will, we shall know the undergirding doctrine.

God humbles us, not by impressing us with our impotence and corruption, but by so animating and absorbing us that we cease to think of ourselves, being neither exalted nor abased by the artifice of humility.

God adds nothing tangible and measurable to what we have without him. His gift is the sense of his reality, which clarifies the mind and augments our power. God is the director of the orchestra we call the cosmos. He plays no instrument himself. Yet his finger brings the orchestra into being, and without making a sound of his own he elicits the mighty volume of the symphony. God is no empirical object ever to be designed or encountered. Nothing in all creation can be a symbol of him. No words can define him or reduce him to the articles of a creed. Still he is creator of all that exists and anything in creation can be a vehicle of his power.

The greatest power within the universe inheres in such a mode of God's being. God's power is supreme. But no man can wield it save him who does actually possess it. And who shall possess it surpasses the power of man to declare.

God spoke these words, saying, Thou shalt not make unto thee any graven image, or the likeness of anything that is in heaven above, or that is in the earth beneath, or that is in the water under the earth: Thou shalt not bow down thyself to them, nor serve them.

These, I bet, were the words Jesus wrote in the sand.